Death Valley SUV Trails

A guide to 46 four-wheeling excursions in the backcountry in and around Death Valley National Park

Roger Mitchell

Two Roads diverged in a wood, and I-
I took the one less travedled by,
And that has made all the difference.

Robert Frost

Death Valley SUV Trails

A guide to 46 four-wheeling excursions in the backcountry
in and around Death Valley National Park

Volume One in the Great Basin SUV Trail Series

Roger Mitchell

All photos by the author except where noted

Track & Trail Publications
Oakhurst California

Published by Track & Trail Publications
P.O. Box 1247
Oakhurst CA 93644

© 2001 Roger Mitchell
All rights reserved
Printed in the United States of America

No part of this book may be reproduced or transmitted in any form or by any means, electronic or mechanical, including photocopying, recording, or by any information storage or retrieval system including the unauthorized posting on the internet or world-wide web, without the written permission of the publisher.

Front Cover: The road into Hanaupah Canyon
Rear Cover: Start of Titus Canyon Road

Library of Congress Cataloging-in-Publication Data

Mitchell, Roger, 1938-
    Death Valley SUV Trails, 1st ed.
    Includes bibliographic references (p.) and index
    ISBN 0-9707115-0-6
    (1) Death Valley National Park (Calif. And Nev.) – Guidebook (2) Death Valley National Park (Calif. And Nev.) – History (3) Death Valley National Park (Calif. And Nev.) – Mines and mining

Printed and bound in the United States of America

Contents

Acknowledgments 1
Introduction 2
Acronyms 4
Backcountry Regulations within the Park 5
Backcountry Regulations outside the Park 6
Archaeological Sites 8
The California Desert Protection Act of 1994 10
The Mitchell Scale 12
A Word of Warning 14
Chapter I: Trails Out of Furnace Creek 15
   1. Echo Pass via Echo Canyon 16
   2. Hole in the Wall 21
   3. Furnace, Kunze and Greenwater 25
   4. Trail Canyon 31
   5. Hanaupah Canyon 36
   6. Johnson Canyon 40
   7. Galena Canyon's "White Gold" 44
   8. Carbonate 47
   9. Mengel Pass via Warm Springs Canyon 50
Chapter II: Trails Out of Stovepipe Wells 57
   10. Grotto Canyon 58
   11. The Tucki Mine 60
   12. Cottonwood and Marble Canyons 64
   13. Jean Lemoigne's Retreat 70
Chapter III: Trails Out of Scotty's Castle 75
   14. A Four Camp Loop Through Yesteryear 76
   15. White Top Mountain 83
Chapter IV: Trails Out of Beatty 91
   16. Phinney Canyon 92
   17. Gold Bar and Currie Well 97
   18. Old Pioneer 101
   19. Down Titus Canyon 105
   20. Chloride City 111
   21. Echo Pass via Lee's Camp 117
Chapter V: Trails Out of Shoshone 121
   22. Deadman Pass 123
   23. Gold Valley 125
   24. The Ashford Mine 129
   25. Ibex and Saratoga Springs 133
   26. Denning Spring 141
   27. Amargosa Canyon 145

Chapter VI: Trails Out of Big Pine 153
    28. Steel Pass from the Eureka Valley 155
    29. The Saline Valley Road 163
    30. Steel Pass from the Saline Valley 175
Chapter VII: Trails Out of Panamint Springs 183
    31. The Big Four Mine 185
    32. Back Door to Darwin 191
    33. Around Hunter Mountain 197
    34. Osborn Canyon 209
    35. Lonely Lookout 213
    36. Snow Canyon 218
Chapter VIII: Trails Out of Ballarat 221
    37. Jail Canyon 224
    38. Panamint City, Paradise Lost 227
    39. Rogers Pass via Pleasant Canyon 233
    40. Rogers Pass via South Park Canyon 240
    41. Mengel Pass via Goler Wash 246
    42. Reilly Was a Company Town 251
Chapter IX: Trails Out of Trona 255
    43. Remi Nadeau's Shotgun Road 256
    44. The Arrondo Mine 264
    45. The Gold Bottom Mine And Beyond 267
    46. Those Curious Pinnacles 273

Appendix A: Glossary of Geologic and Mining Terms 278
Appendix B: Geologic Time Chart 282
Appendix C: The Pleistocene Ice Age in Death Valley 283
Appendix D: Ice Age Lakes of the Death Valley Area 284
Appendix E: Early Man in Death Valley 285
Appendix F: Strange Happenings in Goler Wash 286
Appendix G: Common Wildflowers You May Encounter 289
Appendix H: A Four-Wheeler's Equipment Checklist 291
Appendix I: Some Useful Addresses 294
References 296
Index 302

Acknowledgments

Several women have been particularly helpful in the preparation of this guide. First, I would like to thank my long-suffering wife, Loris, who has been my traveling companion, my scribe, my proofreader and my literary critic. Without her assistance and support this book would not have been possible. Likewise, publication would not have been possible without the technical support of Glenn Harmelin.

Wynne Benti is the senior editor and driving force at Spotted Dog Press. It was Wynne who encouraged me to rewrite and update my books previously published by La Siesta Press a quarter of a century ago. Spotted Dog did not ultimately publish this book; nevertheless, I am greatly indebted to Wynne for getting me back to the typewriter.

Thanks, too, go to Blair Davenport, of the Death Valley Museum, and to Beth Porter of the Eastern California Museum. They were very helpful in providing some of the historic photos. National Park Service personnel who assisted in this publication were Ranger-Naturalist, Charlie Callagan, whose time, advice, and suggestions were invaluable, and Corky Hayes, the Chief of Interpretation, and her assistant, Terri Baldino.

My research for this guide was greatly aided by the patient staffs at the county libraries in Beatty, Bishop, Independence, Trona, and Ridgecrest. I am also indebted to the very professional assistance provided at the Henry Madden Library, California State University at Fresno, the Nevada State Library in Carson City, the California Room of the California State Library in Sacramento, the California Division of Mines and Geology Library in Sacramento, and the library of the U.S. Geological Survey in Menlo Park CA.

I particularly appreciate the help of Remi Nadeau IV, author and noted historian who reviewed the portions of my manuscript involving his great great grandfather's "shotgun road" to Lookout, and who kindly provided the photograph of Mr. Nadeau and his freight team.

Finally, recognition should also go to the staff and volunteers, and the hundreds of people who financially support the Maturango Museum in Ridgecrest and the Eastern California Museum in Independence. These institutions perform a valuable service in preserving the history of the western side of the greater Death Valley region.

RM

Introduction

This is a guidebook to the back roads and jeep trails of the greater Death Valley region. If you are one who simply likes to take his four-wheel drive rig out to push it to the limit, this guide may not be for you. If, however, you are interested in broadening your knowledge and experience of the desert, while enjoying wholesome outdoor activity, then hopefully this guide may be of some assistance. It was not my intent to simply make this an inventory of poorly maintained back roads. Most of the outings I describe have some interesting scenic or other unique feature. Most of the excursions are not really difficult, providing you have a high clearance vehicle and exercise prudence and caution.

Death Valley National Park contains 3.4 million acres, much of it accessible only on foot or by semi-improved dirt roads

I grew up in the shadow of Death Valley and came to have an intimate knowledge of its mountains, hidden canyons, and broad valleys. I have never outgrown the enjoyment of exploring some back road for the first time, or of climbing to the summit of a new peak.

In 1968 I wrote the first edition of *Death Valley Jeep Trails*, followed by *Inyo Mono Jeep Trails* in 1969 and *Western Nevada Jeep Trails* in 1973. All three books covered the region in and surrounding what was then Death Valley National Monument. But a lot has happened in the last quarter of a century. I feared that many of the trails I described in the 1960s had been closed for one reason or another. Some were; however, I was pleasantly surprised to find some of my favorite routes were not only still open, but also virtually unchanged over the last thirty years.

At the time these roads were rechecked between 1997 and 2001, the trail information was current. Conditions can vary, however, so the reader must use common sense and adapt to post-publication changes. Trails may wash out and become virtually impassable, as is the route into Panamint City. Sometimes backcountry roads are upgraded to higher standards, as has been the case in Titus Canyon. Interestingly enough, with the 1976 closure of Death Valley to mining, some roads which had good graded surfaces are no longer being maintained. They are deteriorating to the status of jeep trails once again.

Obviously it would be prudent to inquire about current road conditions at the Death Valley Visitor Center or National Park Service offices in Stovepipe Wells, Scotty's Castle, Shoshone, or Beatty before actually going out to try them. For adjoining areas outside the Death Valley National Park, inquiries can be made at the BLM office in Ridgecrest (Tonopah for Nevada areas) and the Interagency Visitor Center in Lone Pine. Wherever applicable, I have provided those addresses and telephone numbers in Appendix I.

As this book goes to press in 2001, the National Park Service is in the process of formulating a General Management Plan for Death Valley National Park that would guide management during the next ten to fifteen years. Several alternatives are under consideration. None will have a significant impact on any of the routes I have described. The 350 plus miles of backcountry roads would remain open at present levels of maintenance. Changes could occur at Stovepipe Wells, with the minor realignment of State Highway 190. Some campgrounds could be upgraded and have reduced numbers of campsites, while small primitive backcountry campgrounds might be added. It is quite possible that the parking situation at Lower Warm Spring and at Palm Spring in the Saline Valley could be changed, with more formal walk-in campsites established.

The author's first SUV on the Racetrack playa (The National Park Service has subsequently closed the lakebed to all motor vehicles)

Acronyms

In order to economize in the use of words, I have sometimes resorted to the use of acronyms in certain frequently used word groups. Hopefully, these initials will not sound foreign to the reader. We tend to use them this way in everyday speech.

ARPA	Archaeological Resources Preservation Act, a federal law enacted by Congress in 1979 that carries stiff penalties for disturbing and taking of archaeological artifacts.
BIA	Bureau of Indian Affairs, a federal agency under the Department of the Interior responsible for matters relating to Native Americans.
BLM	Bureau of Land Management, a federal agency under the Department of the Interior responsible for the multiple use management of millions of acres of federal land outside of our national parks, national forests, and national wildlife preserves.
CDPA	California Desert Protection Act, legislation passed by the Congress in 1994 which changed Death Valley from a national monument to a national park, greatly expanding its size in the process, and designating 95% of the new park as *Wilderness*.
DFG	Department of Fish and Game, a State of California agency responsible for managing the state's wildlife.
MPA	Mining in the Parks Act, legislation passed by Congress in 1976 that started the process of phasing out mining in Death Valley National Monument.
NAWS	Naval Air Weapons Station (at China Lake), formerly NOTS.
NOTS	Naval Ordnance Test Station (at China Lake) now NAWS, Naval Air Weapons Station.
NPS	National Park Service, a federal agency under the Department of the Interior.
SUV	Sport utility vehicle.
USFS	United States Forest Service, a federal agency under the Department of Agriculture responsible for the multiple use management of millions of acres of federally owned forest lands.
USGS	United States Geological Survey, a federal agency under the Department of the Interior responsible for mapping and geological studies.

Backcountry Regulations within the National Park

The following regulations are applicable within Death Valley National Park:

Off-Road Driving: The routes described in this guide are open to travel by street-legal off-road vehicles. Driving off these routes is not permitted.

Camping: Camping is not allowed along the Grotto Canyon Road, Titus Canyon Road, the West Side Road, the Racetrack Road between Teakettle Junction and Homestake Dry Camp, or the first eight miles of the Cottonwood Canyon Road. Camping is not allowed at the Inyo Mine, the Lost Burro Mine, or the Ubehebe Lead Mine. Finally, camping is not permitted within two hundred yards of any water source, or one hundred feet from any flowing stream. (These regulations are subject to revision, so check with the rangers.)

Fires: Campfires are not permitted, except in fire pits in the developed campgrounds. The gathering of any wood, alive or dead, is prohibited.

Firearms: Firearms are not permitted in Death Valley National Park.

Pets: Pets must be on a leash and restrained at all times. They are not allowed off the roads, on the trails, or in wilderness areas.

Collecting: The collecting of plants, wildflowers, animals, rocks, minerals, fossils, and artifacts is strictly prohibited within Death Valley National Park. The use of metal detectors is prohibited.

Rock hounding: The taking of rocks, minerals and fossils from within Death Valley National Park is prohibited.

Mining: Mining took place in Death Valley long before it became a national park. Even with its national monument status between 1933 and 1994, Death Valley was one of only two units in our National Park System where mining was permitted. That all changed in 1976 when a new law, the *Mining in Parks Act*, was enacted. This legislation permitted existing mining to continue until its validity could be evaluated, but prohibited the staking of new claims, and required an evaluation of nearly 50,000 mining claims. By 1980 mining was allowed to continue on 2,000 of the 50,000 evaluated claims. In 1989, many of the talc mines in Warm Springs Canyon were bought and the land transferred to the National Park Service. Then in 1994 passage of the California Desert Protection Act prohibited the filing of new claims in the newly established Death Valley National Park. Valid existing claims could continue to be worked. Currently only about one hundred valid mining claims remain in the park. The Billie Borax Mine is the only mine operating.

Private Property: Although new mining claims can no longer be located within the national park, there is still private property, including many patented mining claims. Respect the rights of the owners.

Backcountry Regulations outside the Park

In general the lands surrounding Death Valley National Park are federally owned public lands administered by the Department of Interior's Bureau of Land Management. On the western and southern sides of Death Valley, jurisdiction lies with the Ridgecrest Resource Office (part of the Desert Conservation District). BLM lands on the Nevada side of Death Valley are the responsibility of the Tonopah BLM office.

The U.S. Forest Service and the BLM have a mission that is clearly different from that of the National Park Service. The major emphasis of the NPS is resource preservation first and foremost, with recreation secondary. The responsibility of USFS and the BLM is resource management in a broader sense, which may include preservation in places, but also provides for a wide variety of multiple uses, of which recreation is only one.

Off-Road Driving: In recent years, the BLM and the Forest Service have done a pretty good job of posting their lands relative to vehicle use. Essentially, these agencies classify ORV use on their lands in one of three ways: Closed, Restricted Use, or Open.

Closed areas are generally those areas formally designated as *Wilderness*, or less formally as *Wilderness Study Areas*. There are many such areas surrounding Death Valley National Park, including the Piper Mountain, Sylvania Mountains, Funeral Mountains, Resting Spring Range, Ibex, Manly Peak, Argus and Malpais Wilderness Areas. In addition, vehicle use may be prohibited in small areas because of some local resource that might be damaged.

Restricted Use generally means that motor vehicle travel is permitted, but limited to designated roadways. The vast majority of BLM administered land is in this category.

Open areas are generally open to all types of vehicles with no restrictions of any kind. The nearest such places to Death Valley are the Spangler Hills south of Trona, the Dumont Dunes, and the Olancha Dunes.

Camping: Generally camping is permitted anywhere on public lands administered by the Bureau of Land Management and the U.S. Forest Service, unless it is specifically prohibited.

Fires: Campfires at undeveloped campsites are permitted. A California Campfire Permit should be in the possession of the person having the fire. These are available at no charge from any state (CDF) fire station, U.S. Forest Service Ranger Station, or BLM office.

Firearms: Generally the safe discharge of firearms for hunting or recreational purposes is permitted on public land, unless posted or near habitation sites, as specified by state law.

Pets: Generally there are no federal restrictions on pets on USFS or BLM lands.

Mining: Outside the national park boundaries, public lands under USFS and BLM administration are generally open to mineral entry, unless they lie within designated *Wilderness Areas*. In the last few years many new regulations have been added that apply to the staking of mining claims. Contact the nearest BLM office for the details.

Collecting: The collecting of Indian arrowheads, pots, grinding stones, petroglyphs, pictographs, and any other artifact is prohibited on public lands by the National Antiquities Act of 1906 and the Archaeological Resource Protection Act of 1979. The collecting of rocks and mineral specimens for home use and personal collections is generally permitted on lands administered by the BLM.

BLM regulations prohibit the taking of plant or invertebrate fossils for commercial purposes; however, reasonable quantities may be picked up for personal collections. Individuals may collect petrified wood, such as that mentioned in Excursion #27. The limit is 25 pounds per person per day plus one piece, with a 250-pound limit in any calendar year.

Dead wood for campfires may be gathered. The taking of a wildflower specimen, while discouraged, is nevertheless permitted as long as it is not a rare, endangered, or otherwise protected species.

Archaeological Sites

Death Valley, Panamint Valley and the Saline Valley are rich in archaeological sites, many of them unmapped, and still unknown to archaeologists. Of those that are known, only a handful have been systematically excavated and studied. Unfortunately over the years, and in spite of the National Antiquities Act of 1906 and the Archeological Resources Protection Act of 1979 which outlaw private collecting and the looting of archaeological sites, arrowhead collectors and pot hunters have made their way along the ancient shorelines and into the canyons, plundering these irreplaceable resources. Without any harmful intentions, many citizens have deprived science of answers to the questions of anthropologists and archaeologists about where we came from and when we got here.

The debate as to when man came over the Bering land bridge into North America has been going on for nearly a century. The answers are slow to come. Some like Ruth Simpson and her African protégé, the late Dr. L.S.B. Leaky, believe they have uncovered in the Calico Hills, near Barstow, evidence that man was in North America 50,000 years ago. Others in the field have been very skeptical about the Calico "stone tools", arguing that they are products of nature, not man. Until recently many scientists believed that man has only been in the New World since the last glaciers retreated some 10,000 to 12,000 years ago. The argument goes on; however, there have been some startling new finds in recent years in some very unlikely places. A cave in Pennsylvania has yielded man-made artifacts with a reasonably accurate date of about 15,000 years ago. Radiocarbon dates from a site in central Mexico have revealed that man killed mammoths there 20,000 years ago. A cave in Peru strongly suggests human occupation 24,000 years ago.

So what does all this have to do with back roads and jeep trails in the Death Valley country? As you take many of these routes, you will pass through, or very near, a number of archaeological sites. Most park visitors will not recognize them as such, but you may, if you have a keen eye. I would urge that anyone reading this guide not disturb any artifacts or sites that you might come upon. If you find an arrowhead, please leave it where you find it. It might have been made, and lost, by a Timbisha Shoshone just a few generations ago. It may have no particular significance. On the other hand it might be an early Archaic fluted point of the San Dieguito Culture from 9,000 to 11,000 years ago and thus extremely important. Stone tools from these people have been found in Death Valley, Panamint Valley, Owens Valley and at China Lake. It seems likely to assume that many more artifacts are out there waiting to be found. Please let their discovery help unlock the secrets of the past. They are of no scientific use to anyone if you take them home and put them in a drawer.

With these thoughts in mind, I will not point the way to petroglyphs, pictographs, chipping sites, house rings, cave sites, or other archaeological features, except in general terms. Unfortunately, too much vandalism has occurred already.

If, in your backcountry wanderings, you find something you think is unusual or significant, do not disturb it. Take a photo or two, carefully diagram its position, and report it to National Park Headquarters behind the Visitor Center at Furnace Creek. The National Park Service has staff archaeologists trained to evaluate and follow-up on such citizen reports. If your find is outside the park, notify the Bureau of Land Management's Ridgecrest Resource Office at (760) 384-5400, or write to the BLM's Desert District Office at 6221 Box Springs Blvd., Riverside CA 92507, (909) 697-5200.

The California Desert Protection Act of 1994

Death Valley has been a part of our National Park System since February 11, 1933, when President Herbert Hoover made it a national monument. With the passage of Public Law 104-433 in 1994, *The California Desert Protection Act*, the California desert was changed forever. This legislation was passed in the waning days of the 104th Congress, after an eight year long debate. Passage was primarily along partisan lines, opposed by the local Republican House member in the affected district, and supported by the Democratic Congressional leadership. President Bill Clinton enthusiastically signed the measure. Passage of the bill had been heavily lobbied by a number of environmental organizations and opposed by off-road user groups, who correctly feared they would be shut out from using millions of acres of land. The passage of the bill had profound consequences for backroad explorers who were net losers in this process. Both Death Valley National Monument and Joshua Tree National Monument were upgraded to National Park status. To most visitors this had little meaning; however, in the process 234,000 acres have been added to the new Joshua Tree National Park, 70% of which is to be managed as *Wilderness* (meaning vehicle access is prohibited).

In the case of Death Valley, the old national monument was expanded by the addition of 1.3 million acres. The new Death Valley National Park contains 3.4 million acres of which 3.1 million or 95% is now *Wilderness*. Death Valley National Park is now the largest national park in the contiguous 48 states, although a half dozen parks in Alaska are larger.

In addition to the two new national parks mentioned above, a new Mojave National Preserve was carved out of 1.4 million acres of desert lands. Management was transferred from the hands of the Bureau of Land Management to that of the National Park Service, both entities of the Department of the Interior. Visitors are not likely to see many changes in the immediate future. Under BLM control this area was their East Mojave Scenic Area. The existing campgrounds, hiking trails and visitor information centers will remain open. Motor vehicles will be restricted to existing roads only. The historic Mojave Road will remain open, but only for "street legal" vehicles (*Green Sticker vehicles* prohibited). Firewood, vegetation, and hobby rock and mineral collecting are not allowed. Target-shooting and plinking are not allowed.

Together the 17,475 square miles of Death Valley National Park, Joshua Tree National Park, and the Mojave National Preserve contain as much land as the entire States of Massachusetts and New Hampshire combined! Government bureaucrats, over whom the public in general has little influence and certainly no control, make resource management and land use decisions in these parklands.

The CDPA also created 69 new *Wilderness Areas*, covering 3.6 million acres in the public lands still under BLM management.

Over the years backcountry explorers, like myself, have suffered significant losses in the Death Valley country, although certainly not all of these road closures can be attributed to the CDPA. In the 1970s and 80s we lost a number of backcountry roads. The National Park Service closed Wingate Wash to vehicles because the Navy was having a problem with illegal trespassers on NOTS Range B. One of nature's gully washers closed the road between Trail Canyon and Aguereberry Point. Well before the CDPA was enacted by Congress, putting Greenwater Canyon in the expanded park, the BLM closed the road through it because of increasing vandalism and theft of the petroglyphs there. Passage of the CDPA did close roads in Lemoigne and Happy Canyons, as well as the spectacular switchbacks going over the ridge between Jail Canyon and Hall Canyon. Still, the damage could have been worse. We still have an off-road vehicle corridor between the Eureka Valley and the Saline Valley by way of Steel Pass. We can still drive into Cottonwood Canyon and lower Marble Canyon. Most of the canyons on both sides of the Panamints remain open to vehicle travel. Phinney, Titus, and Echo Canyons remain open as does Hole in the Wall. The passage of the CDPA then did then result in some curtailment of permitted activities in the California desert. The good news is that many favorite four-wheel drive trails are still open and as enjoyable as ever.

The Mitchell Scale

Everything seems to have its standard of measurement. Earthquakes have their Richter Scale. Temperature has its degrees. Sound has its decibels. Thus it is that I have attempted to quantify the degree of difficulty to the various SUV trails that I describe. This scale, which I modestly call *The Mitchell Scale,* was blatantly stolen from rock climbers and mountaineers who have their own peculiar brand of madness. It goes from Class I, the easiest, to Class VI, the impossible.

CLASS I: This is of only slightly worse condition than a graded road. It includes just about any kind of semi-improved and unmaintained dirt road over which you can safely maneuver a standard automobile. A Class I route should cause no one problems. The road into Chris Wicht's Camp in lower Pleasant Canyon is a good example.

CLASS II: This road is a bit more rough than Class I, and may have a high center or deep potholes requiring vehicles with greater clearance. Four-wheel drive may not be absolutely necessary, but extreme care should be taken if you don't have a vehicle with high clearance. A good example of this is the road into the Tucki Mine.

CLASS III: Here high clearance and four-wheel drive are a necessity, and perhaps low range gears and limited slip differentials, too. But the route is not so difficult that your SUV should be damaged if reasonable care is taken. The trail going up the Amargosa Canyon from the Dumont Dunes is a typical Class III route.

CLASS IV: The going gets rougher still. If you are not a skillful and experienced off-road driver, the body of your vehicle may suffer a little. You may wish to have a passenger outside the vehicle to act as a spotter, guiding you through the tight places. Taking the trail through Goler Wash or the Lippencott Grade will give you an appreciation for Class IV.

CLASS V: Most people will turn back before attempting a road of this severity. It is highly questionable whether the abuse your vehicle is taking is really worth the effort. Skid plates under everything are a must. The upper part of Echo Wash has two short Class V pitches, as does the last half mile of the Big Four Mine road. The western ascent of Echo Pass, and Goler Wash, have a few challenging, but short sections of Class V.

CLASS VI: This is for the foolhardy only. The route is so extreme that the use of a winch or two is often required. "Road building" and other creative feats of engineering are a likely necessity. You certainly don't want to try this trail without a second vehicle along, one equipped with a master mechanic, a welding torch, a complete set of spare parts, and a world-wide satellite communications system. Originally I had no Class VI in my system. That changed when I saw the magnitude of the washouts in Surprise Canyon below Panamint City. Getting a vehicle up those rock barriers is technically possible, but a challenge without equal.

Typical Class I Road

Typical Class II Road

Typical Class III Road

Class IV Road (going down)

Class V may require a winch

Class VI is extreme 4-wheeling

A Word of Warning

Although most of the roads and trails described herein have been used by the author for the last forty or more years, all were nevertheless re-scouted from 1997 to 2001 in the preparation of this publication. The route descriptions were accurate at that time.

Conditions change, however, sometimes in a matter of minutes. Bad roads can become graded. Graded roads can quickly develop an awful washboard surface. Good roads can become flooded, washed out, or buried by landslides or the ever-shifting sands. High standard roads once used by heavily laden ore trucks can deteriorate rapidly once mining stops. A section of trail that has been Class I or Class II for the last fifty years may deteriorate very quickly to Class V. A single thunderstorm may make a road suddenly dangerous or impassable.

The reader must exercise great caution and use common sense when traveling any of these routes. It is always best to let someone know where you are going and when you expect to return. Never drive anyplace where you cannot see ahead, and when in doubt always stop and scout the route ahead on foot. Remember that if your vehicle gets stuck or breaks down, you are on your own. Help may be a very long distance away. Backcountry patrols by rangers are random and sporadic. Go prepared!

In addition, be aware that public land management agencies such as the National Park Service, the Bureau of Land Management, and the Forest Service can administratively close a road or area with little or no advance notice. One must always heed the signs placed by these agencies.

In summary then, be vigilant, be cautious, be prepared, and be safe. Remember - No guarantee is made that the reader will find the trail as described.

There are thousands of old mine shafts in the Death Valley country **(Consider them all dangerous and stay out of them!)**

Chapter I
Trails Out of Furnace Creek

The Furnace Creek Ranch area is the heart of Death Valley National Park. Not only are the park's administrative offices here, but there is also a Death Valley Visitor Center complete with museum, theater, and bookshop. Slide shows and films in the theater augment the visitor's introduction to Death Valley. In addition, ranger-guided tours add to the understanding and appreciation of this unique place. There is a second museum in the ranch complex, which highlights borax and hard-rock mining, as well as early transportation in the Death Valley area.

Facilities provided by concessionaires include a general store, a restaurant, a gas station, a golf course and a 3,000-foot paved airstrip (but no AV gas). The elegant hospitality of the Furnace Creek Inn has been well known for more than half a century. For the less affluent there are three campgrounds here: Furnace Creek, Texas Spring, and Sunset (the latter for self-contained trailers and motor homes only).

1

To Echo Pass via Echo Canyon

Primary Attraction:	Interesting scenery and geology, historic mines and mining camps, and a very challenging route across the Funeral Mountains into Nevada.
Time Required:	Half a day to Schwab and the Inyo Mines and return, or all day to cross Echo Pass into Nevada.
Miles Involved:	It is fourteen miles from Highway 190 to Echo Pass; add another 3.1 miles from Furnace Creek Ranch.
Degree of Difficulty:	The road past Eye of the Needle and on to the Inyo Mines is generally Class II. Beyond Saddle Cabin it is mostly Class III for three miles, until bedrock in the canyon narrows creates one hundred feet of a very challenging Class V ascent. Once you are over that obstacle, the last mile is all Class III to the summit of Echo Pass. (The eastern side of the pass is generally Class III and IV as the route enters Nevada).

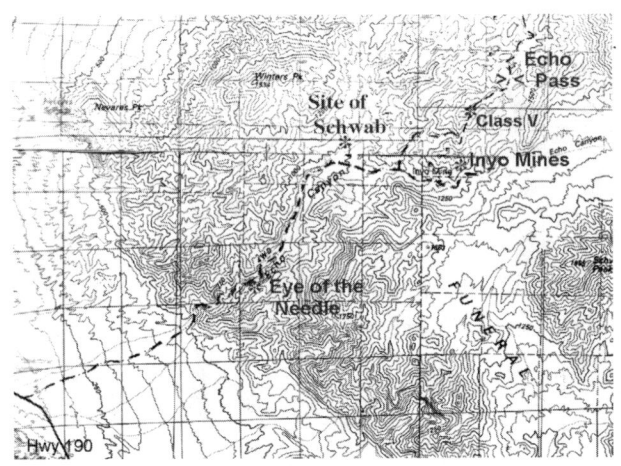

To Echo Pass Via Echo Canyon

Lower Echo Canyon is one of the easiest and most delightful jeep trails in Death Valley National Park. Because of its close proximity to the Furnace Creek Ranch and Texas Spring Campground, it can easily be visited in half a day. This outing offers typical "canyon scenery" of the Funeral Mountains, as well as an old mine with its ghost town thrown in as a bonus. Upper Echo Canyon, on the other hand, is the third or fourth most difficult route described in this guide.

The start of the route is off State Highway 190 at a point two miles east of the road junction opposite the Furnace Creek Inn. Look to the left for a small sign displaying the jeep symbol and reading *"Echo Canyon"*. Start up the wash; there should be tracks to follow. The first ten miles are generally Class II.

The predominate plant at first is creosote, *Larrea tridentata* var. *glutinosa*, a hardy shrub well adapted to its desert environment. The creosote commonly has shallow roots that spread out many feet beyond the plant. Nature causes these bushes to be spaced well apart to reduce competition for moisture, and as the days grow longer, warmer, and drier, the creosotes drop many of their leaves to further reduce moisture loss. The veteran desert naturalist, Edmund Jaeger, once documented creosote bushes that went 32 months without a single drop of rain.

The flat lying beds of rocks on either side of the wash are part of the Furnace Creek Formation, a fanglomerate deposited in the late Pliocene or early Pleistocene, a mere two or three million years ago. The appearance of those layers containing well-rounded rocks suggests that conditions then may have been very similar to those forming the alluvial fans in Death Valley today.

After ascending the gentle slope of Echo Wash for three miles, you will enter the Lower Echo Canyon, and in the canyon the geology changes and becomes very complex. Echo Canyon has eroded through old Cambrian marine sediments that are highly faulted. The Wood Canyon Formation, as it is known, has layers that range from sandstone to dolomite. These rocks were being deposited as silt at the bottom of a once great seabed more than 500 million years ago. The upper layers contain trilobite fossils, some of the very oldest and most primitive marine animals to be found in the fossil record. (Remember that collecting fossils within our National Parks is prohibited.) The older, lower layers of the Wood Canyon Formation are barren of fossils here, suggesting that they might have been deposited at the very dawn of sea life.

The road twists and turns as it winds its way up the canyon. Watch your odometer, because at a point 4.6 miles in from the pavement you will reach *The Eye of The Needle*, a natural window eroded out of the canyon wall to your right. If you take the time to climb to the window (easiest on the western side) you will find that the opening is more than ten feet from top to bottom.

Eye of the Needle

The canyon remains narrow for another half mile, and then it opens into a small valley. At a point 7.8 miles from the highway, a faint set of tracks goes up a wash to the left. This was once the way to the site of Schwab. That road is now closed, but it is just an easy walk of 0.7 of a mile to the old townsite.

The book *Death Valley, A Guide*, published in 1939 as part of the WPA Federal Writers Project, describes Schwab as follows:

> *"Schwab is an old mining camp with a few deserted and tumbling houses and one or two that are still inhabited."*

That may have been the case in the 1930s, but, alas, little is left today. You have to look close or you will walk right by the old townsite. It is the rusty tin cans strewn about that mark the site. Named for Charles M. Schwab, President of Bethlehem Steel and a noted financier of Rhyolite fame, Schwab was a typical Turn of the 20th Century gold camp. Like at its sister cities of Lee and Furnace, the veins of gold here proved to be as elusive as the hopes and dreams upon which they were built. The typical cycle of birth, boom and bust did not take long at Schwab.

To continue on, stay to the right following the clearly defined Class II tracks. A few prospect holes are passed, and in 1.3 miles the road forks. Here a slab foundation is all that remains of a structure once known as *Saddle Cabin*.

By taking the right fork for a half mile, you will come to the camp and millsite of the Inyo Mine. This mine was discovered as part of the Greenwater Excitement in 1905, which caused prospectors to pour over every inch of the Funeral and Black Mountains. The actual mines are high on the hillside to the north; it is the camp and millsite that are in this canyon bottom.

If you take the left fork at Saddle Cabin, the road immediately crosses a low ridge and forks again. The National Park Service has closed the left fork that once went 0.8 of a mile down the wash to Schwab; stay to the right.

Soon the country closes down into a canyon once again, and the road deteriorates to Class III. In a little less than two miles, you will see a cable stretching from the canyon bottom to the ridge top high above. This was once a crude device used to drag machinery up to the Furnace Mine some four hundred feet above. Another cabin site is passed on a knoll to the right.

Jaw Crusher and ball mill
at Inyo Mines in 1968

At a point 2.9 miles above Saddle Cabin, the canyon narrows to a series of three dry waterfalls. The first of these is Class IV; the second and third are an even more challenging Class V. The second obstacle is the worst, but fortunately there is a handy anchor rock above it for those who need to winch themselves up.

Caution: stop and scout the route on foot before attempting to drive any farther. This Class V pitch should not be underestimated. I would not recommend that the drivers of pickups or long wheelbase vehicles attempt these dry falls. When I last scouted this route, a Jeep CJ5 with large tires went up and down the obstacle with ease; however, a Land Rover got hung up on the rocks, and its driver had to winch himself up and over the last half of the ledge. A short bobtail rig can probably make it if the driver first scouts the route and is a skillful and experienced off-roader. This is not a place you would wish to get stuck or have a breakdown.

Beyond the dry falls, it is a relatively easy Class III road to the old 1907 mining camp of Echo, atop 4400' Echo Pass on the crest of the Funeral Range. If you thought Schwab was short lived, Echo was a mere flash in the pan. There are two rusting tin cans at Schwab for every one remaining at Echo.

From the summit of Echo Pass, it is 5½ miles down to the site of Lee, and another 7.4 miles to Valley View Road, the nearest paved road in the Amargosa Valley. For the route description coming up to the pass from the opposite side, see the trail description coming out of Beatty (Excursion #21).

A difficult Class V pitch
in upper Echo Canyon

2

Hole in the Wall

Primary Attraction:	Rugged austere scenery of the Funeral Range, interesting geology, and nature's cactus garden.
Time Required:	Three to four hours out of Furnace Creek Ranch and return.
Miles Involved:	It is 3.7 miles from Highway 190 to Hole in the Wall, 2.4 miles more to the wilderness boundary near the old quarry.
Degree of Difficulty:	Mostly Class II, but Class III conditions may exist in sandy spots.

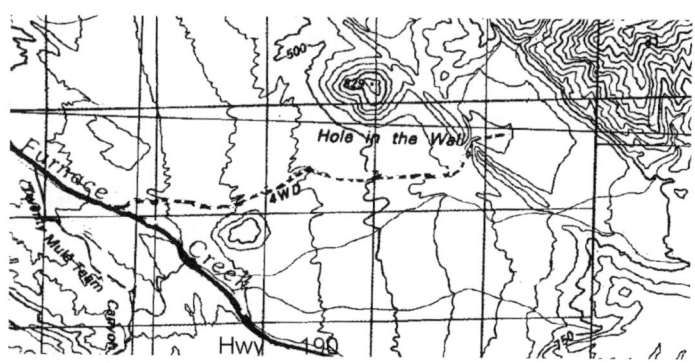

   Hole in the Wall is an easy excursion out of Furnace Creek Ranch, generally no more difficult that Class II unless the sand is soft. The route goes up an unnamed wash, through Hole in the Wall to end at an old rock quarry. Along the way you'll see some fascinating geology.

   From the road junction opposite the Furnace Creek Inn, start eastward on State Route 190, ascending Furnace Creek Wash. At a point five miles up the wash and 0.7 miles above the entrance to Twenty-Mule Team Canyon, look for a sign with the jeep symbol on your left. Turn left here, starting up this side wash. There are usually tracks that have been left by previous vehicles, depending on how recent the last rain was. (Yes, Virginia, it does rain in Death Valley. The average precipitation at the Furnace Creek Ranch is 1.92 inches per year.) There is no established roadway; simply make your way up the wash following the tracks of previous vehicles. The sand is soft in places, but that is why you have four-wheel drive.

The road into Hole in The Wall is
usually no more severe than Class II

At first the most noticeable desert plant is the creosote bush. This shrub spreads its roots out wide in search of moisture. After periods of rainfall, the creosote will quickly react, producing tiny yellow blossoms.

Notice, too, the very abundant growth of Desert Holly, *Atriplex hymenelytra*, thriving in the wash. With its whitish or pale green spiny leaves, this hardy little shrub often grows quite well in soils that are much too salty for other plants. For this reason it is common in the bottom of Death Valley, particularly on the eastern side.

As you proceed up the wash, also notice the gently dipping beds of light brown sandstone that is capped with a darker colored alluvium. The lower layers are part of the Furnace Creek Formation deposited during the Pliocene epoch, just before the massive glaciation of the Pleistocene which made lakes in many of these desert valleys. The Furnace Creek series of sediments is one of the more important geologic formations in Death Valley, because the borate mineral colemanite is found in these layers of compressed mud. The capping layer of desert alluvium was deposited in much later times.

At a point 3.7 miles from Highway 190, you will encounter a fascinating geologic phenomenon called *Hole in the Wall*. As the name implies, a small gap bisects a natural wall of rock some four hundred feet high. It is immediately apparent by the color, texture, and composition that this wall of rock is very much different than the other sediments back down the wash. This formation is the Funeral fanglomerate, and it is older than the Furnace Creek Formation. This band of sediments is composed of both smoothly rounded as well as angular rock fragments, all laid down together in an ancient alluvial fan during the Pliocene some one million years ago. The Furnace Creek Fault on the eastern side of "the wall" has caused these deposits to be pushed upwards, so that the once nearly horizontal layers are now standing on end.

This gash in the Funeral conglomerate
is called the "Hole In The Wall"

After passing through the Hole in the Wall, turn sharply to the right and you will see the remnants of an old road. Driving farther up the wash, you can easily observe five of the thirteen species of cactus to be found in Death Valley. While cacti do not like the salty soils on the floor of Death Valley, they seem to thrive on the alluvial fans and in the washes. Perhaps the most conspicuous cactus here is the so called cottontop or many headed barrel cactus, *Echinocactus polycephalus,* which typically has six to ten barrels growing out of single root mass. The solitary barrel cactus, *Echinocactus acanthodes,* is much less common, but also present. Two species of cholla cactus can be seen here: the Strawtop cholla, *Opuntia echinocarpa,* and the other spiny fruited cholla, *Opuntia erinacea.* Equally abundant are the prickly pear or beaver tail, *Opuntia basilaris.* Present in smaller numbers is the mound cactus, *Echinocereus mojavensis.* Cacti have done a remarkable job of adapting to arid climates. They have the ability to retain moisture when it does rain, and their waxy skins retard moisture loss when it is dry.

Follow the old roadway up the fan. After going 2.4 miles from Hole in the Wall, you will find an old rock quarry. Here slabs of nicely layered travertine were cut and split into convenient sizes for shipping. They were then transported by truck and rail to Los Angeles, where they were used in the construction of the Pacific Coast Borax Building on Shatto Place. Vehicles are now prohibited beyond the quarry, but at one time there was a Class III jeep trail that continued up the wash for another three miles to dead-end in the Red Amphitheater.

3

Furnace, Kunze, and Greenwater

Primary Attraction:	Three Turn of the 20th Century mining camps in the Black Mountains.
Time Required:	This outing can be done in a half day out and back from Furnace Creek, or it can be combined with the Deadman Pass Route, or a Gold Valley excursion for a full day of historical backroad wanderings.
Miles Involved:	It is no more than thirty miles out of Furnace Creek Ranch to the three camps.
Degree of Difficulty:	Generally Class I and II, with only a little easy Class III between Kunze and Greenwater.

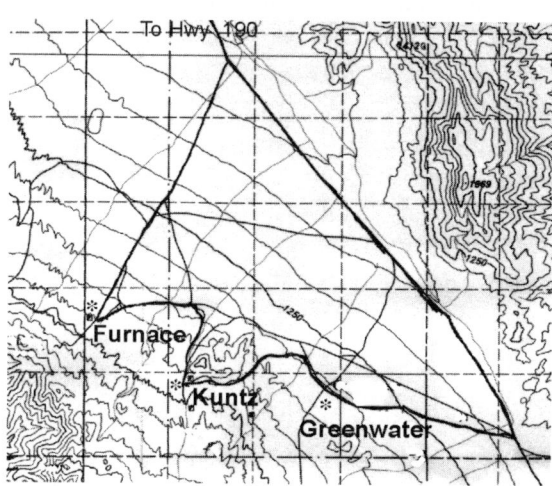

It has been said that the Yukon gold rush of 1898 was the last great gold rush in this nation's history. Don't tell that to Shorty Harris. His discovery at Bullfrog touched off a whole series of gold rushes. In his excellent book *"Nevada's 20th Century Mining Boom"*, Russell Elliott chronicles the major boomtowns of Tonopah in 1900, followed by Goldfield in 1903, Bullfrog and Rhyolite in 1905, Silver Peak, Ramsey, Wonder and Fairview in 1906, and lastly Rawhide in 1908. In 1907 Goldfield was the largest city in the entire State of Nevada!

These mining booms created enormous transportation needs in an area where roads were primitive at best. Half a dozen railroads were built to fill this need. Not only could they bring in heavy mining and milling equipment, but they could also carry out the ore concentrates and bullion. The Tonopah and Goldfield Railroad made connections with the Carson & Colorado near Candalaria. In the other direction, the Las Vegas & Tonopah Railroad came up from the south, as did the Tonopah & Tidewater. The Bullfrog Goldfield Railroad laid some track, too. These railroads created their own prosperity in towns like Las Vegas and Reno, but also spawned new supply points like Beatty and Gold Center. Places like Shoshone and Tecopa were mere sidings, somehow managing to hang on and survive long after the rails were pulled up.

While all of this activity was going on, prospectors were pouring over every mountain and canyon in western Nevada and Eastern California. A few were lucky, finding mineral wealth overlooked in the previous half century of prospecting. These finds gave rise to new, smaller camps. In Nevada, towns like Round Mountain, Manhattan, Silver Peak, Kawich, and Fairview suddenly sprang up overnight. The same was true in Eastern California. In the Death Valley region places like Lee, Echo, and Schwab briefly sprang up out of nowhere and had their day in the sun. In this easy outing, we will visit the sites of three such camps: Furnace, Kunze, and Greenwater.

We start by taking Highway 190 southeast out of Furnace Creek Ranch, ascending Furnace Creek Wash. At a point 10.8 miles above the Furnace Creek Inn, a paved side road turns south towards Ryan and Dante's View; turn right here. Soon the modern-looking works of the Billie Mine are passed on the left. It is the only working borax mine in the Death Valley area. After 2.4 miles a paved road to the left goes to Ryan, an important borax producer between the years of 1915 and 1927. It was the terminus of the seventeen mile long Death Valley Railroad, which connected with the Tonopah & Tidewater at Death Valley Junction.

Continue south on the Dante's View Road. At a point 7.5 miles south of Highway 190, keep to the left on the graded Greenwater Valley Road, rather than following the pavement on to Dante's View. After 2.8 miles of the moderately washboard surface, you will be glad to turn off to the right onto a more comfortable Class I desert road, which makes its way to the southwest into the Black Mountains. Simply follow this road straight up the bajada, and after 3.5 miles you will be in what once was downtown Furnace.

The cycle of birth, boom, and bust all took place in Furnace in three years' time, 1905 to 1907. One is tempted to say that Furnace was a suburb of Greenwater, but that is not entirely true. Furnace had its own industry (copper mines) and its own surveyed townsite, complete with a downtown business district composed of the usual enterprises: a saloon, restaurant, boarding house, stable, and even a post office. The largest structure in Furnace was the Miner's Hospital with eight rooms. (A few months after it was built, the building was cut into thirds and moved to Zabriskie, where it was pieced together and used as a boarding house for the next eleven years. It was then dismantled again and moved to Shoshone, where it still stands to this day.) Furnace also had stage service to Amargosa, a stop on the Tonopah & Tidewater Railroad. Alas however, there was no bank in Furnace. For such financial transactions, one had to go to Greenwater.

The fact that most of the structures in Furnace consisted mainly of tents is irrelevant. The good citizens of Furnace took pride in their community, right up until the time that they shut the town down and moved to Greenwater!

As you might expect from a tent camp, there are no Rhyolite-like ruins to mark the townsite, rather just a few stone walls and flat areas where tents were once pitched. High up on the ridge, several hundred feet above the townsite are most of the copper mines which briefly gave life to the community. The largest block of claims were the Furnace Creek Copper Company, financed by Seattle businessman, "Patsy" Clark, who had made a fortune in the Yukon Excitement. There are several Class II roads that go from one mine to the next. Specimens of copper ore minerals can be found on some of the mine dumps. The bright green mineral is malachite; the blue mineral is azurite. (Note, however, that rock hounding and mineral collecting in Death Valley National Park is prohibited.)

To continue on to the old camps of Kunze and Greenwater, keep right on the road below Furnace, heading east. In about a mile, look for a Class I road going to the right up a canyon. In 1.2 miles a side road to the right turns south, climbs the fan, and within a mile you will come to stone ruins marking the lower residential district of Kunze, a camp even more obscure than Furnace. Continue driving up the wash another quarter of a mile to reach the downtown district.

In his little book, *"Greenwater"*, noted desert writer, Harold O. Weight, retells the controversy as to who it was that first found copper in this part of the Funeral Range. By some accounts it was Arthur Kunze, right here in this little canyon early in 1904. Others say it was late in 1904 that Phil Creasor and Fred Birney, who had been grubstaked by "Patsy" Clark, found copper. That argument aside, there is no doubt that Arthur Kunze sold his claims to eastern steel magnate Charles Schwab in July of 1906, and it was this action that set off the stampede to the Greenwater Mining District.

Of the three camps Kunze was the smallest, perhaps doomed by its close proximity to Greenwater just to the south. The founding fathers had drawn a plot map with streets laid out and lots subdivided, but the camp didn't have time to develop much more than a city of white canvas tents. Ironically however, the stone structures put up in Kunze have lasted far longer than the wooden buildings of Greenwater. Of this trio of camps, more history survives in Kunze, but admittedly, that is limited to mine dumps, a few stone walls, and a lot of broken glass.

The last surviving building in Kuntz

From downtown Kunze, a Class II road goes east over a saddle in the hills, where it passes a mine tailings dump, and briefly deteriorates to Class III as it makes its way down the hillside. From the last mine in Kunze, it is only 1.5 miles on to the site of Greenwater. Alas, there is little left to mark the site today. Some rascal has created a monument of rusty metal to artistically mark the major intersection of downtown Greenwater.

Named after a small spring on the hillside two miles to the south, Greenwater was laid out on the bajada where it had room to grow. Situated at an elevation of nearly 4,300 feet, Greenwater had everything a town could want: fresh desert breezes, a great view, and of course, the promise of great mineral wealth that would rival and exceed the great copper deposits of Butte, Montana. Oh sure, Greenwater had its shortcomings, too. There was no water within miles, and the nearest railroad was nearly twenty miles away. But surely Greenwater sat upon the greatest copper deposit in the world, and all of those problems would be quickly resolved.

As word of Schwab's investment leaked out, the saloons and boarding houses of Goldfield and Tonopah emptied overnight. In late 1906 and early 1907 the population of Greenwater went from seventy to more than one thousand. More than 2,500 claims were staked in the surrounding hills in a matter of weeks.

Staking claims was no easy task. This is Inyo County, and in order to record a claim, one had to go to the Inyo County Courthouse in Independence. This meant getting a seat on one of the automobiles that carried passengers north to the southern end of the Bullfrog Goldfield Railroad, which would take you north to Goldfield. From there one had to next get on the northbound train of the Tonopah & Goldfield Railroad, taking it to McSweeney Junction east of Tonopah. Here there was another train change which would take you west to Tonopah Junction, where a southbound train of the Carson & Colorado would take you to Kearsarge Station. From here a buckboard took passengers the last five miles into Independence. Altogether, the four hundred-mile trip from Greenwater to Independence was a journey of two days by rail. The only alternative was an arduous 180-mile trek across Death Valley and Panamint Valley to Keeler, where one could catch a train north to Kearsarge.

Nevertheless, Greenwater prospered for a year, even though not a single ounce of copper had been smelted. No less than fifty companies were formed, each burrowing in the ground and issuing stock fast and furiously. Stock in the Furnace Creek Copper Company went from an initial offering of $.25 a share to $5.50 in a matter of weeks. The Greenwater & Death Valley Copper Company did not do as well. It too went to $5.50 a share, but it had an initial offering price of $1.00. Altogether an estimated thirty million dollars was invested in Greenwater mining ventures in a three-month period.

Greenwater started as a tent city, but by late 1906 more substantial buildings appeared, built with lumber carried by train from Tonopah to Death Valley Junction and then by mule-drawn freight wagon over Deadman Pass (see Excursion #22). At its peak, Greenwater had the usual mining town amenities: several saloons and general stores, a drug store, a livery stable, a bank, many boarding houses, and of course, a red light district. The Tonopah & Tidewater Railroad even opened an office here anticipating that a spur line would be brought in. The people were so keenly interested in the goings on here, that Greenwater soon had two newspapers, "The Greenwater Miner" and the "Chuck-Walla". They sold as many copies in San Francisco, Tonopah, and Goldfield as they did in Greenwater.

Main Street in Greenwater circa 1906
(Photo courtesy of Nevada Historical Society)

Alas, it all came crashing down in the summer of 1907. By then it had become clear that while Greenwater had copper, it simply was not in concentrations high enough to make it worth mining. With the mines closing down, there was no longer a reason for anyone to live here. The population left as rapidly as they had come. In January 1907, Greenwater had a population of seven hundred; by September it was down to one hundred. One of the last to leave was Deputy Sheriff Charles Brown, who departed in 1909. Desert freight-hauler, R.J. Fairbanks, bought most of the abandoned houses for a song, had them dismantled and then rebuilt in Shoshone. Thus it has often been said, "If you want to see Greenwater, look in Shoshone!"

There is a good Class I road heading northeast from the Greenwater "monument" 1.8 miles down the fan to rejoin the graded Greenwater Valley Road. This takes you back to the paved Dante's View Road. Or you can choose the fork that heads southeast, and after nearly twenty miles come out onto State Highway 178 at a point six miles west of Shoshone. Still another alternative is to head for Shoshone as described above, but to turn off to the left off the Greenwater Valley Road at a point 12.2 miles from Greenwater. This will take you over lonely Deadman Pass (as described in Excursion # 22) and put you on State Highway 127 at a point 7.6 miles south of Death Valley Junction. Yet another possibility is to proceed southeast 2.4 miles down to the Greenwater Valley Road and then on another 9.3 miles where a right turn will head you into Gold Valley (as described in Excursion # 23).

If you are a history buff, a day spent in the old mining camps of the Black Mountains can be rewarding and interesting.

This monument of rusted cans marks
the site of downtown Greenwater

4

Trail Canyon

Primary Attraction: Of all the well-watered canyons that you can drive into on the east side of the Panamints, Trail Canyon is the most northerly and easily accessible from Furnace Creek Ranch. The road has been in use by miners for nearly a century.

Time Required: If you hurry, and who wants to do that, this outing can be done in half a day out of Furnace Creek Ranch.

Miles Involved: The one way distance from Furnace Creek Ranch to the end of the road in Trail Canyon is 23 miles. All but seven of those miles are over dirt roads.

Degree of Difficulty: Most of the roads are of graded dirt or are Class I. Once you get into the canyon proper, it is mostly Class II, with only a little easy Class III.

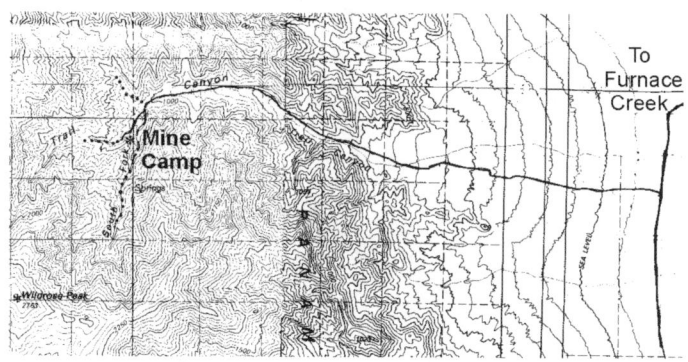

At one time it was possible to drive up Trail Canyon all the way to Aguereberry Point and Harrisburg Flats. In that eleven-mile journey you were able go from 276 feet below sea level to 6,240 feet above sea level on Class II and III roads. You can still drive into Trail Canyon, and you can still drive to Harrisburg Flats and Aguereberry Point, but the four miles of spectacular road in between the two points have been washed out, and the National Park Service has decided not to restore it. Even with the heart cut out of this breathtaking route, a trip into Trail Canyon is still interesting.

Trail Canyon is found by taking the Badwater Road six miles south of the Furnace Creek Inn to where the West Side Road goes off on the right. Turn here and follow this wide graded road south across the salt flats of the Devil's Golf Course for another five miles. Here a National Park Service sign saying *"Trail Canyon"* points west to a road heading towards the still distant Panamint Mountains; turn right here. This easy Class II road begins its climb up the alluvial fan. No camping is permitted along the first two miles. At a point three miles up from the West Side Road, our route crosses the main wash and soon enters the canyon proper. The road deteriorates in the wash, and while four-wheel drive is not absolutely necessary, there are some easy Class III sections.

The road into Trail Canyon
is mostly Class I and II

In the springtime after a wet winter, the wild heliotrope, *Phacelia*, can put on an awesome display of colorful purple splendor here in Trail Canyon. A word of warning, however; the genus *Phacelia* is very large and some of its species, like *crenulata,* can cause a reaction on human skin similar to poison oak! Not only is it against National Park regulations to pick the wildflowers, but if you do so, your punishment may swiftly come from Mother Nature, if not from Smokey The Bear!

Another plant you do not want close contact with is known as cottontop, Mohave Redhead, or many-headed barrel cactus, *Echinocactus polycephalus*. Its spines are very sharp. Growing in clusters of from five to thirty barrels in a bunch, it is very abundant on the hillside to the left, a mile into the canyon. There are thirteen different species of cactus in the park, representing four different genera. The cottontop is one of the most common, and where you see one, you are likely to see many. Trail Canyon is no exception. To catch its fragrant flower you must see it in the heat of summer. The fruit produces seeds that were a staple in the diet of the Shoshone Indians.

Another common cactus in the canyons of the Panamints, although not present in as many numbers, is the Engelmannn's hedgehog or calico cactus, *Echinocereus engelmanni*. This species and its cousin the mound cactus, *Echinocereus mojavensis,* can both be seen in Trail Canyon. Look for them on the left, two miles inside the canyon.

Notice the bedrock geology as you make your way up the canyon. These are largely marine sediments ranging from the late Precambrian Period, some 560 million years old, to the late Ordovician, 435 million years old. This is a time span of more than one hundred million years. Tilted at a steep angle Ordovician age rocks of the Ely Springs dolomite are encountered as you enter the canyon. These are the youngest rocks in the sequence you will see. As you go up the canyon, the rocks will become older. The next formation is Eureka quartzite, once a very white sand deposited at the bottom of an ancient sea during the middle of the Ordovician Period. In sharp contrast to the white Eureka sandstone, the next sequence is the Pogonip Series of shale interspersed with dolomite. Its layers were deposited very early in the Ordovician times. The upper most layers of the Pogonip sometimes contain fossil gastropods and brachiopods, shellfish that lived on the sea bottom. The Cambrian layers begin in the time sequence below the Pogonip and are encountered as you go farther into Trail Canyon. Representing the late Cambrian Period is the Nopah Formation, which was once limestone, and has now mostly metamorphosed into dolomite. The next oldest is the Bonanza King Formation consisting mainly of shale, limestone and dolomite. Older yet in Cambrian times come the various layers of silt, shale and limestone of the Carrara Formation. In places this formation is rich in trilobite fossils, the very first hard-shelled animals to scurry about the sea bottom. Next comes its slightly older cousin, the Zabriskie Point Formation, a quartzite that never contains fossils. Finally, where Trail Canyon forks into three, we find the Wood Canyon Formation. These early Cambrian layers of shales and limestones contain the oldest fossils found in Death Valley National Park. They represent a time in the earth's history when marine animals made the transition from soft organisms like worms and jellyfish to hard-shelled bottom dwellers. Beyond the forks you come to the oldest layer yet, the Sterling quartzite that goes back into the late Proterozoic Era when life forms on earth were extremely primitive, leaving no fossil record.

So, it was not until the early Paleozoic Era that sea life began to evolve to the point where traces of them can be easily found in the fossil record. Even then sea life consisted mostly of hard-shelled creatures such as trilobites, brachiopods and gastropods, and soft tissue organisms like sponges and worms. Can some of these marine fossils be found in the strata of Trail Canyon? Yes. Can you collect specimens? No. Fossil collecting is prohibited in our National Parks.

After you have ascended the canyon for five miles, the canyon divides into three branches. At a point 9.4 miles in from the West Side Road the Aguereberry Point road once turned off to the right. The road now has one of those ugly *NO VEHICLES* signs posted on it. If you wish to walk up it for a half-mile or so, you will come to the Tarantula Mine.

During the Korean Conflict era of the early 1950s, tungsten was in great demand for use as an alloy to harden steel. California was a major producer of tungsten, with mines at Atolia near Randsburg, Coyote and Pine Creeks near Bishop, and several locations in the High Sierra above Bass and Shaver Lakes. The Tarantula Mine in Trail Canyon was Death Valley's contribution to meet the demand for tungsten. The mineral scheelite, the most common tungsten ore, was first found here during World War II in quartz veins in a metamorphosed zone between limestone and granite. At that time, the property was named The Victory Tungsten Mine. Because of its remote location and difficulty of access, the mine shipped but one ton of ore. That was in 1943. A decade later when the price of tungsten shot way up, the access road switch-backing down from Aguereberry Point was built, and the mine was reopened under the name of the Tarantula Mine. This time hundreds of tons of ore with assay values of from 2 to 12% tungsten were shipped. Production peaked in 1958, although continued exploration of the orebody is said to have gone on until as recently as 1971.

Scheelite gives off a unique sheen under ultra violet light. If you should have a battery powered UV light, you might look over the mine dump after dark. The scheelite will be obvious. You might also find the copper minerals of azurite (blue), malachite (green) and bornite (bronze looking) although they do not fluoresce under a UV light. Remember that with the passage of the Mining in the Parks Act of 1976, rock hounding and mineral collecting are no longer permitted in Death Valley.

If you are really ambitious, you can continue to hike the remaining 3.5 miles

Trail Canyon

up to the graded road, then another 1.5 miles out to Aguereberry Point. Such a walk involves a vertical gain of 2,400 feet.

Leaving this one time fork in the road, today's road swings to the left and within fifty yards forks again. The left fork is in a wash and can be easily missed. This fork soon deteriorates to Class IV as it goes up the south fork of the canyon another mile to where there are some springs and, with them, the new Wilderness boundary. Further vehicle traffic is prohibited. Originally the road went on another mile to the McBride Camp, called the Morning Glory Camp by some, where several buildings still remain. In this heavily mineralized area was the Old Dependable antimony mine, and high on the hillside, the Morning Glory Mine whose tramline brought down lead, silver, zinc and copper ores.

At this second fork, the main road keeps to the right. The Tarantula Mine Camp is reached within a quarter of a mile. This makes a good campsite, particularly for groups, as there are adequate flat places among the deteriorating buildings, and it is far enough from the nearest water so that camping is not prohibited. The road continues up the middle fork a short distance and soon ends. Beyond are a series of mines and prospect holes.

The Tarantula Mine Camp

5

Hanaupah Canyon

Primary Attraction: Interesting geologic features and old mines.

Time Required: Hanaupah Canyon alone can be seen in half a day out of Furnace Creek, but when combined with jaunts into Trail Canyon to the north, or Johnson Canyon to the south, a full day of back road exploration is required.

Miles Involved: It is 17.8 miles from Furnace Creek Ranch to Shorty's Well. From there to the end of the road in Hanaupah Canyon is another eight miles.

Degree of Difficulty: Mostly Class II or better, except for the last mile and a half which are Class III.

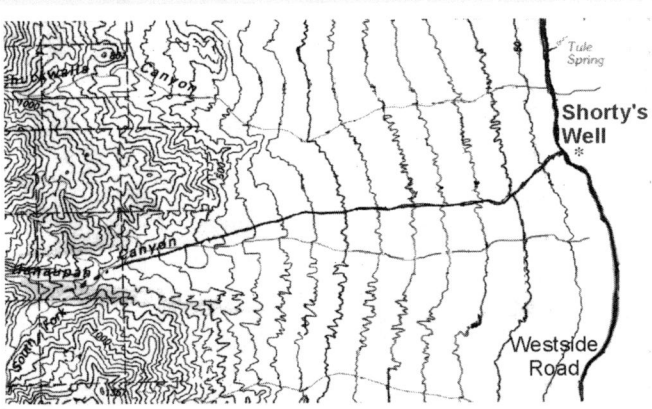

Hanaupah Canyon is one of a score of canyons in the east slope of the Panamint Range that contain reliable year around water. The presence of this life giving liquid has not only attracted wildlife, but also early Indians in Death Valley. In later years, it was sourdough prospectors who were scrambling over every inch of these mountains in search of that elusive rich vein.

Hanaupah Canyon is accessed off the West Side Road. Go south down the valley from the Furnace Creek Inn 6.1 miles to the West Side Road. The turnoff to the right is well marked. This graded road goes down the western side of Death Valley for some 35 miles to rejoin the paved Badwater road near the Ashford Mill ruins.

Hanaupah Canyon

For Hanaupah Canyon, however, we are taking the West Side Road only 10.2 miles to Shorty's Well. The site of the well is a few hundred yards east of the West Side Road. The story is that Alexander "Shorty" Borden (not to be confused with his contemporary, Frank "Shorty Harris" of Bullfrog fame) dug this well by hand. Although it was a shallow well at the edge of the salt flats, the water was said to be fresh. I first sampled the water in 1956 and the notes I scribbled on my topo sheet were *"hand-pump, brackish"*. Since then, the well has all but disappeared.

While you are looking around, notice the mounds of pickleweed, *Allenrolfea occidentalis,* a low sprawling shrub very common at the edge of the salt flats all along the West Side Road. This is the most salt tolerant of all the desert plants, even more so than the two exotic tamarisk species introduced into Death Valley by man around the turn of the 20th century.

At Shorty's Well a Class I road heads westward up the alluvial fan. You reach sea level at a point 0.8 miles from the West Side Road, and a tenth of a mile beyond, cross a north/south trending earthquake fault. The escarpment can be clearly seen, but perhaps best when backlighted in the late afternoon sun. The vertical displacement along this fault scarp measures between twenty and fifty feet.

Geomorphologists have closely studied the Hanaupah fan, because at least four surface depositional layers can be identified: one at 550-800 thousand years, one at 120-190 thousand years, one at 15-30 thousand years and the most recent surface laid down a couple of thousands of years ago. The layer of patina on the rocks, so-called desert varnish, has dated the most recent layers. The older surfaces have been dated by a more complex carbon isotope method.

As you make your way up the alluvial fan, you might appreciate the road a little more to know that all nine miles of it were built solely by Shorty Borden, using only simple hand tools, with his two burros as his only companions. He had found a lode of silver in Hanaupah Canyon and needed a road to properly work it, even though he himself owned no vehicle. He started the project in September of 1932 and completed it six months later in March of 1933.

When I last scouted this road in the spring of 1998 to update this book, I was struck by the vast quantity of orange dodder that covered all of the native vegetation. Dodder is a parasite because it contains no chlorophyll and, hence, cannot manufacture its own food like most green plants do. Once established on another plant, it relies on its host plant for its nutrients, and eventually kills its host. In the spring of 1998 dodder seemed to be much more widespread throughout Death Valley than I ever recall seeing it before. One wonders if its spread was related to the unusually heavy El Niño rains that fell during the winter of 1997/98.

Curiously, as you make your way up Hanaupah Canyon, the cactus is noticeable by its absence. How can this happen when Trail Canyon just to the north has lots of it, as does Johnson Canyon just to the south?

As you drive up the fan, one cannot help but notice Telescope Peak, the highest point in Death Valley National Park. The elevation at the summit is 11,049 feet. It typically carries a mantle of snow from November well into April. A few hardy souls attempt to climb the peak from the end of the road in Hanaupah Canyon. It is a grueling two-day siege involving a vertical ascent of 7,500 feet. I always preferred the conventional route, by trail from Mahogany Flat, which involves a still respectable climb of 3,000 feet.

At a point 4.8 miles from the West Side Road, Shorty's old road drops down into the wash. Before descending this short grade, stop a moment and look around. To the west, of course, Telescope Peak dominates the skyline. Behind you, to the east are good views of the salt flats 2,000 feet lower in the bottom of Death Valley. But looking to the south and west notice as well how the old alluvial fan surface coming out of Hanaupah Canyon has been deeply cut into by today's wash. This suggests that sometime after this older fan was deposited, the Panamint Mountains began a new cycle of uplift, causing more recent flash floods of the last ten thousand years to cut down through the older fan surface. The new floods have caused erosion, rather than deposition. Studies of the old levels of Ice Age Lake Panamint on the western side of the range confirm this recent uplift theory. Geologists say that the Panamint Mountains are 67 feet higher today than they were 15,000 years ago when Lake Panamint was full and overflowing down Wingate Wash.

The road drops into the wash and at the bottom of this short but steep grade Chuckawalla Canyon comes in from the right. This is probably the best place in Hanaupah Canyon where camping is permitted, particularly if you have a group of several vehicles. At a point 6.8 miles in from the West Side Road, the canyon makes a turn to the south, and with it the road turns to Class III. In a mile the canyon swings west again and soon, you may see your first trickle of water upon the sand. Today's road ends at a point eight miles in from the West Side Road. At one point, the road continued on up another mile to a fork in the canyon, and to Shorty's mine in the northern fork. Camping is not permitted here because of the close proximity of water at the road's end. The ground is very rocky and there are not really any good places anyway. Better to return to Chuckawalla Canyon for that.

Archaeologists have excavated sites in Hanaupah Canyon, which show Indian occupation well over 1,000 years ago. In the Death Valley context this may not be so remarkable, because stone tools from other sites go back 9,000 years or more. Nevertheless, Hanaupah Canyon suited the Indians well, providing not only water, but also game and natural plant foods ranging from wild grapes to pinyon pine nuts.

If you are of a mind to climb Telescope Peak, avid Death Valley hiker Michael Digonnet recommends a trailless ascent of the ridge between the south and middle forks of the canyon to the 10,000 foot level, where you can pick up the trail from Mahogany Flat. Good luck!

Hanaupah Canyon Road

6

Johnson Canyon,
Where Hungry Bill Once Lived

Primary Attraction:	Of all the canyons on the eastern slope of the Panamints, Johnson is my favorite because of its scenery and historical connection with Panamint City.
Time Required:	This is an all day's outing from Furnace Creek, even if you don't leave your vehicle. The hike up to Hungry Bill's Ranch is highly recommended, however, and to do that, you had better plan on a two-day excursion and camping in the canyon.
Miles Involved:	From Furnace Creek Ranch to the start of the Johnson Canyon Road is 27.8 miles, plus another 10.4 miles to the end of the road.
Degree of Difficulty:	The first six miles are mostly Class I and Class II. The last four miles are both Class II and Class III.

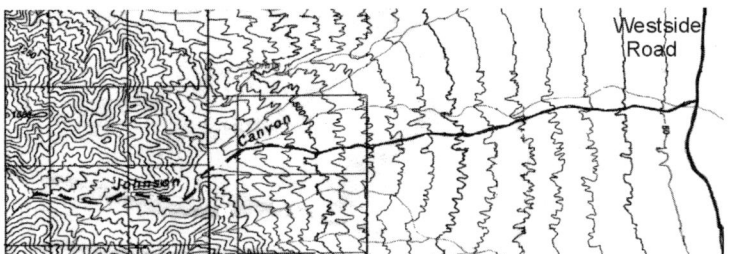

Those interested in history, hiking, nature, and wildlife photography will all find the trip into Johnson Canyon a worthwhile endeavor. Take the Badwater Road south of the Furnace Creek Inn. After going south 6.1 miles, take the graded West Side Road turning off to the right. Soon you will be crossing the barren salt flats known as "The Devil's Golf Course". Five miles from the pavement, the Trail Canyon Road is passed, and after four more miles you will come to Tule Spring. This is probably the site of "Bennett's Long Camp",

Johnson Canyon, Where Hungry Bill Once Lived

where in January of 1850 the exhausted and starving Bennett-Arcan Party of emigrants could go no farther. They sent two of their younger men, William Manly and John Rogers, ahead with meager rations and $60 in coin. "The Boys" were to scout the way to civilization, buy fresh horses and supplies, and return. They did just that, going to San Francisquito Ranch (near today's Newhall) and back in only 26 days.

Continue south on the West Side Road heading towards Shorty's Well. Notice the prominent fault scarp on the Hanaupah alluvial fan about three quarters of a mile to your right. This twenty-foot embankment was caused when the eastern side of the fault dropped in relation to the western side. The escarpment is still fresh, exhibiting only minor erosion. This suggests the faulting took place relatively recently, perhaps even within the last thousand years.

Along the West Side Road a mile and a half south of Shorty's Well are the graves of two noted Death Valley sourdoughs, Jim Dayton and Shorty Harris. Dayton died here in the summer of 1898. Harris died three decades later in 1934, and at his own request, Shorty Harris was buried here beside his friend.

A half-mile farther to the south are the ruins of the Eagle Borax Works, the very first borax mining operation in Death Valley. Unfortunately for its owner, it was also the first such operation to go broke. A sign and an unsold pile of borax, still awaiting shipment, mark the site.

Finally, after you have gone south on the West Side Road for 19.7 miles, a Park Service sign points the way to Johnson Canyon; turn right here. As you start up the alluvial fan, a groan of protest from your engine advises you that the grade is steeper than it appears. The road surface hovers someplace between Class I and Class II. Notice how barren and devoid of life the bajada surface is. Only a few hardy creosotes manage to grow in the small gullies. In the loose and disturbed soil along the road, however, the curious Desert Trumpet, *Eriogonum inflatum*, has managed to find a foothold. Some people use the tender tips of the stems to add zest to salads, but, of course, picking native plants is not permitted in our National Parks. If you want to sample this morsel, plenty can be found outside of the park in Panamint Valley and Searles Valley.

At a point 6.4 miles up from the West Side Road, the Johnson Canyon Road drops down into the wash and deteriorates. Sometimes the route is Class II, sometimes an easy Class III. At a point 8.7 miles from the West Side Road, the canyon forks. At one time it was possible to drive up the left or south fork for a short distance. The National Park Service has now closed that road, so you must keep to the right in the north fork.

At a point ten miles off the West Side Road you encounter the first flowing water. The canyon is alive with wildflowers if you venture into here in the springtime. The "P's" are well represented by phacelia, primrose, phlox, popcorn, paintbrush, and pentstamen. Other blossoms you are likely to see come from chia, fiddleneck, gilia, and mallow.

The road forces its way upstream through a thicket of willow, and ends beneath a large cottonwood tree where a corral was once located. Over the years a lot of people have camped in this inviting spot. Although it is close to water, camping is still permitted here.

By walking a quarter of a mile beyond the end of the road, you will see an old arrastra on the south side of the trail. Miners commonly used this crude device in the 1850-80s to crush and pulverize ore so that the gold could be extracted. A single horse or burro would walk around and around, pulling a horizontal beam that pivoted on a vertical shaft. The beam would drag a large boulder around within a circular rock-lined race. Ore and water were added occasionally and the pulverized ore, now the consistency of fine sand, was drawn off so that the gold could be panned out. While this simple method was not very efficient, the device was relatively easy to construct and cheap to operate.

A short distance up the trail are the rock outlines of a second arrastra, an aqueduct, and what appears to be a primitive reduction furnace. Beyond, the trail climbs the south wall of the canyon to avoid the willow-choked streambed. After hiking an hour or so, a little less than two miles, you will come to the massive stone walls that mark the site of Hungry Bill's Ranch.

Death Valley historian, Richard Lingenfelter, says that the site of Hungry Bill's Ranch was once the site of the Shoshone village of *Puaitungani* (said to mean "Mouse Cave"). During the boom days of Panamint City's heyday, a Kentuckian by the name of William Johnson moved in, cleared, terraced, and irrigated land, and grew a variety of vegetables which he sold for a good price to the hungry residents of Panamint City. He made so much in his first growing season that he terraced even more land and started orchards of apples, pears, peaches, apricots, and figs. Alas, the boom at Panamint City died before his fruit trees were mature. No longer having any customers for his crops, Johnson abandoned his works and moved on to the Kern River country. Upon Johnson's departure, Hungry Bill, a Shoshone chief of immense size and appetite, moved onto the land and filed a homestead claim. He lived there off and on until his death in 1919. Although Hungry Bill's Ranch has been abandoned for years, some of the orchards, vineyards, and terraced and fenced lands remain. When I first visited the site in the 1950s, the trail in was reasonably good. I recall picking enough of the stunted and half worm-eaten apples to make a pie. There were a few figs, too. The last time I was in there, the trail had become overgrown and I didn't see any edible fruit. If you don't mind a little hike of a couple of miles, the trip into Hungry Bill's Ranch is one of the more interesting walks in the park.

For the really ambitious, one can continue on up the canyon to 8,070'

Panamint Pass. Even forty years ago this trail was badly washed out in places and sometimes hard to find. It has only deteriorated further in recent years. Nevertheless, if a car shuttle can be arranged, a two or three day traverse of the Panamints from Johnson Canyon to Christ Wicht's Camp in Surprise Canyon is a memorable experience.

End of the road in Johnson Canyon

7

Galena Canyon,
The Home of "White Gold"

Primary Attraction:	An opportunity to see, close-up, how talc was once mined.
Time Required:	Because of its semi-remote location and distance from the major areas of the park, Galena Canyon will be an all day excursion, but one that can be combined with Warm Springs Canyon.
Miles Involved:	The Galena Canyon Road leaves the West Side Road at a point 32.6 miles south of Furnace Creek Ranch, or 41 miles west of Shoshone. The distance up the canyon is another 5.6 miles.
Degree of Difficulty:	The Galena Canyon Road is mostly Class I; however, in order to visit some of the mines off this road, Class III roads will be encountered.

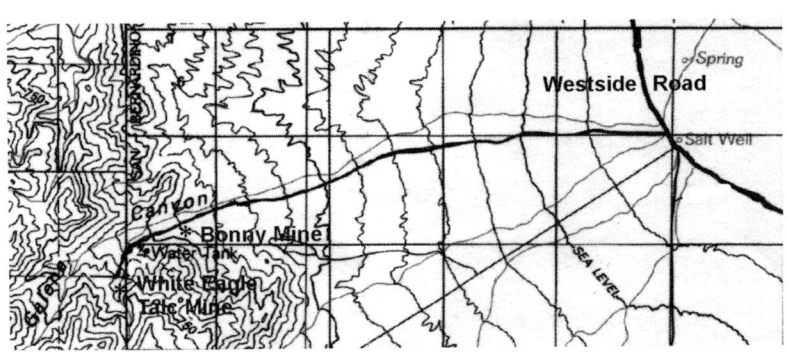

The mineral *galena* is the major ore mineral of lead. Presumably then, in a place called Galena Canyon one might understandably expect to find lead and lead mines. Right? Wrong. Galena Canyon in Death Valley is not noted for the heavy dark gray lead mineral, but a soft, lightweight, sparkling white mineral that is used to dust a baby's bottom - talc! You figure it out. I can offer no explanation.

The lack of lead notwithstanding, Galena Canyon nevertheless makes an

Gallena Canyon, The Home Of "White Gold"

interesting destination for an outing in the southern end of Death Valley. The Galena Canyon Road leaves the West Side Road 10.2 miles north of the south intersection of the Badwater Road and the West Side Road. This is 25.5 miles south of the north intersection of those same two roads. Clear enough, huh?

Turning west off the West Side Road, the Galena Canyon Road gradually starts up the alluvial fan. At one time this road saw heavy traffic from fully loaded ore trucks. Since the mines closed, road maintenance has also ceased, and the roadway has deteriorated a bit to Class I.

If you elect to visit Galena Canyon, try to do so in late April or early May. Once you leave the salt flats of the valley floor, there is a mile or so along the north side of this road where the Beavertail Cactus, *Opuntia basilaris*, grow in great abundance. In the springtime, their deep rose color blossoms are quite beautiful. This is a good place to see and enjoy them.

There were four major talc mines in Galena Canyon, all operated at one time or another by the Minerals, Pigments, and Metals Division of a major pharmaceutical firm, Pfizer, Inc. As you come to them, they are the Bonny Mine, the Mongolian Mine, the Mammoth Mine, and finally, the White Eagle Mine.

At a point 4.4 miles in from the West Side Road, the first of these talc mines can be seen off to the left. It is here that the road to the Bonny Mine's giant open pit left the Galena Canyon Road. Although intentionally scarified by Pfizer, the Bonny Mine Road remains a passable Class III. The Bonny Mine was the largest producer of talc in Galena Canyon in the period 1970 to 1975, when it produced 29,645 short tons of talc worth $1,612,000. **Use extreme caution in wandering around these mines**.

You cannot help but notice two large rusting tanks standing upright on the hillside just a quarter of a mile up the Galena Canyon Road. A steep, but otherwise good Class III road goes up to them. The route is a tenth of a mile beyond the tunnels of the Mammoth Mine. Unlike those of its neighbors, the Bonny and Mongolian Mines, the Mammoth orebody was worked from underground tunnels. **These tunnels, or adits, remain open today, but obviously, they should not be entered under any circumstances**. The talc came out of the underground works in small ore cars that were pushed onto a platform over the twin tanks, where the ore was stored for truck transport to market.

What is talc and what is it used for, other than the obvious talcum powder? Pure talc is hydrous magnesium silicate, affectionately known as $Mg_3(Si_4O_{12})OH_2$ to the chemist. It is used by a number of industries including auto, paint, paper, ceramic, plastic, rubber, roofing, and petroleum manufacturers. Commercial talc is classified in four categories: "Soft platy talc", used in more products than any other type, "Steatite", the most pure, and the most expensive for its excellent insulating properties, "Tremolite talc", and "Mixed talc" (most commercial talc products are a mix of these four types).

All of the talc deposits in Galena Canyon and from adjoining Warm Springs Canyon (see Excursion # 9) come from the Crystal Spring Formation, which are among the oldest layers of the larger Pahrump Group. The talc was formed when diabase, an igneous rock, was intruded into limestone and dolomite beds in the middle of the formation. The heat and pressure created by the diabase altered the carbonate beds to talc.

The Crystal Spring Formation is Precambrian in age, and often 3,000 to 4,200 feet thick. I was once talking to a Johns-Mansville geologist in Warm Springs Canyon, who made the comment: *"You show me an outcrop of the Warms Springs Formation, and I will show you talc"*. The Crystal Spring Formation is very widespread in the southern part of Death Valley. For years, Inyo County was a major producer of talc.

Talc mining in the Death Valley area began in 1910, although the Galena Canyon Mines are not that old. The White Eagle is probably the oldest mine in Galena Canyon, and it was first opened in 1939.

From the turnoff up to the Mammoth Mine, the main access road passes two cabins of the Mammoth Mine camp. A Class II road turns off to the right, heading up Galena Canyon at a point 0.9 miles beyond the cabins. These tracks dead-end within a half-mile. The main road curves to the left and it, too, soon dead-ends at the enormous ore bunker of the White Eagle Mine. Again, stay out of the underground workings; they are no place for amateurs. Specimens of steatite grade talc can be found around the ore bunker. As strange as it may sound, prior to passage of the Mining in the Parks Act of 1976, talc miners could lawfully haul away thousands of tons of this material; however today, the collecting of even one small piece is illegal.

Ore bunker of the White Eagle Talc Mine

8

Carbonate and the Queen of Sheba Mine

Primary Attraction: An obscure and short-lived Turn of the 20th Century mining camp.

Time Required: This excursion can be done in half a day out of Furnace Creek Ranch, but because of the distance it would be better to combine it with another west side outing for a full day's activity.

Miles Involved: This site is 37 miles south of Furnace Creek Ranch via the West Side Road. It is 44 miles from Shoshone via State Route 178.

Degree of Difficulty: The roads are all good, except for the last 3.9 miles which are Class II and III.

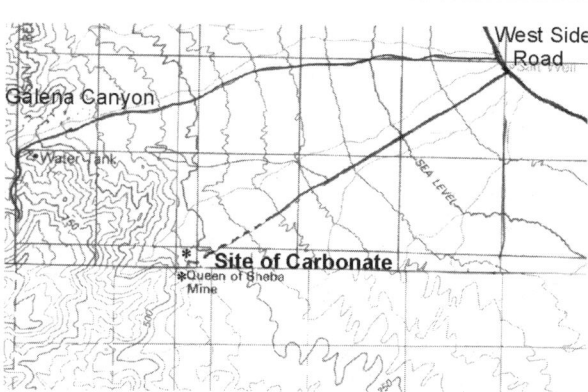

The site of Carbonate is reached by taking the West Side Road south through Death Valley. At a point 32.6 miles south of Furnace Creek Ranch, the Galena Canyon Road goes off to the right. Continue south on the West Side Road another 0.1 miles. On the left are two rusting steel tanks. On the right a road heads south and west, straight up the bajada toward the distant hills. This is the road to Carbonate.

When Goldfield Consolidated Mines was doing exploration work in the Queen of Sheba Mine back in 1952-53, this road was in much better condition. Since that time the road has deteriorated and it has had several minor washouts. Today the road up from the valley floor is Class II for the first two miles, and then turns into a very easy Class III for the last two miles.

The Queen of Sheba Mine camp is reached at a point 3.9 miles up from the West Side Road. This mine was the last to be worked and only a couple of its buildings and an ore bunker survive to this day. The old camp of Carbonate was situated down in the wash, just north of the Queen of Sheba Mine. Although the camp consisted mostly of white canvas tents, Carbonate was said to have had a saloon and a couple of stores. Practically nothing has survived. Up on the ridge above the camp was Chester Pray's Carbonate Mine.

Curiously, Carbonate was the only mining camp on the east slope of the Panamint Range. In 1908 a drifter from Nevada named Chester Pray stumbled upon the mineral cerrusite (lead carbonate) on the mountainside just south of Galena Canyon. His find was in the Noonday dolomite, 700 million-year-old marine sediments of the Precambrian age. Pray dug several tunnels and otherwise explored his find for several years, but shipped no ore. In 1913 he approached Jack Salsberry, a big promoter from Tonopah. With Pray and one other partner, Salsberry formed the Carbonate Lead Mines. Pray had ore blocked out, but no means to ship it to a smelter. He began the arduous task of building a road for forty miles to the Tonopah & Tidewater Railroad station at Zabriskie. Pray shot himself in the head before the road was completed.

Jack Salsberry completed the road late in 1913. Much of it is still there in the form of today's State Highway 178. The 3,315-foot high point still carries the name Salsberry Pass. Nevertheless, after building all that road, Salsberry found the price of lead depressed. The value of the lead produced did not exceed the high cost of extraction, shipping, and smelting. Then a fortuitous event happened for Salsberry. World War I came along and the price of lead doubled from 3½ cents a pound to seven cents. By the summer of 1915, Carbonate Lead Mines employed sixty men. There were just a handful actually working at the mine, because they could put the ore in the bunker faster than it could be hauled away. Most of those workers were engaged in transporting forty tons of ore per week. Mule drawn wagons were first used to haul the ore to Zabriskie siding on the Tonopah & Tidewater Railroad. From there it went by rail to Midvale, Utah for smelting. Later a fleet of sixteen trucks was utilized for the first leg of the journey. There was no water at the mine, so the otherwise empty ore trucks carried water on the return trip.

The price of lead continued to rise, reaching a peak of twelve cents by 1917. World War I ended with the armistice of November 11, 1918, and with this, the bottom dropped out of the price of lead. In its first four years of production, however, the Carbonate Mine had produced 6,500 tons of ore worth about a third of a million dollars.

Gallena Canyon, The Home Of "White Gold"

The story of the Carbonate Mine did not end there. Between 1923 and 1926 optimism was running rampant across the country. Salsberry worked a couple of stock deals with the mine that artificially inflated the value of the stock, and then, of course, he sold out, leaving others holding the bag. After the stock market crash of 1929 many people lost their jobs, and the wages for what work was available were low. Under these circumstances, Salsberry was able to reopen the Carbonate Mine and the adjoining Queen of Sheba Mine in 1930. Another 4,000 tons of ore was shipped between 1930 and 1935.

Queen of Sheba Mine

The Carbonate Mine was reluctant to close for good. It was leased out and worked again in 1948-49, when a new mill was built, and again in 1952-53. The neighboring Queen of Sheba Mine was worked as recently as 1972. Much of the machinery left on the sites dates from this later period. Historian Richard Lingenfelter says the Carbonate and Queen of Sheba Mines were the second most productive and profitable lead mines in the Death Valley country. State records indicate that, in their sixty year lives, the Carbonate and Queen of Sheba Mines produced five million pounds of lead, 146,000 pounds of copper, 100,000 ounces of silver, and 1500 ounces of gold.

Warning: The underground workings are not safe and the visitor would be well advised not to attempt to enter them.

9

Mengel Pass via Warm Springs Canyon and Butte Valley

Primary Attraction:	Talc mines, interesting geology, unusual scenery, and a little history all come together to make this outing one of the most interesting in the park. Smart backroad explorers make the traverse of the Panamint Range, going up Warm Springs Canyon and down Goler Wash, which is somewhat easier on your nerves and your vehicle than going in the opposite direction.
Time Required:	It is an all day trip to Mengel Pass and back, or over the top and down. Three days could be spent exploring the various side roads.
Miles Involved:	It is forty miles from Furnace Creek Ranch to the beginning of the Warm Springs Canyon Road, and then another 24 miles to the Summit of Mengel Pass. If you choose to go on, add another 25 miles down Goler Wash to Ballarat.
Degree of Difficulty:	The route through much of Warm Springs Canyon is Class I. Beyond the road deteriorates to an easy Class II as far as Greater View Spring. The last mile to the summit of Mengel Pass is Class III. **For those planning on going over the pass, be aware that the Goler Wash side has several short Class IV and V sections (see Excursion #41).**

To find the Warm Springs Canyon Road, take the Badwater Road 6.1 miles south of the Furnace Creek Inn, then turn right and continue south on the graded West Side Road another 33 miles. Watch for a sign pointing to the west that reads "*Butte Valley*"; turn right on this graded road. For years, heavily laden ore trucks used this road. Then it was then a high standard road. Since the last talc mine in Warm Springs Canyon closed in the 1980s, the road has deteriorated some, but it still generally meets the Class I criteria of *The Mitchell Scale*.

Mengal Pass via Warm Springs Canyon and Butte Valley

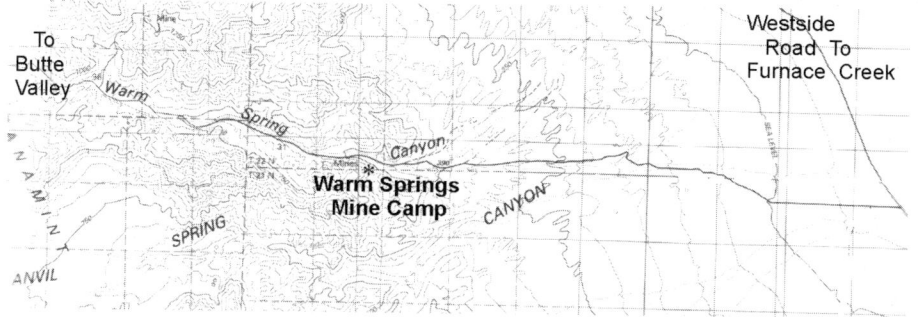

Shortly after turning off the West Side Road, a side road to the left once went over to Wingate Wash, where a four-wheel drive route followed the path of the 20-Mule Team borax wagons up the wash on the long road to the railhead at Mojave. This road was closed by the National Park Service in the early 1980s, because the United States Navy was having trouble with trespassers on N.O.T.S. Range "B". Wingate Wash is still open to hikers and backpackers willing to carry sufficient water.

At a point seven miles from the West Side Road, Anvil Spring Canyon appears off to the left. Fifty years ago there was a road through here going all the way up to Butte Valley. It was not Congress or some faceless government bureaucrat that closed this route. It was closed by one of Mother Nature's gully-washers in the 1940s.

In a little more than seven miles, our road enters Warm Springs Canyon. As you start up the wash, notice the rocks on the south side of the canyon. These old pre-Precambrian rocks are part of the Crystal Spring Formation. Millions of years ago these already formed limestone and dolomite layers were profoundly altered by heat and pressure when a dike of molten igneous rock was intruded into these sediments. As a result of this metamorphism, a band of talc was formed next to the dike. This band is two miles long and up to 25 feet thick. You can get a close look at the mineral in numerous abandoned workings on the south side of the road. **Warning: Stay out of the underground workings. They are unsafe!**

The first mine encountered is the Big Talc Mine. The access road to it is 9.1 miles in from the West Side Road. The next mine, also on the left, is the Number 5 Mine. It and the Big Talc had underground workings that connected and were all part of what was known as the Grantham Mine.

Of the one hundred or so women who have trod Death Valley's barren hillsides in search of mineral wealth, Louise Grantham was by far the most successful. In 1931 she and Ernest "Siberian Red" Huhn recognized the potential of the talc deposits and started staking claims up and down the canyon. These were the depression years, however, and the demand for talc was not great; nevertheless talc mining began in 1933. With the advent of World War II, talc became an important commodity, and by 1943 it was a commodity crucial to the war effort. The mine's output was continuous in the post war years. In 1972 Johns-Manville Products purchased the property, and they operated the mine another fifteen years.

In those later years both mines had extensive underground workings on sixteen different levels. Many of the tunnels were big enough to accommodate the use of rubber-tired diesel haulers and front-end loaders. The ceilings of the tunnels and stopes were supported in one of three ways. At times extensive heavy timbers were utilized. In other areas, roof bolts were driven into the "hanging wall" (the ceiling). In yet other areas, room-and-pillar mining was employed, where large columns of ore were left in place to support the ceiling. As these levels were worked out, the last areas to be mined were the pillars themselves leaving a very dangerous unsupported void. **None of these underground workings are now safe to enter!**

The third mine encountered off to the left is the Warm Spring Mine. It had an enormous open pit eight hundred feet long by four hundred feet wide by eighty feet deep. The access road to this mine is 9.6 miles in from the West Side Road.

At a point 10.8 miles in, a side road left goes to the Warm Springs Mine Camp, a worthy stop and a good overnight campsite. The Paiutes had camped at Warm Springs long before the first prospectors came this way. The Shoshone village of *Pabuna* was here when the Bennett-Arcan party made their long camp at Mesquite Well just a few miles to the north. The remnants of this village are said to have been destroyed by a flash flood in 1897. Only the fig trees planted by Panamint Tom in 1890 remain.

Warm Springs has served as a comfortable base camp for the many talc miners who have come and gone since the 1930s. In her book *A Mine of Her Own: Women Prospectors in the American West, 1850-1950,* Dr. Sally Zanjani of the University of Nevada in Reno postulates that it was the "woman's touch" brought by Louise Grantham that brought these amenities to Warm Springs Canyon. I recall that when I was in here during the early 1970s, the place looked more like a mobile home park than a mining camp. While the last mobile home was pulled out nearly twenty years ago, many of the camp buildings remain in good condition, thanks in part to The Mojave River Valley Museum of Barstow, which has sort of adopted the place. They have placed a sign telling a little about the camp, and have a register for visitors to sign. The imported giant salt cedar trees still provide cool shade on a warm summer's day, and the spring of lukewarm water still feeds the swimming pool. Camping is permitted here, and there are even a couple of picnic tables. Campfires are not permitted.

Mengal Pass via Warm Springs Canyon and Butte Valley

Talc was not the only mineral commodity handled here at Warm Springs. In 1939 gold miners erected a mill here to process gold ore from the Gold Hill Mine. The mill has suffered relatively little vandalism in recent years and looks very much like a reconstructed museum piece designed to display various types of ore dressing. Through a series of belts and gears, a single, horizontal-cylinder gasoline engine drives three different kinds of ore crushers. There is an arrastra, one of the most primitive ways of crushing ore, a small jaw mill, and a more efficient ball mill. Once it was reduced to sand-size particles, the ore and water combination flowed across shaker tables. Here the free gold was concentrated at one corner of the vibrating table, with the lighter waste material flowing off at another corner.

Gold Hill Mill

Beyond Warm Springs the road deteriorates to Class II, but it poses no problem for vehicles with high ground clearance. At a point 15.5 miles from the West Side Road, Warm Springs Canyon is left and Butte Valley is entered. It will be a couple of miles yet before the Striped Butte, from which the valley gets its name, is visible. The road gradually turns to the south and the scenery becomes dominated by Striped Butte, rising some nine hundred feet above the valley floor. The colorful layers of sediments in this butte make it geologically unique, for the surrounding country is made up of largely granitic rocks. When prospector Hugh McCormack passed through here in the 1860s, he named it "Curious Butte". Through the years, however, the name has changed to "Striped Butte".

At a point 20.7 miles in from the West Side Road, the main road goes straight; however, a Class II side road turns off to the right. By following it to the west

1.8 miles, the crest of the Panamint Range can be crossed at an elevation of 4,626 feet. On the other side, a deeply rutted Class III and Class IV road descends into Redlands Canyon all the way down to Redlands Spring nearly 2,000 feet below. Historian and tireless researcher Leroy Johnson thinks Redlands Canyon is the route used by Manly and Rogers in February of 1850, when they rescued the ill-fated Bennett-Arcan Party that was stranded in Death Valley.

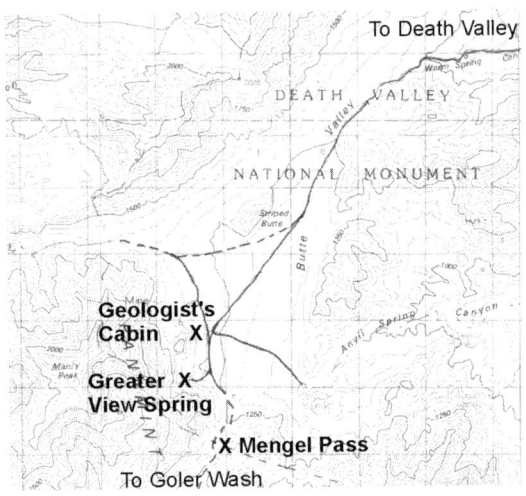

A side road to the left off the Redlands Canyon trail takes you into an old miner's camp in Wood Canyon. It is in this general area that Panamint Russ claimed he found, and then lost, a fabulous vein during a prospecting trip in 1925.

Continuing ahead on the main road for 1.8 miles, a lone cottonwood tree marks the site of Anvil Spring. The stone cabin above it is sometimes known as *"Geologist's Cabin"* after one of its original occupants. Supposedly Anvil Spring got its name from Lieutenant Charles Bendire, whose United States Army scouting party found an anvil here in 1867. Historian Richard Lingenfelter says that it had been thrown into the spring in disgust seven years earlier by Charles Alvord's prospecting party, after Alvord was unable to locate a rich vein of gold that he had found only five months previously.

The stone Geologist's Cabin is weather tight, stocked with food and water by passersby, and kept unlocked and available for public use. It is one of several such emergency shelters in the high Panamints. Use it if you wish, but please keep the place clean and restock any food you might use. There is a register for visitors to sign. On occasion the backcountry ranger stays here, as do National Park Service volunteers. If the flag is flying, the ranger is in residence.

Mengal Pass via Warm Springs Canyon and Butte Valley

The "Geologist's Cabin" at Anvil Spring
with Striped Butte in the background

Less than a mile south of Anvil Spring is Greater View Spring, once the home of veteran prospector Carl Mengel, a buddy of Frank "Shorty" Harris and Pete Aguereberry. He also had a close relationship with Bill and Barbara Myers, who lived on in a little ranch just over the pass in Goler Wash. Mengel, who lost a leg in a mining accident in Nevada, settled at the spring here in 1912, rebuilding an old preexisting cabin left by Mormon prospectors in 1869. In 1912 he also bought the Oro Fino Mine in Goler Wash. While trying to find a better route for his mules to haul ore out, he discovered a lode of high-grade ore that is said to have assayed as high as $35,000 per ton! Unfortunately, the deposit was small. Except for his financial interest in the nearby Lotus Mine, Carl died penniless of tuberculosis in 1944. His cremated ashes lie within the monument at the summit of what is today called Mengel Pass.

Mengel's cabin, too, is left unlocked and stocked with water and some food. It may be weather tight, but it is not rodent-tight like the Geologist's Cabin. Camp here if you wish, but if you stay inside, you will most likely have little four-footed visitors during the night. One convenience that Mengel's cabin has, and the Geologist's Cabin does not, is an outhouse!

Carl Mengel's cabin at Greater View Spring

Beyond Mengel's cabin, the first 0.3 miles is Class II, but soon that turns to Class III as the last 1.3 miles of climb to 4,800 foot Mengel Pass is made. If you have difficulty getting up this last mile, go no further. **Although downhill all the way, the descent through the Goler Wash side of Mengel Pass is much worse than the Warm Springs side.**

Carl's ashes rest in this monument
at the summit of Mengel Pass

Chapter II

Trails Out of Stovepipe Wells

Today's Stovepipe Wells is a convenient creation of the 1930s when President Herbert Hoover created Death Valley National Monument. It was then that Civilian Conservation Corps crews realigned the old Eichbaum toll road over Towne Pass to bypass the real Stovepipe Wells. Its original namesake is actually six miles to the northeast just across the sand dunes.

Stovepipe Wells is a secondary tourist center within Death Valley National Park. There is a Ranger Station here, where the latest road and visitor information can be obtained. Concessionaire services include a motel, a restaurant and bar, a gift shop, a general store, a service station, and an RV park with full hookups. There is also a campground operated by the National Park Service. There is even a paved airstrip (no AV gas).

During the winter season Ranger Talks are given in the evenings in the campground. Check at the Ranger Station for a schedule of events.

Bungalette City at Stovepipe Wells circa 1932
(Photo courtesy of Nevada Historical Society)

10

Grotto Canyon

Primary Attraction:	Access to a narrow canyon carved into a fantastic grotto by infrequent desert storms.
Time Required:	The mouth of the canyon is only a twenty-minute drive from Stovepipe Wells.
Miles Involved:	The jeep trail ends 2.1 miles from Highway 190.
Degree of Difficulty:	While signed for jeeps, the road is generally an easy Class II.

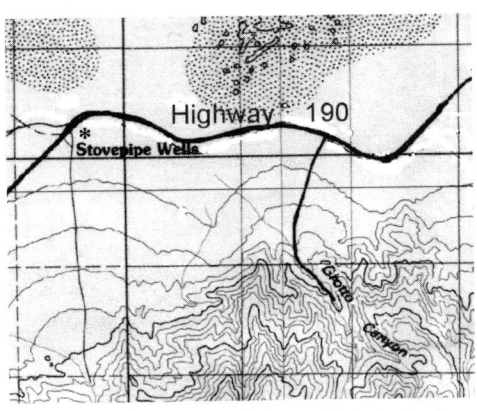

Grotto Canyon hardly qualifies as an honest to goodness jeep trail because it is so short, and while a high clearance vehicle is needed, four-wheel drive usually is not. I have, nevertheless, included it in this guide because most visitors to Death Valley will never drive in there. That is a shame, because the canyon offers some interesting geology and scenery. The Grotto Canyon excursion is just minutes from the Stovepipe Wells resort, and should take no more than an hour to see if you choose not to hike much beyond the road end. Camping is not permitted in the lower canyon.

From the Stovepipe Wells Hotel, drive east on Highway 190 for 1.4 miles. Look for a National Park Service sign showing a jeep; pointing to the right, it reads *Grotto Canyon*. Turn south here, starting up the alluvial fan. Within a mile, the Class II road drops down into the wash coming out of Grotto Canyon. Depending on the conditions of the moment the tracks may remain Class II, or they could deteriorate to Class III if the sand is soft.

The flat lying conglomerate rocks at the canyon's entrance are part of the Nova Formation of Tertiary age. This same formation is found in Telephone Canyon on the way to the Tucki Mine (see Excursion #11). Soon you will come to another rock sequence that seems to be standing on end. These are marine sediments, part of the very old Bonanza King Formation of Cambrian Age. There is a hiatus of five hundred million years between these two rock sequences.

The tracks make an "S" turn and before you know it, the canyon pinches down to the narrows preventing further vehicle travel. A short walk brings you to the First Grotto, where the narrow water-smoothed walls of the canyon reach upward to the sky. A couple of dry waterfalls bar easy passage by foot, although skilled rock climbers can get over these to progress to several more grottos and dry falls further up the canyon. If you want to hike up this canyon, see Michel Digonnet's excellent book *Hiking Death Valley*.

From the road's end, Grotto Canyon is only accessible by foot

11

The Tucki Mine

Primary Attraction: Interesting geology and canyon scenery.

Time Required: This is a half day excursion out of Stovepipe Wells at a minimum, but it would be a much better plan to spend the entire day.

Miles Involved: It is ten miles one way from the Wildrose Road to the Tucki Mine, 21 miles from the Stovepipe Wells Resort.

Degree of Difficulty: Much of the route is Class II, with only a few sections of easy Class III.

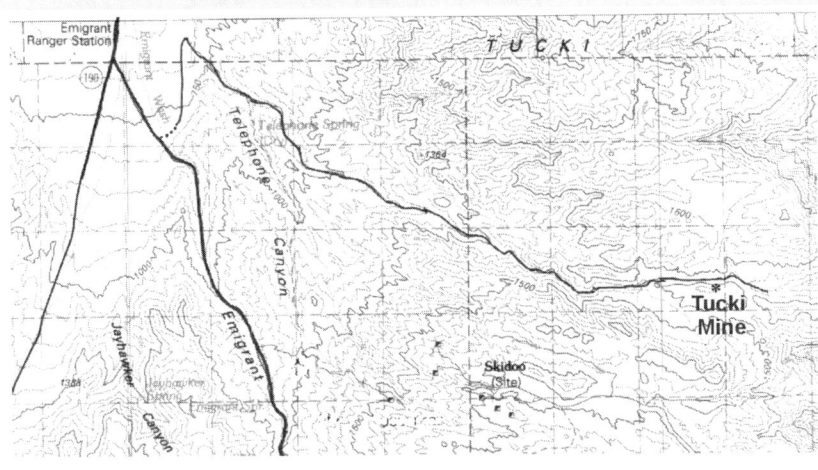

   As this book is being published, the National Park Service has not placed a sign at the beginning of this jeep trail. You will have to look close or you might miss it. From Stovepipe Wells, drive south on State Route 190 some 9.2 miles to Emigrant Junction. Turn left here on the Wildrose Road and proceed 1.5 miles to the entrance to Emigrant Canyon. Just before entering the confining walls of the canyon, watch carefully for wheel tracks going to the left across the wash. If the sand is dry, you may need four-wheel drive to get across the wash. If recent flooding has washed the tracks away, the route can be seen climbing up onto the bajada across the wash. Get there the best way possible. The way is clear from there on.

Tucki Mine

The jeep trail heads north crossing the flat desert surface, with good views of the northern portion of Death Valley. At a point 1.3 miles from the pavement, the jeep trail makes a sharp turn to the left, and in another 0. 4 miles enters Telephone Canyon. This drainage has its headwaters below the old mining camp of Skidoo. In 1907 a telephone line came through here to connect Skidoo with the outside word at Rhyolite, then a booming metropolis situated on the railroad. The telephone line is long gone, but the name has stuck.

As you proceed up the canyon, you cannot help but notice the horizontal beds of reddish brown conglomerate rock on either side. This is part of the Nova Formation, a fanglomerate of the late Tertiary era. It was formed about ten million years ago under similar circumstances as those under which the Emigrant Wash fan is being deposited today. At one point the Nova Formation is so undercut that you can drive your vehicle under it.

The Nova Formation overhangs the
road in the lower Telephone Canyon

The canyon forks at a point 0.7 miles above the mouth, with Telephone Canyon continuing to the right. When I first published *Death Valley Jeep Trails* in 1969, it was possible to drive up Telephone Canyon another mile and a half, where it left the wash to rejoin the Wildrose Road. The California Desert Protection Act of 1994 imposed *Wilderness* classification on that route, so it is now unlawful to drive through. If you don't mind a short hike of less than a mile round trip, you can walk up the right fork to a natural arch and Telephone Spring, now dry, just beyond. The spring was the site of an old miner's cabin and an arrastra, a crude device to crush ore into sand size particles so the fine gold could be extracted. Just who it was that operated this small mill has been lost in the sands of antiquity.

Natural arch in Telephone Canyon

From this fork in the canyon, the jeep trail keeps to the left, gradually making its way eastward as it climbs ever higher into the northern Panamints. As you climb higher, the younger Nova beds are left behind and you enter the metamorphic core of the range. Here are steeply dipping slate and schist which, in the Proterozoic era some 750 million years ago, were laid down as sea-bottom sediments.

At a point seven miles from the mouth of the canyon, the walls dissipate and the road improves as the country opens up. In a half-mile the crest of the Panamints is crossed at an elevation of 4,900 feet. Since entering the canyon, the road has gradually climbed some 2,500 feet. From the pass it is an easy 0.6 miles down the eastern side to the Tucki Mine.

The quartz veins of this area are thought to have first been claimed by a Henry Britt in 1909, as part of the Skidoo-Harrisburg frenzy. The first serious mining efforts were in the 1930s, with a little ore being shipped between 1937 and 1941. With the start of World War II, the gold mines were closed by Executive Order in 1942. When I was first in here in the 1960s there was less to see than there is now. Russ Journigan reopened the mine in 1975 and built a new carbon filtration mill to rework the old tailing dumps. Alas, the new operators put more money into the project than the few ounces of gold and silver they got out.

If you want to see the ore, look for odd pieces on the tailings dump. **Warning, the old tunnels and inclined shafts may look inviting to explore, but are in dangerous condition and should not be entered under any circumstances.**

Two older structures remain and one from the latest period of operation. The building in the middle is an unlocked cabin, maintained as an emergency shelter and stocked with food and water. Look around if you wish, but please leave it as you find it.

The jeep trail continues eastward down the canyon beyond the mine, but dead-ends in less than a mile. A trip down the canyon might interest the geologist, for here can be seen a reddish brown dolomite of the Cambrian age.

From the end of the trail one gets only a glimpse of the floor of Death Valley, some ten miles and nearly 5,000 feet below.

The Tucki Mine

12

Cottonwood and Marble Canyons

Primary Attraction: Two interesting, well-watered canyons with a few archaeological sites. In recent years these canyons have become a very popular destination for visitors with SUVs, looking for a more secluded campsite. (Camping is not permitted along the road for the first eight miles out of Stovepipe Wells, or once inside the canyon, within a quarter of a mile of surface water.)

Time Required: This is an all day excursion out of Stovepipe Wells.

Miles Involved: It is 19 miles from Highway 190 to the end of the trail in Cottonwood Canyon. Add another five miles for the round trip into Marble Canyon.

Degree of Difficulty: It is graded washboard, then Class I for the first 8.5 miles. Once in the canyon it is mostly Class II, with a little Class III in places going up the sandy boulder-strewn wash.

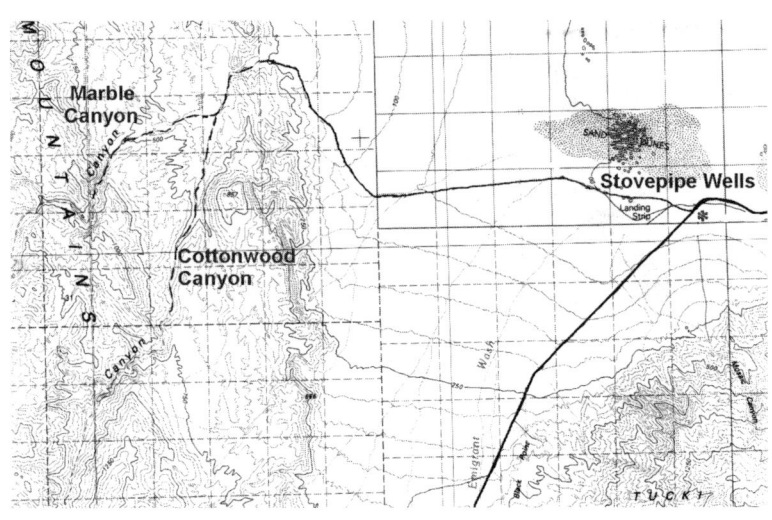

Cottonwood and Marble Canyons

As everyone knows, Death Valley is as hot and dry and desolate as a place can be. Yet here is a paradox, for amid the sun-bleached sands flow streams of sparkling water supporting a wide variety of plant and animal life. One such spot lies hidden deep within Cottonwood Canyon near the floor of Death Valley, only a few miles west of Stovepipe Wells. Here a rare desert stream is forced to the surface by layers of bedrock. In its brief life of only a few miles, the life-giving stream supports a small forest of cottonwood trees and an untold variety of native wildlife. Exploration of this isolated region is not for everyone. Soft sand and boulders make it difficult to get close in a standard automobile. Four-wheel drive vehicles, particularly those with high clearance, should have little trouble.

The route begins on the western side of Highway 190 just south of the General Store. Take the road past the entrance to the campground and the north end of the airstrip. Here there is the customary jeep symbol with a sign reading *Cottonwood Canyon.* A graded desert road heads west across the valley floor. It is difficult to understand why the National Park Service made the decision to grade this jeep trail, an act which created a washboard surface, making the road far worse than it was originally. After 6.5 miles the washboard surface finally ends, and the road turns into a more comfortable Class I.

After 8.5 miles you will begin to enter a gorge cut from beds of dolomite comprising the massive front wall of the mountain's face. This is the gateway to Cottonwood Canyon and its secrets.

A Sierra Club outing explores Cottonwood Canyon. The Park Service requires large groups to obtain a permit

Upon entering the gorge, the road deteriorates further from Class I to Class II, perhaps even a few short areas of Class III. Indeed, the "road" may actually cease to exist at all, depending on conditions at the moment. Nevertheless, start up the canyon being careful to pick your way through the maze of half buried boulders. Cottonwood Canyon has become a popular off-road destination in recent years. It is very likely that a number of previous vehicles have left tracks for you to follow. It was also a popular place with the ancient Indians who occupied the Death Valley area for the last two thousand years. They left their marks pecked into the rocks of the canyon walls.

In 1998 while re-scouting these jeep trails, my wife and I were camped on a sandy bench at the entrance narrows in Cottonwood Canyon. Just after sunset when it was still light, the air became alive with motion as hundreds of bats emerged from the pock marked rock walls above us. Within fifteen minutes they had all disappeared up the canyon.

As soon as you become accustomed to the confining walls of the gorge, the canyon opens into a large flat and forks. When I was first here in the 1960s an old metal *Automobile Club of Southern California* sign was still standing, and without a single bullet hole in it! (The Auto Club placed hundreds of these signs in the California desert in the 1930s.) The sign is no longer there. I hope it found a good home.

As soon as the canyon opens up, there is the temptation to turn to the right in order to go to Marble Canyon; resist the temptation. You must go up Cottonwood Canyon nearly a mile after the first narrows before a sign points right to the Marble Canyon Route. This turnoff is 10.8 miles from Highway 190.

Marble Canyon has a much different ambiance than Cottonwood Canyon. There is no water along the road and no cottonwood trees. The canyon narrows with towering walls of solid rock on either side. At least part of the route is Class III. At a point 2.6 miles above the turnoff from Cottonwood Canyon, the canyon narrows to a seven-foot width. Here the National Park Service stops further vehicle traffic, although the road once continued on another 1.1 miles to a point where a house size boulder rolled off the hillside to make an impassable obstacle.

The reason for this arbitrary and premature cessation of the jeep trail is that the Park Service wants to keep some space between visitors and the Indian petrogylphs found further up the wash. The Park Service is reluctant to reveal the exact whereabouts of these sites because of past incidences of theft and senseless vandalism. One need look no farther than the mouth of Cottonwood Canyon for that. Indeed the one time jeep trail through Greenwater Canyon was closed entirely because people were destroying irreplaceable archaeological sites.

Rock art buff Geron Marcom says there are at least 158 prehistoric rock art sites in Death Valley National Park, with about a third here in the Northern Panamints. With the new lands added to the park in 1994, I am sure those figures are very low. Donald Martin, who cataloged and studied the Death Valley rock art sites for 25 years, thinks they had magical or religious significance associated with hunting. Many, but by no means all, were near water or game trails. Rock art takes on three forms: petrogylphs, designs pecked into the rock surface; pictographs, designs painted on rocks with primitive pigments; and geoglyphs, stone alignments on the desert floor. Petrogylphs are the most common, and are likely to be the best preserved. Some were made long enough ago that the *desert varnish*, a natural patina that develops with time, covers even the etched surfaces within the rock. Such petrogylphs could have been made as long ago as 3,000 years. Of the 158 known rock art sites, only seventeen contain pictographs. These sites are particularly sensitive to the weather and the elements, and in spite of man's best efforts, are slowly being weathered away. Other very sensitive sites are those locations in Panamint Valley and elsewhere where Archaic man has aligned stones on the desert floor in mysterious patterns. While none of those in the Death Valley area compare to those on the Colorado River near Blythe, California, they nevertheless remain an archaeological mystery just as much as the famous ones at Nazca, Peru.

If you leave your vehicle at the end of the road and walk up Marble Canyon a ways, you might be rewarded by one of these rock art sites. Keep your eyes open! For those who can arrange a car shuttle, Goldbelt Spring (see Excursion # 33) is a vigorous hike of twelve miles up the Marble Canyon.

The Marble Canyon narrows

Once you leave Marble Canyon and return to Cottonwood Canyon proper, you will want to turn right. Cottonwood Canyon generally heads south now. Soon the vertical walls of the highly metamorphosed limestone will once again enclose the main wash. At a point four miles above the fork, look for a large cave hollowed out of thick layers of fanglomerate. Carved out by floodwaters coming down the canyon, it is difficult to estimate the age of this cave. The cave is the most popular place in the canyon to camp today. It seems reasonable to assume that it has in its past provided shelter for the ancient and more modern Indians who lived and farmed in this canyon.

This cave is a popular place to camp

A short distance up the wash from the cave, the canyon walls suddenly turn from fanglomerate of Tertiary age to limestone of Mississippian age. You can climb up and put your hand on the contact point of the two vastly different rock types. When doing so, your hand will cover a missing gap of 340 million years in the earth's history.

Almost immediately the road passes a second set of narrows cut through the marine sediments of the Perdido Formation. At a point 17.4 miles from Highway

190, the first surface water from Cottonwood Creek may be encountered in wet years. A mile beyond is the first cluster of cottonwood trees from which the canyon gets its name. The road deteriorates to Class III and a little Class IV in its last 0.8 miles.

By all means hike up the stream a ways from the end of the road. Watch the moist soil along the creek for various animal tracks. When I would come in here thirty and forty years ago, feral burros were everywhere. Thanks to the National Park Service's relocation program, they are rarely seen today.

Cottonwood Canyon teems with wildlife. Less conspicuous dwellers of the canyon are various kinds of small rodents, rabbits, foxes, and of course, the ubiquitous coyote. Keep your eye on the high ridges, too. Desert bighorn sheep, *Ovis canadensis nelsoni,* have been seen here. Birdwatchers in particular will find Cottonwood Canyon fascinating. At almost any time of the year, the huge spreading cottonwood trees are alive with the flutter and chatter of various birds. Here the normally hushed desert is so noisy that nature seems unbalanced somehow.

Whether you spend a day or a week in Cottonwood Canyon, you will find the trip both rewarding and pleasing.

Cottonwood trees line a small stream in Cottonwood Canyon

13

Jean LeMoigne's Retreat

Primary Attraction:	A hiker's trailhead to the one time camp and mine of one of Death Valley's *old timers*.
Time Required:	It is about an hour to the present end of the jeep trail near the mouth of the canyon. Add another four to five hours to hike up to LeMoigne's mine camp and back.
Miles Involved:	From Highway 190 to today's road end is only 4.7 miles.
Degree of Difficulty:	The route is Class III most of the way.

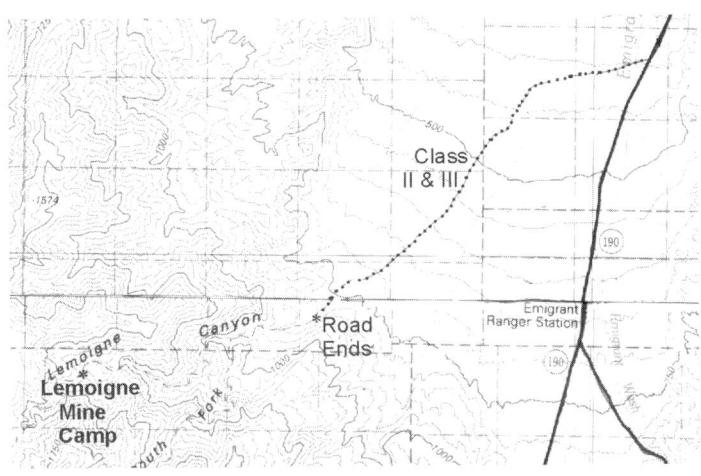

If you thought Cottonwood Canyon was off the beaten path, you should visit LeMoigne Canyon just to the south. This largely forgotten spot was once the home of a spunky little Frenchman named Jean LeMoigne. Prior to passage of the California Desert Protection Act of 1994, it was possible to drive right up to LeMoigne's mine and home site, but, with that legislation, both have been classified as *Wilderness*. Nevertheless, it is still possible to take a Class III route a short distance into LeMoigne Canyon; however, you will have to walk the last several miles to see Jean LeMoigne's retreat.

From the Stovepipe Wells Resort take Highway 190 south starting up

Emigrant Wash. At a point 6.1 miles from the hotel, (coming the other way go 2.7 miles beyond the Emigrant Ranger Station) you will have to watch carefully to see some wheel tracks leading off to the right. This is where you leave the pavement. Engage your four-wheel drive here, for you will need it the rest of the way.

For the first mile and a half, the roadway cuts across the grain of the drainage pattern coming down Emigrant Wash. This is an endless series of ups and downs. Eventually high ground is reached and the road swings to the south to climb the bajada. Here among patches of reddish brown basalt boulders are textbook examples of *desert pavement*, that tightly packed surface of largely soil-free rocks which seems to have been laid out and compacted by a steam roller.

The road gradually climbs the alluvial fan, and 4.3 miles from the pavement there is a good flat campsite high above the wash. The road drops from here down into the wash and continues on another 0.4 miles before coming to an abrupt end. This is today's *Wilderness* boundary. Further vehicle travel is prohibited. For those who want to continue on, Jean's camp is a walk of nearly four miles in which the elevation gain is some 1800 feet.

Jean LeMoigne's life seems to be a series of contradicting stories. The tale told most often is that in 1883, Isadore Daunet wrote to his friend and fellow Frenchman, Jean LeMoigne, enticing him to come from Paris to America. LeMoigne was a chemist and engineer, and Daunet needed help operating his Eagle Borax Works. LeMoigne accepted his friend's offer, but, by the time he got to Death Valley in 1884, the bottom had fallen out of the price of borax,

Daunet had gone broke, his wife had left him, and pal Isadore had committed suicide. There was no job for Jean LeMoigne. Some Death Valley historians doubt that version because LeMoigne's name is mentioned as part owner of a mine near Panamint in 1880, three years before Daunet ever started mining borax. Whatever the story, Jean, or Cap as he was known to his many friends, liked the desert and spent the next 40 years prospecting in the Death Valley country.

The legend persists that Cap had a silver mine that supported his modest needs and on occasion grubstaked his friends. Here again however, stories differ as to where this mine was. Some think Cap found the "Lost Gunsight Lode", which was found by a group of Georgians in 1849. Was it this lode that kept Cap in beans and bacon? Author John Southworth, who wrote *Death Valley in 49*, contended that Cap's mine was right here in what is known today as Lemoigne Canyon. However, friend and fellow prospector, Frank Crampton, claims LeMoigne's silver mine was just north of Skidoo and his lead mine was in LeMoigne Canyon. Again, the stories differ.

Jean LeMoigne and his friends in 1915
(Photo courtesy of National Park Service)

We do know that Cap built a small stone cabin and was mining lead in LeMoigne Canyon in 1918. However, his mine was a long way from markets and transportation was difficult. With the World War I armistice on November 11, 1918, the price suddenly dropped and Cap stopped mining lead.

In August of 1919, 71 year old Jean LeMoigne decided to make a fateful trip to the outside world. Cap was camped near Salt Creek between Stovepipe Wells and Furnace Creek, when he went down. He crawled under a mesquite bush and died, leaving his two faithful burros tied nearby. Death Valley Scotty claimed that he discovered Jean's body, together with those of his two animals. Scotty said that he buried Cap there on the spot. Another account is that Shorty Harris and Frank Crampton found Jean's body. Harry Gower also claims that he and Tom Wilson buried Jean in one grave and his two burros in their separate graves. Thus the list of people who claimed to have buried Cap is endless. A pile of rocks and bleached wooden cross marking Cap's grave can still be seen to this date, if you know where to look.

Cap's grave down near Salt Creek

After Cap's death a couple of local boys, Bill Corcoran and Bev Hunter, quietly went into Lemoigne Canyon and relocated all eight of Cap's claims. Twice they tried to sell the property, only to have the buyers die before the deals could be consummated. In 1924 they finally did sell the property. The new owner shipped 200 tons of lead ore between 1925 and 1927. Since then further exploration has been sporadic with activity as recent as 1975, but little ore has been shipped.

This well norished coyote hung around Scotty's Castle seeking hand-outs from visitors. The Park Service asks that you not feed the wild animals.

Chapter III

Trails Out of Scotty's Castle

Scotty's Castle is the principle attraction in the northernmost part of Death Valley National Park. It is sort of a Hearst Castle in the desert. As a young boy, Walter Scott ran away from his home in Kentucky to join his brother on a ranch in Nevada. He bounced around doing odd jobs, including a twelve-year stint in a Wild West show. He apparently honed his con man skills there, for he started telling potential investors that he had a rich gold mine in Death Valley. He must have been a smooth talker, because they put up the money and he spent it. Scotty lived a lifestyle far beyond his own limited means. This lifestyle included the building of a palace in the desert. Construction on Scotty's Castle started in 1922, seemingly with money provided by Scotty's friend and benefactor, Albert Johnson, an insurance magnate from Chicago. The project never really was completed, but what you see today was finished in 1931.

The National Park Service conducts tours during the peak winter season (sign up as soon as you arrive) and they will tell you the whole story.

Visitor services at Scotty's Castle are limited to a snack bar, gift shop and gas pump, all of which are only open from 9:00 a.m. to 5:30 p.m. There are no overnight accommodations. The nearest campground is at Mesquite Spring 4.8 miles to the south. In between Scotty's Castle and Mesquite Spring is the Grapevine Ranger Station, where park and road information can be obtained.

Scotty's Castle shortly after it was built
(Photo courtesy Nevada Historical Society)

14

A Four Camp Loop through Yesteryear
(Gold Mountain, Oriental, Tokop & Gold Point)

Primary Attraction: A tour of four historic, picturesque mining camps.

Time Required: This is an all day journey back through time.

Miles Involved: The entire loop from the Grapevine Ranger Station to Gold Point and return is 88 miles. Be sure to top off your gas tank at Scotty's Castle before starting off.

Degree of Difficulty: When I re-scouted and updated all of these roads for this book in 1998, I found them to be generally Class I, with a little Class II between Old Camp and Tokop. However, for much of its one hundred-year history, the route up Oriental Wash has been Class III because of soft sand. One good flash flood and it could easily be Class III again. Check conditions with the Rangers at Scotty's Castle.

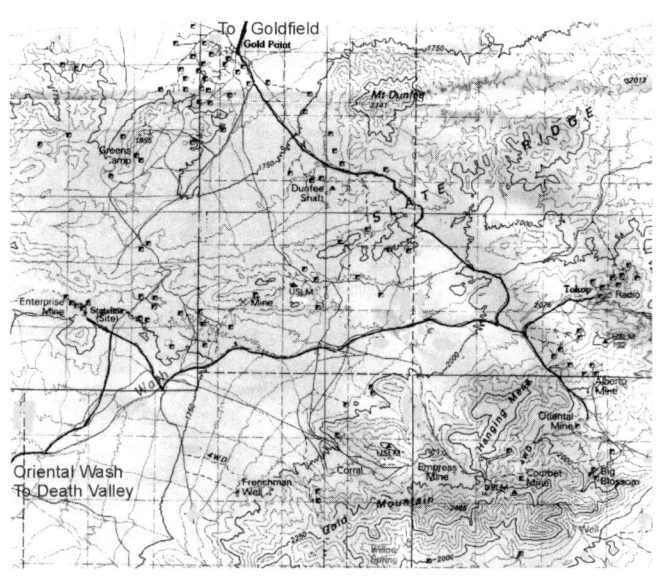

Four Camp Loop

From the Grapevine Ranger Station, three miles south of Scotty's Castle, take the paved road north towards Ubehebe Crater. After 2.8 miles the paved road to Ubehebe Crater goes off to the left (see Excursion #15). You will want to stay right on the graded dirt road. This is the start of 13.4 miles of the most awful washboard road in the entire park. It is bone jarring at any speed! My only suggestion to make it more pleasurable would be to take this road in May when the cottontop and prickly pear cacti are in bloom.

Just before reaching Little Sand Spring, 13.4 miles from the last pavement look for an unsigned graded road going off to the right. After 4.3 miles, Death Valley National Park is left behind, and you enter Nevada. This is now federal land administered by the Bureau of Land Management's Tonopah Field Office. Rock hounding, camping, and campfires are permitted here, but please do not burn wood from historic sites. A quarter of a mile beyond the state line, a side road goes right; stay to the left on the main road. A mile from the state line a remote weather station is passed and a tenth of a mile beyond it, the road from Tule Canyon comes in from the rear. Stay right going up Oriental Wash. In a couple of miles, as you gain elevation, yuccas and their close cousins, the Joshua trees, will begin to appear.

The next key intersection is 7.2 miles ahead. At this desert crossroads, the left fork goes 0.8 miles to the remains of the old mining camp of Gold Mountain, later called Stateline after the principal mine of the area.

The armies of blue and gray had just laid down their arms when Leander Morton first found gold-bearing rock on what would become known as Gold Mountain. Morton did not feel the lode was rich enough, so he sought his fortune elsewhere. He robbed a train in 1870, was caught and sent to prison, escaped, was caught again and then hung by a posse at what is now Convict Lake. So much for Morton's judgment!

A fellow named Tom Shaw came along in 1868 and discovered a quartz outcrop twelve feet thick and nearly a half-mile long. He and his partners staked four claims along the ledge. They pecked away for several years but had no way to mill the ore. In 1871 Shaw built a mule-powered arrastra at a spring some five miles away, and with that he was able to eke out $9.00 per day, about twice the wage of a working miner. Historian Richard Lingenfelter says Shaw's State Line Mine was the first profitable mine in Death Valley. The State Line Mine passed through several hands, and then a con man by the name of George D. Roberts bought the mine in September of 1880. He broke it up into quarters, one for each claim, formed four companies and set out to sell stock in each one. He enlisted the aid of various experts who promptly called it "the greatest gold mine on this continent". All the activity at State Line attracted a lot of attention. Investors in the east were lining up to buy Roberts' stock, the price of which he was carefully manipulating. Out west people began pouring into State Line, hoping for a piece of the action. By November of that year Taylor had laid out a townsite, called it "Gold Mountain", and was selling lots for $50 to $500 each.

By March of 1881 a small mining camp had sprung up, complete with the usual assortment of saloons, stores, livery stables, bawdy houses, boarding houses, blacksmith shops, a bakery, butcher shop, post office and other essential services needed at the time. He set about building an impressive forty-stamp mill. At the same time he bought some 65,000 feet of six inch spiral wrapped pipe and began to lay a twelve mile long pipeline in from upper Tule Canyon.

The stock in Robert's venture soared, even though not a single ton of ore had been crushed. When the stock reached a peak of around $25 a share, Roberts began to quietly sell off his substantial holdings. By August, with the pipeline still miles away and the mill not yet complete, Roberts slipped away. He knew full well that the ore in the State Line Mine was worth only about $10 per ton, not the exaggerated $100 per ton the experts had proclaimed a year before. By December of 1881 the Roberts' stock transactions were recognized for what they were, a swindle of gigantic proportions.

Some mining continued around Gold Mountain, but by 1891 the post office closed. The Goldfield Excitement of 1905 brought renewed interest and the mines of Slate Ridge briefly reopened. The mines have closed and reopened several times since then, once even with the construction of a new mill. As you enter Gold Mountain you pass the stone ruins of many miners' cabins. The lonely headframe of the State Line Mine is halfway up the hillside. Just below it are the foundations of the Enterprise Mill. If you look around you will find several dugouts and several wooden structures in various stages of decay. The camp's sole resident occupies the best house in Gold Mountain. **For your own safety, stay out the tunnels and shafts!**

The Stateline mill in 1915
(Nevada State Historical Society photo)

Four Camp Loop

By turning right at this desert crossroads, it is just four miles to Gold Mountain's sister city, Oriental, later called "Old Camp". Tom Shaw, the same guy who first found gold veins at Gold Mountain, also found gold here in 1864. Once again Shaw was unable to take advantage of his findings and it was not until 1871 that the Oriental Mine was developed on one of the more promising veins. The Oriental Mine produced some very rich *specimen ore*, several pieces of which were put on display at the 1876 Centennial Exposition in Philadelphia. Oriental, too, had a post office that lasted until 1900.

With the Oriental Mine, a small camp of the same name sprang up two miles to the west on the northern slope of Gold Mountain at an elevation of 7,000 feet. Unlike the town of Gold Mountain, Oriental had a small well nearby to service the residents' needs, but it was insufficient to run an ore mill. At least one could get a drink of water here and the pinyon forest just above town provided firewood for heating and cooking. Somewhere along the line, the name of the community changed its name from Oriental to Old Camp, the name used on the 1911 1:250,000 topographic map, and the current Automobile Club of Southern California *Death Valley National Park* map. Today the site consists of the ruins of eleven stonewalled structures, plus several wood cabins and an old boiler.

Oriental today

The miners of the 1870s were by no means the first humans to call this country home. With its dark basalt lava, Hanging Mesa was frequented by the Indians, who left petroglyphs and obsidian chips on its summit and around its perimeter.

The camp of Tokop lies a few miles to the northeast, and it is also at 7,000 feet. Mineral exploration did not begin here until the 1890s, but it took the Greenwater Excitement of 1904 before serious attempts at mining were made. Gold was indeed found, but the orebodies were too low grade to turn into anything great. Today only one wooden building marks the site of Tokop. There is a good graded road from Tokop past the Senator Mine, over Slate Ridge and into Gold Point, the fourth camp on our journey. This is the only camp to survive into modern times.

Tokop was a busy place in 1926
(Nevada State Historical Society photo)

Gold Point started as Lime Point in 1868, when a short-lived lime quarry was established here. It became re-established and was re-inhabited in 1880 under the name of Hornsilver when a silver mine opened. That operation lasted only two years, primarily due to its then remote location and the long ten-mile haul to Lida for milling and ore dressing. The Goldfield-Greenwater Excitement of 1903-05 rekindled mining interests in the area with the opening of the Great Western Mine in 1905. With the railroad now only fourteen miles away at Cuprite, silver mining was less expensive. In 1908 new silver discoveries created yet another stampede and overnight Hornsilver gained its place on the map of Nevada. In May and June of 1908 Hornsilver grew from a small collection of tents to a townsite complete with mapped streets, the usual saloons, sporting establishments, restaurants, general stores, boarding houses, livery stables, a gasoline pump, and even a post office. The newly established *Hornsilver Herald* proclaimed the community would be the brightest star in Nevada's crown.

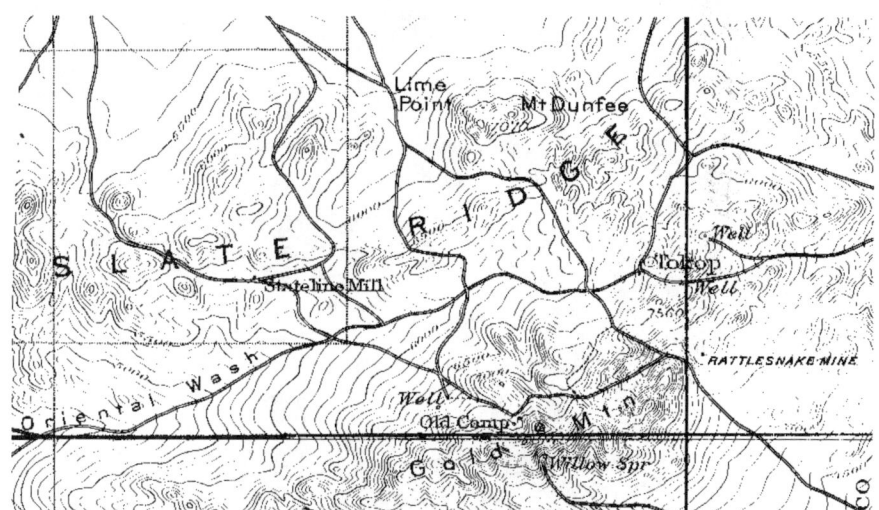

On the 1913 topographic sheet, Gold Point is shown as "Lime Point" and Oriental is shown as "Old Camp"

The largest mine, the Great Western, had legal as well as ore milling problems which caused on and off operations for several decades. As the mines grew deeper, gold began to become more important than the silver. By the 1930s the community changed its name to Gold Point, seeming more appropriate under the changing circumstances. The Great Western Mine was closed in 1942 by President Roosevelt's proclamation that all gold mines were to be closed so that the workers could be better utilized in the war effort. At that point Gold Point was abandoned, leaving its fifty-some wooden buildings to bleach in the sun.

Fortunately for history buffs like myself, Gold Point has not changed much in the last forty years. However, I am sure that with the passage of each year the wooden buildings will weather and deteriorate a little bit more, and it will only be a matter of time before the site returns to the sand. Gold Point is not a *ghost town*. In 1998 there were still 22 mailboxes in use on a rail in the center of town. When asked why they choose to live here, many of the local residents said they wanted to stay away from the hustle and bustle of Goldfield, the seat of county government for Esmeralda County. Here in Gold Point, life proceeds at a more leisurely pace.

Gold Point today

15

White Top Mountain

Primary Attraction: Recent volcanic craters, some interesting sedimentary geology, old mines, and some very remote country with nice views down into Death Valley make this an outstanding back-country drive.

Time Required: This is an all day outing from Scotty's Castle or anyplace else.

Miles involved: From the parking lot at Scotty's Castle to the end of the road at the Silver Crown Mines is 45 miles.

Degree of Difficulty: The 21 miles from Ubehebe Crater to Lost Burro Gap are generally Class I. The remaining 14.5 miles are generally Class II, but may contain a few short sections of Class III.

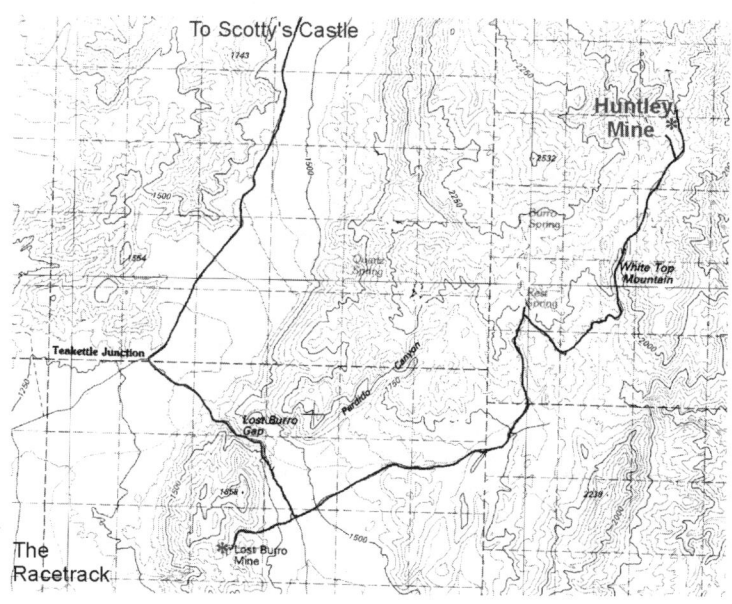

Take the paved road from Scotty's Castle down the canyon three miles to the road junction just north of the Grapevine Ranger Station; turn right. As you drive north up the valley, notice the line of mesquite trees at the base of the hills to the right. A geologic fault runs along here and in that zone of weakness and sheared rocks, ground water seeps to the surface. It was at one of these springs that Walter Scott, Death Valley Scotty, had a small bungalow that he far preferred over the "castle". (Scotty's Castle was actually the elegant vacation home of Albert and Bessie Johnson, not Scotty.) At a point 1.5 miles north of the Grapevine Ranger Station a side road right goes to Scotty's bungalow. The National Park Service has closed the site to visitors.

A road junction is reached at a point nearly three miles north of the Grapevine Entrance Station. To the right a graded dirt road with a washboard surface goes north up the valley, ultimately reaching Big Pine. At this intersection, stay left on the pavement another 2.5 miles to Ubehebe Crater.

Ubehebe Crater

There are more than a dozen distinctly separate volcanic craters at the site generally known as Ubehebe Crater. All seem to be explosive events, with little or no lava emitted away from the craters. Explosive events like these typically occur when magma deep within the earth rises and comes in contact with groundwater. The water flashes to steam and, in the expansion process, the force of the explosion is directed upwards. In all likelihood, the entire eruption cycle from beginning to end takes only a few minutes. In the case of Ubehebe Crater, the resulting hole is 750 feet deep and 2,000 feet across. Cinders and ash were thrown out from two to five miles in every direction. As noted geologist Tom Clements pointed out, the emitted cinders lie on top of, not within, the sediments formed in the bottom of Pleistocene Lake Rogers. This would suggest that the first eruption occurred after the lake dried up some 10,000 years ago. The lack of erosion around the crater suggests that the event occurred a few hundred, or perhaps only a few thousand, years ago, although ash found with archaeological artifacts suggests an age of 6,000 years. If you have the time, take the 1.5-mile foot trail that circles the rim of Ubehebe Crater, or walk at least the half mile trail over to Little Hebe Crater.

Beyond Ubehebe Crater, a graded dirt road heads south up the Racetrack Valley. The first two miles of road cross a thick mantle of volcanic ash that was thrown out by the volcanic explosions. Soon the countryside returns to sandy alluvium as one begins the ascent up the valley. In the twenty miles from Ubehebe Crater to Teakettle Junction, the road very gradually climbs from 2,600 feet to 4,100 feet.

To the left is an impressive high ridge of mostly limestone and dolomite layers, which culminates in 8,953' Tin Mountain. As you allow your eyes to climb up the mountainside from the bottom, you look through sediments of the Cambrian, Ordovician, Silurian, Devonian, and Mississippian Ages. The time span represented in these layers is some 250 million years. The rock layer on the summit is appropriately named the Tin Mountain limestone. It was deposited in the sea bottom about 325 million years ago.

The summit of Tin Mountain is garnished with a scattering of pinyon and juniper trees. A light sprinkling of snow can often be seen here after winter storms. I have never climbed this summit, but I know people who have done so. From the road the four-mile walk with a vertical gain of 4,100 feet took four hours one way.

Teakettle Junction is reached at a point 19.8 miles south of Ubehebe Crater. This road junction gets its curious name from the variety of teakettles which people have placed on the road sign over the years. Turn left here. The right fork goes to the Racetrack Playa (see Excursion #33).

Teakettle Junction

The road remains Class I for the next mile, and then deteriorates a little as it passes through a little canyon known as Lost Burro Gap. While this canyon is only a mile long, the steeply dipping limestone rocks here represent one hundred million years of the earth's history. The first and youngest rock stratum encountered is the Tin Mountain limestone of Mississippian age. After 0.2 miles the Lost Burro Formation of Devonian age is reached. Once out of the canyon, off on the right, a small exposure of the Hidden Valley dolomite of Silurian age can be seen. All three of these formations contain fossils of the primitive animals that lived in the sea at that time, although this is not the best place to look for them.

A crossroads is reached at a point 3.2 miles beyond Teakettle Junction; this is Lost Burro Junction. To the right a Class II road goes 1.2 miles to the Lost Burro Mine. If you have the time, the quick side-trip visit is recommended. A gold bearing vein was found here at the contact point where the Cretaceous granitic rocks forced their way up through the Tin Mountain limestone. The main vein averaged about two feet in width and contained *free gold*. The first claims were staked in 1907 and between then and 1912, the mine is said to have produced $85,000 in gold. Some estimate the mine's production from 1935 to 1942 to have been in excess of $100,000. Built in 1917, the mill has been salvaged for use elsewhere; however, the timber frame remains. There is a weather-tight cabin at the mine, which can be used as an emergency shelter in a storm if you don't mind sharing your quarters with the mice and packrats.

For the White Top Mountain area, turn left at Lost Burro Junction and note your odometer reading. The Class II road heads east up the bajada. After a mile and a half, the gently dipping limestone beds of the Andy Hills are on the right. They are more of the Lost Burro Formation that you saw a few miles back. At a point 3.3 miles in from Lost Burro Junction, faint tracks go to the right. Stay left as the road swings to the north.

Soon you will be entering Rest Spring Gulch. At first the Tin Mountain limestone of early Mississippian age will be off the road to the left and right. But as the gulch narrows, the road enters the next strata up, the Perdido Formation of late Mississippian age. This dark rock strata contains a variety of fossils including the *Cravenocerus* genus of ammonite, a rounded nautilus type shell. Also present are crinoid stems, the only hard part of a plant-like animal that lived on the sea bottom. While these 320 million-year-old marine critters are interesting to look at, keep in mind that fossil collecting in the park is strictly prohibited.

At a point 4.9 miles in from Lost Burro Junction, the road goes up and over a few feet of bedrock in the canyon bottom. This dry waterfall or cascade should cause no real problem, although caution should be exercised, and the use of four-wheel drive might be prudent but not usually necessary. Once over that obstacle, the Perdido Formation is topped and the road enters the Rest Spring Shale strata. These soft and easily eroded layers of shale are thought to be of early Pennsylvanian Age. The road forks a tenth of a mile above the bedrock cascade. For White Top Mountain stay right on the main road.

To the left a Class III road goes up the narrow gulch a half mile to Rest Spring. Here a short tunnel dug into the soft shale has produced a seep of brackish water. As uninviting as this water may appear, wildlife in the surrounding hills depends on it. When I approached the spring on foot in December of 1998, I startled a huge covey of fifty or more chukar partridges. They took to the air in one mass, flapping their wings and making quite a racket. They landed again a few hundred feet down the wash and quickly seemed to loose interest in me, although a few curious birds did watch me walk back to my car.

Back in 1932 some 52,000 chukars were imported from India by the California Department of Fish and Game. Those placed in the high deserts adapted readily to their new habitat and flourished. Like the burro, the National Park Service considers them to be an exotic species, and thus to have no place in Death Valley National Park. Unlike the burro, however, there are no current plans to eradicate the chukar. There are simply too many of them. They are found everywhere in the park where there is year around water.

At one time the jeep trail continued up the draw to Burro Spring, about a mile to the north. The Park Service has closed this road. Please do not camp within a quarter of a mile of Rest Spring.

From the turnoff to Rest Spring, the main road turns east, crossing a rolling ridge top. From here the first views down into Death Valley can be seen. To the north is 7,607' White Top Mountain. This is a bit of a misnomer. The light colored dolomite and quartzite rocks near the summit are not actually white, but they look so much lighter than the dark summits of surrounding mountains that the name was chosen.

The road winds around through the soft shale, drops down into a wash, and once again heads north up a canyon. This canyon was eroded out of the broken and crushed rocks along a north-south trending fault where one side has slipped in relation to the other side. As you enter the canyon, and for nearly the next mile, the rocks on the east side of the narrow canyon are different from those on the west. At first the stratum on the right is the Ely Springs dolomite, followed by the Hidden Valley dolomite. At the same time, the rocks on the left are first the Perdido Formation, followed by the Tin Mountain limestone, and then the Lost Burro Formation.

Eight miles in from Lost Burro Junction strangely eroded pinnacles appear in the Ely Springs dolomite high on the ridge to your right. Here, too, the first pinyon and juniper begin to appear. No matter what time of year you visit, the air should be getting cooler. The elevation is 6,600 feet.

At a point 8.5 miles in from Lost Burro Junction, the road forks. The left fork went to some mining claims in existence prior to the creation of the national park; stay right. In another 0.4 miles a side road right winds its way up the hillside. This was one of several roads put in to access the Huntley claims. The remains of the camp set up by Huntley Industrial Minerals are another 0.6 miles up the main road. The site consists of a wooden cabin and several metal tanks.

The carbonate rocks in this area have been intruded by a younger granite-like, igneous rock called syenite. Where these two rock units come in contact, the carbonate sequence, particularly the Ely Springs dolomite, have developed lenses containing the amphibole suite of minerals. One of these minerals is tremolite, an ore of asbestos. It was this commodity that the miners had been seeking since the deposit was first worked in 1900. Prospect pits are everywhere. A few hundred tons were shipped, but in general the impurities were too great and the asbestos fibers too short to warrant the long haul to the mill and market. Being careful not to raise any dust, the author did find a single specimen of long fiber chrysotile asbestos in one of the test pits years ago before Death Valley National Park was created. Today mineral collecting is prohibited.

White Top Mountain

Huntley Mine Camp

Beyond the Huntley Mine Camp, the road forks after another 0.3 miles; some call this Syenite Junction. The left fork is a Class III route, which after a couple of miles ends at the Silver Crown Claims in O'Brien Canyon. Veins containing copper and fluorite minerals were discovered in 1912 in the Tin Mountain and Perdido Formations. Although one 75-foot tunnel was dug and several shafts sunk, no real production has ever taken place here. **Warning: Do not enter any underground workings. They are not safe!**

From Syenite Junction the right fork proceeds up the draw another half mile to where there are many spur roads to prospect pits. The syenite rocks of this area are somewhat unique in that they contain the mineral nepheline. While rocks of this type are common in Ontario, Canada, this is the only such locality ever reported in California.

There are some waterless, but otherwise fine campsites here among the pinyon pines. The elevation here is 6,800 feet. On the ridge to the right are nice views down into Death Valley. If you want to escape the crowds in other parts of the park, this is the place to do it.

Beatty in 1905 before any permanent structures had been built
(Nevada Historical Society photo)

Chapter IV

Trails Out of Beatty

Of all the Turn of the 20th Century mining camps in the Bullfrog Mining District, Beatty is the only one to survive to modern times. The Beatty of today has a population of about 1800 people. For the traveler, the town is pretty much open 24 hours a day, offering motels, restaurants, towing service, auto parts, and of course, a casino or two for Nevada-style entertainment. The Phoenix Inn and the Rio Rancho RV Park have laundry facilities.

Prior to 1904 there was nothing in this remote part of Nevada except for a few scattered ranches. Then in the summer and fall of 1904 that all changed when the mining excitement from Tonopah and Goldfield moved south. Rich discoveries were made in what would soon become the boomtowns of Rhyolite and Bullfrog. Beatty was born of necessity, a regional center where freight was brought to be redistributed to the nearby mines and camps. Streets were laid out in an orderly manner by 1905. It didn't matter that most people here were still living and doing business in tents. Beatty had its own newspaper by April of 1905. By fall that same year, the town's founder, Bob Montgomery, had built a fine two-story hotel that quickly became the center of social life. For the next few years Beatty had a population of one thousand people and was served by three railroads: the Bullfrog Goldfield Railroad, (1906-1928), the Las Vegas & Tonopah, (1906-1918) and the Tonopah & Tidewater (1907-1940).

Beatty was given a rebirth after World War II when it became home to thousands of workers involved in the Nuclear Weapons Test Programs conducted just to the east at Frenchman Flat, Yucca Flats, and later Yucca Mountain. As those programs have wound down, Beatty continues to hang on, relying on servicing the needs of travelers going between Reno and Las Vegas, as well of tourists going to Death Valley from Nevada locations. Until the Bullfrog Mine closed in December of 1998, laying off 280 miners, mining had still been important to Beatty's prosperity. With the development of the nearby nuclear storage facility, Beatty's future seems assured.

The National Park Service maintains an information office on State Route 374 near Beatty's main intersection.

16

Forgotten Phinney Canyon

Primary Attraction:	A peek at a remote and seldom visited portion of the Grapevine Mountains.
Time Required:	This is pretty much a full day's outing.
Miles Involved:	From downtown Beatty it is 11.8 miles up Highway 95 to the dirt access road and then another 21 miles to the summit of the Grapevine Mountains.
Degree of Difficulty:	The dirt roads are mostly Class I and II, with a little Class III as you near the crest of the range.

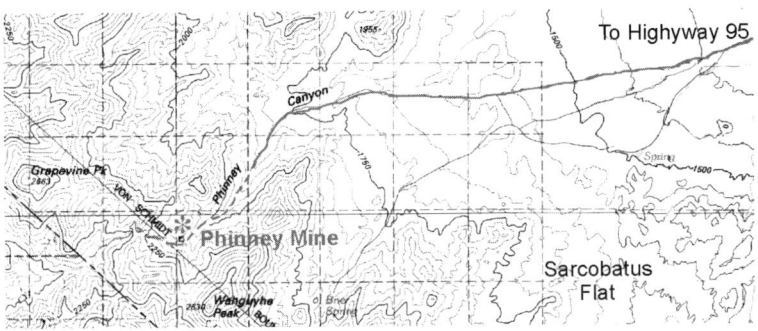

If you are one who comes to the desert to find peace and quiet, free from the hustle and bustle of the megalopolis, then a visit to Phinney Canyon should be your goal. There certainly are no crowds here. Indeed, this particular corner of Death Valley has never really been "discovered", much less visited. You will probably have to share the solitude with only an occasional pinyon jay. Much of its "undiscovered" nature lies in the fact that it is off the beaten tourist path, coupled with the fact that it is really not near anything else.

From downtown Beatty, take U.S. Highway 95 going in the direction of Goldfield and Tonopah. After 9.5 miles you will pass the small settlement of Springdale. Then 1.6 miles beyond, an unmarked dirt road goes left off the highway heading west. This is 0.3 miles north of highway milepost 71. Turn off here, closing the gate as you pass through. This is rolling rangeland where cattle pretty much roam at will. Good at first, the road gradually deteriorates to Class I as it makes its way across the vast expanse of Sarcobatus Flat. This geographic name with a tongue-twisting name comes from the plant species *Sarcobatus vermiculatus,* common greasewood that grows in great abundance here. Do not confuse greasewood with the creosote bush; they are two distinctly different plants that live in two different habitats. Greasewood thrives on alkali soils and tolerates very cold temperatures. It is common around the saline sinks of Nevada. Creosote on the other hand prefers the more southernly environment of the Mohave and Sonora deserts.

In the first 6.5 miles, there are four side roads going off to the left. Always go straight ahead on the main road. However, at 6.6 miles the road forks; this time go left. Soon you will enter Death Valley National Park. After another 4.2 miles, a crossroads is reached. The fork to the left goes 2.4 miles south to Currie Well. If you are following the route description in Excursion # 17, this is where you will come in to join the Phinney Canyon Road.

Continue heading west. At a point 1.5 miles from the last crossroads, you will cross the grade of the old Las Vegas & Tonopah Railroad whose tracks were pushed across Sarcobatus Flats in 1907. However, it is still another four miles before the road enters Phinney Canyon. Before long the brush covered hillsides turn into a forest of pinyon pine and juniper.

The scattered junipers give a distinctly *high desert* atmosphere to the countryside. Junipers are well adapted to arid lands. Two species of juniper grow within the park. The species most common in California is the *Juniperous californica.* Those growing here, however, are their eastern cousins *Juniperous osteosperma,* which grow throughout the Basin and Range province. During lean times, the native Americans sometimes dried the berries to be later ground and roasted, often making them into mush or cakes. Tea and other beverages were also made, as were medicines used for colds and fever.

Another plant in this part of the Grapevine Mountains that was utilized by the Indians is the hardy ephedra, often called Squaw tea or Mormon tea. When boiled in water, its tender young shoots produce an astringent tea said to cure intestinal ailments. I have brewed some from time to time, but always find it more palatable with some sugar or honey to offset the bitter tannic acid it contains.

At a point 19.5 miles from Highway 95 a side road, now closed by the National Park Service, branches off to the right. This leads to the Phinney Mine, a short hike up the canyon. Two brothers from Beatty, Charles E. Phinney and F.C. Phinney located this mine in 1930. The two men toiled away for several years, with a net production of some 50 tons of ore worth about $17.00 per ton. The tattered remains of their tent cabin still cling to the top of the tailings dump.

The Phinney Mine in 1968

Continue up the main canyon, which by now is Class II. In a half mile there will be another old mine shaft on the right side of the road. From here on it is mostly Class III.

After another 0.7 miles you will discover that you are on the crest of the Grapevine Mountains. Below to the west is the floor of Death Valley. Beyond, peaks of the High Sierra are clearly outlined on the skyline, even though they are seventy miles away. Prior to the California Desert Protection Act of 1994, one could drive down the other side to a spring. The area is now designated as *Wilderness* and vehicles are prohibited. If you wish to get out and stretch your legs, look for Doe Spring, a small seep on the north side of the canyon. This is one of the few places in Death Valley National Park where mule deer can be found. Remember that our national parks are game preserves where hunting is prohibited.

For really ambitious hikers 8,738' Grapevine Peak is a modest climb of 1,200 feet, about two hours and two false summits to the north. At the highest point in the Grapevine Mountains, the view is superb. On your way up, keep an eye open for a tree which has needles in bundles of fives and looks very much different from the pinyon pines all around you. This new tree is the limber pine, *Pinus aristata,* whose habitat is limited to only the highest peaks in the Basin and Range Province. Very old sheltered packrat middens reveal that the Limber pine was very widespread during the Pleistocene Ice Age. But as the southwest became warmer and drier, the habitat of the Limber pine retreated uphill so that today these trees are only found near the tops of the highest peaks.

And speaking of unusual plants, Phinney Canyon has another interesting story to tell. In 1890 the U.S. Department of Agriculture sponsored a *Death Valley Expedition* in which nine scientists from various areas of natural science spent months looking for new species and surveying the geographical distribution of plants and animals. The expedition was a success in one respect. It identified two dozen new genera and 150 new species, but it failed to reveal much in the way of potential new farmland.

On June 9, 1891, one expedition member, botanist Frederick Funston, came into Phinney Canyon. At the time it was called Wood Canyon. Funston found a new species of wild pea, although he failed to recognize it as such. He incorrectly identified the plant as *Lathyrus paluster,* a pea that is common along the California coast. Nevertheless, a specimen was sent to the National Herbarium in Washington, D.C., where it was forgotten for the next eighty years. (Funston later fought in the Spanish American War as a brigadier-general and died of a heart attack in 1917 while chasing Pancho Villa with Blackjack Pershing on the Mexican border.)

Then in 1970 a modern day botanist, James Reveal, found in the Bullfrog Hills a wild pea that he could not identify. He suspected that he might have discovered a new species, the dream of every field biologist. After months of research it was discovered that Reveal's specimen matched Funston's specimen in the National Herbarium. However, in the process it became recognized that Funston's find was not *Lathyrus paluster* after all. Funston had discovered a new species and did not know it. The new species was named *Lathyrus hitchcockianus* in honor of Dr. Leo Hitchcock, who pioneered study of the genus *Lathyrus.*

In the early 1980s the Strategic Air Command was looking at the Bullfrog Hills as a potential MX missile site. Being sensitive to rare and endangered species, the U.S. Air Force, through the U.S. Fish & Wildlife Service, asked Mary DeDecker, a noted Inyo County botanist, to determine if the wild pea was still growing and if so, to what extent. Mary and her husband Paul searched Phinney Canyon from top to bottom. All of the plants that Funston had found eighty years earlier were still there, all that is, except for this elusive little pea. She then moved on to Sawtooth Mountain near where Reveal had made his discovery. Sure enough, a healthy population of *Lathyrus hitchockianus* was found growing on the volcanic soils. The 1980 edition of *"Inventory of Rare and Endangered Vascular Plants of California"*, which listed this little pea as *presumed extinct,* was wrong on two counts. The pea was certainly not extinct, and while it may have once grown in California's Phinney Canyon, today's population was now entirely in Nevada.

17

Gold Bar and Currie Well

Primary Attraction: An obscure and long forgotten stage stop, which in later years became a watering point for steam locomotives on the Las Vegas & Tonopah Railroad.

Time Required: Currie Well can be done in a half day out of Beatty, or better yet, it can also be combined with an outing into Phinney Canyon for a full day of backroad exploration.

Miles Involved: From Beatty to Currie Well by the route described, it is seventeen miles. Add another twelve miles if you elect to go up Phinney Canyon to the crest of the Grapevine Mountains.

Degree of Difficulty: Most of the route is Class I or II, but you may encounter some short sandy areas that are briefly Class III.

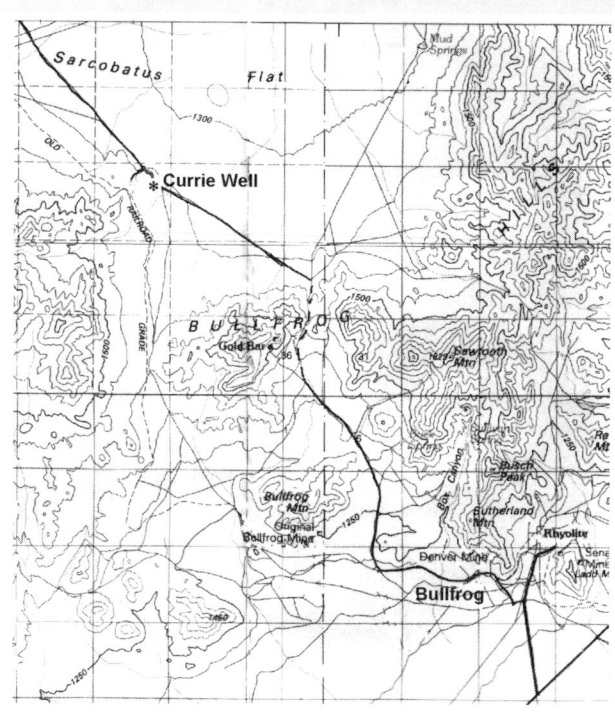

Our journey starts in downtown Beatty, where you will want to head west on Nevada State Highway 374 towards Daylight Pass and Death Valley. After nearly four miles you will pass the enormous tailing dump of the modern day Bullfrog Mine. Just beyond, the paved Rhyolite Road turns off to the right. Leave the highway here and go up this road 0.8 miles to a wide graded dirt road going off to the left. If you have never seen Rhyolite, by all means continue on another mile to see the sights, but note this intersection, as you will need to return here.

Rhyolite today

Rhyolite's "Bottle House"

Gold Bar and Currie Well

After leaving the pavement, you will soon be passing through downtown Bullfrog. Unfortunately only a couple of structures remain from its 1907 heyday. Bullfrog was the first of the Turn of the 20th Century mining camps around what would soon become Beatty. When Shorty Harris and Ed Cross discovered the Bullfrog lode in August of 1904, the first camp to spring up was called Orion. Soon it was renamed Amargosa City. Meanwhile the tent camp of Bonanza also sprang up three miles to the east. Both camps were at the base of steep hills where future growth was limited. Thus it was that both camps merged and relocated on the flat where proper streets and utilities could be laid out in an orderly manner. The new town was then named Bullfrog. By early 1906 Bullfrog had a population in excess of 1,000, with permanent buildings and connections with the outside world by telephone and automobile. The Las Vegas & Tonopah Railroad bypassed Bullfrog a half a mile to the north, and had their station in the competing town of Rhyolite.

Continue westward on this wide road of graded dirt. At a point 3.2 miles from the Rhyolite Road, the National Park boundary appears and for the next 1.6 miles, the now Class I road is on the old roadbed of the Las Vegas & Tonopah Railroad. Upon reaching a washed out trestle, today's road comes down off the railroad right of way. It is here you will leave the Class I road and head north up a sandy wash which skirts around the western side of Bullfrog Mountain. The tracks are sandy in places, but remain an easy Class III.

The road makes its way north, leaving Bullfrog Mountain behind. At a point 6.8 miles from the Rhyolite Road, a "T" intersection is reached. Turn left here and after a tenth of a mile, keep to the right. On the mountainside to the left was the Gold Bar Mine and camp. A quarter of a mile to the north, high on the hillside, were the Homestake Mine and its enormous 25-stamp mill. Both mines were opened in 1905 and shared the same orebody on the hillside. As was often the case, more money was poured into these mines than was ever taken out. The Gold Bar Mine closed in 1908, the Homestake in 1909.

Passing the Homestake mill site, the road climbs to a low pass with a few easy Class III places along the way. From the pass, the vast expanse of Sarcobatus Flat lies spread out before you to the north. At a point 0.6 miles north of the pass in the hills, the road descends to the valley floor where the roads fork. The right fork goes to Mud Springs. For Currie Well and Phinney Canyon, keep left.

One fine spring day in 1998, my wife Loris and I were in our Toyota 4Runner creeping over Sarcobatus Flat heading toward Currie Well. We were well within the national park by several miles. I had absent-mindedly left the radar detector on my dashboard on. Suddenly the device went crazy making all sorts of sounds I had never heard before. Then the sound stopped as suddenly as it started. An instant later there was a deafening roar. A shadow flashed over us, and it was then that we could see the rear of an Air Force A-10 Warthog, about one hundred feet above the ground. The pilot wiggled his wings at us in passing. I then realized what had happened. That clown had illuminated and locked onto us with his weapon's radar. The pilot was no doubt pretending we were an enemy tank, buzzing us in a mock strafing run with his 30 mm Gatling gun. Thus Loris and I made our small contribution to that pilot's flight proficiency skills and to our national defense.

From the fork in the road that is a half-mile north of the low pass, keep left heading northwest for the next 2.8 miles to where there is a desert crossroads. Here spread out over dozens of acres are thousands of rusted cans and broken bottles. The National Park Service has closed the right fork. The road straight ahead continues northwest another 2.1 miles to where it crosses the Phinney Canyon Road. The left fork goes a quarter of a mile up to the site of Currie Well.

The history of Currie Well remains obscure. In 1909 the U. S. Geological Survey published its Water Supply Paper #24, entitled *"Some Desert Watering Places in Southeastern California and Southwestern Nevada"*. In that publication, the following notation is made:

> *Currie Wells, Nye County: This watering place is 10 miles northwest of Bullfrog, on the road to Goldfield, at an elevation of 4,401 feet. Water is obtained from three wells, 10, 12, and 14 feet deep, yielding about 200 barrels of excellent water daily. There is a stage station here, at which meals and forage for animals can be obtained.*

Although not mentioned in the Water Supply Paper, in 1907 Currie Well was also the site of a construction camp for the Las Vegas & Tonopah Railroad which was being built just a few hundred yards up the hillside.

Today none of the structures from the stage stop or railroad days remain. Water still seeps out of the ground in several places and one of the three shallow wells can still be seen. A pile of century old, riveted and spiral wound iron water pipe lies rusting amid the sage. This may even be odd bits and pieces of George Robert's pipeline to his State Line mill. A quarter of a mile to the north are the remains of two rock furnaces, surrounded by rusting 25-pound black powder cans. These were probably used as forges by blacksmiths in the railroad construction gang.

Beyond Currie Well, the Class II road continues north across Sarcobatus Flat to join the Phinney Canyon Road (see Excursion # 16.)

18

Old Pioneer

Primary Attraction:	The site of another Turn of the 20th Century mining camp, although little remains.
Time Required:	Pioneer can easily be seen in a half-day's outing from Beatty.
Miles Involved:	From downtown Beatty to downtown Pioneer is only twelve miles.
Degree of Difficulty:	None of the main dirt roads involved are worse than Class II, although the exploration of nearby mines can produce more challenging routes.

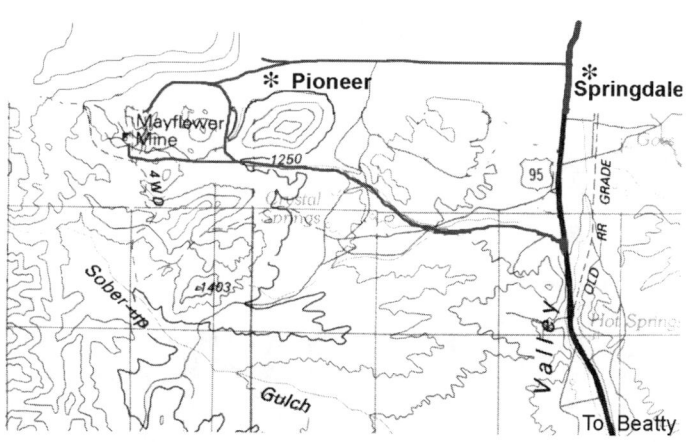

To find the site of Pioneer from Beatty, take U.S. Highway 95 north 6.6 miles. Here a sign marks the beginning of Pioneer Road, which at this point is a wide graded road going off to the left; turn here. A few modern day houses are passed, and the road forks after 1.1 miles. Keep right on the main road. After 0.4 miles a second fork is reached; again stay right. In another 1.5 miles a third fork is encountered. By this time there are mines on the hillsides to the left and right. The Class I left fork goes on for a mile to the Mayflower Mine. The right fork goes to Pioneer. At the third fork in the road, keep right. After 0.7 miles, yet a fourth fork is reached. This time keep left. In less than a half-mile, the piles of old tin cans will mark the beginning of what was once Pioneer.

Pioneer's Main Street in 1909
(Nevada Historical Society photo)

One of Pioneer's many mines in 1908
(Nevada Historical Society photo)

Old Pioneer

Pioneer was the last of the Turn of the 20th Century mining camps along the western side of the Amargosa River. Although promising veins had been found in the hills north of Sober-up Gulch as early as 1905, none proved worthy of serious mining efforts until 1908. At that time some of the old Bi-Metallic claims were leased, and the Pioneer Mine opened. A short distance away, investors opened the Mayflower Mine. By this time Bullfrog was dead, Rhyolite was dying, and only Beatty could still be called any sort of town.

Upon hearing of activity at the Pioneer and Mayflower Mines, out of work miners, merchants, and assorted providers of odd services began to flock to Pioneer. Between December of 1908 and February 1909 the camp swelled from a few hundred to twenty-five hundred. A townsite was laid out, with lots selling for more than $1,000 each. Structures appeared overnight with some, like the two story Montgomery Hotel, moved in from Beatty. Soon Pioneer had telephone service, taxi service connecting it with the railroad at Beatty, and two competing weekly newspapers.

There was a temporary setback on May 7, 1909, when a fire spread through one block of downtown destroying many businesses. The bank and the red-light district were spared, however, and by the Fourth of July things were back to normal. Alas, prosperity was a fleeting commodity. Long simmering litigation turned the boom in Pioneer off like a light switch on July 24th, when one of the litigants got an injunction against the operators of the Pioneer Mine. The mine promptly shut down and within a week people were drifting away. The operator of the Mayflower Mine had his legal problems, too, when he cooked the books causing his stockholders to sue. The resulting lawsuits closed that mine in December. Thus, the cycle of birth, boom, and bust all took place in the twelve-month period from December of 1908 to December of 1909.

The remains of the Mayflower Mine's mill.

There were later attempts to continue mining. The Mayflower Mine reopened under new management in 1911, as did the Pioneer Mine the following year, and once again the sound of dropping stamps could be heard from the Mayflower's fifteen-stamp mill and Pioneer's ten-stamp mill. Most of the good ore had been extracted during those heady days in the spring of 1909, however, and the years just prior to World War I were a disappointment to all. Clearly the glory days of Pioneer were over and would never return.

Admittedly, not much remains at Pioneer today, save for thousands of rusting tin cans and a few lonely utility poles. South of town the ore bunker of the Mayflower Mine remains as a mute reminder of Pioneer's glory days.

If you wish to return to Highway 95 by a different route, there is a Class I and II road that makes its way out to Springdale, some three miles away. From here it is ten miles back to Beatty.

Pioneer Today

19

Down Titus Canyon

Primary Attraction:	Titus Canyon has a little something for everyone: interesting geology, the site of a short-lived mining camp, and some very colorful desert scenery. Do not go into Titus Canyon seeking solitude. It is one of the most popular dirt road destinations in the park. Do check with a ranger before attempting Titus Canyon. Because of the flash flooding hazard in the narrows, the National Park Service tends to close the road during the summer months, and at the slightest hint of rain. During the winter, snow on White and Red Pass summits can close the road. This is a one way road only. You must start at the Nevada end going downhill into Death Valley.
Time Required:	You will want to allow at least a half a day for this outing.
Miles Involved:	The distance is about 33 miles from Beatty down to the floor of Death Valley. The dirt road portion is 26.4 miles in length.
Degree of Difficulty:	The first nine miles of dirt road have a wash-board surface, but the entire Titus Canyon road is generally Class I, with perhaps only a few Class II spots. Drivers should be watchful for large rocks in the roadway.

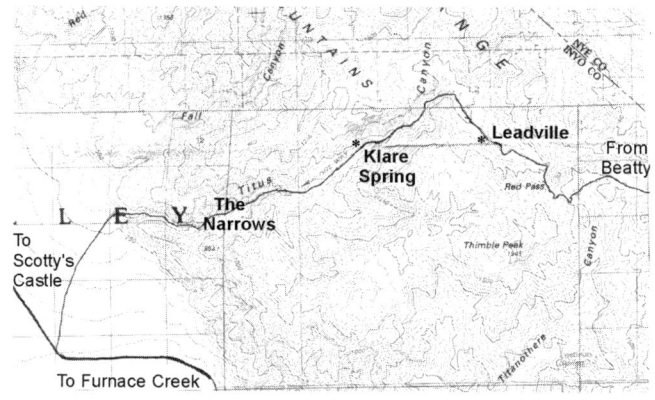

I had great reservations about including Titus Canyon in this book about jeep trails and back roads. The National Park Service has posted the road with a jeep symbol, recommending the route for high clearance vehicles with four-wheel drive. In reality, however, this is a very good road by backcountry standards. You will be disappointed if you seek a "challenge" in your route selection. By all other standards, Titus Canyon is an outstanding excursion worthy of your time.

The canyon takes its name from Morris Titus, a tenderfoot-mining engineer who perished here in the summer of 1906 while prospecting with two companions.

From Beatty take Nevada State Route 374 southwest towards the park. Four miles from town, just past the modern day Bullfrog Mine, a paved side road right goes to the ghost town of Rhyolite. A visit to this historic camp is highly recommended.

At a point 2.1 miles beyond the road into Rhyolite, watch for a graded dirt road turning right, heading westward. Turn right here, and note your odometer reading. Within two miles you will enter Death Valley National Park. A park service sign announces that camping is not permitted anywhere along the Titus Canyon Road.

In its first six miles the graded road gradually climbs 800 vertical feet up the alluvial fan before entering the Grapevine Mountains. Once the wash is entered, the country becomes more interesting. The surrounding mountains are Tertiary volcanic rocks, representing several phases of volcanism occurring over a span of five to eleven million years ago. Many of the peaks are actually volcanic plugs, the hardened material in the throat of a volcano left exposed after the cone has weathered away.

A very common plant along the roadside here is ephedra, sometimes called Squaw Tea or Mormon Tea. There are seven species of ephedra in California, five of which are found within the park. Three of those five species are found here on White Pass: the very common *Ephedra viridis*, the less common, but still abundant, *Ephedra nevadensis*, and *Ephedra funerea*, which is on the California Native Plant Society's list of rare and endangered plants. Originally it was thought to grow only in the Funeral Mountains near Ryan, but in recent years it has been found here in the Grapevine Mountains and in San Bernardino County as well.

At a point 12.8 miles from the pavement, the summit of White Pass is reached. The elevation here is slightly over 5,100 feet. Winter snows can sometimes cause the Park Service to close this road for a few days.

In the next two miles, the road descends some five hundred feet through layers of green, red, and black sediments. This is the upper basin of Titanothere

Canyon, so named for a large rhinoceros-like animal that roamed this area during Oligocene times. The 32 million year old fossilized remains of this critter were excavated from the red sandstone member of the Titus Canyon Formation near Leadville in 1933. The Oligocene landscape was much different than what you see today. In those prehistoric times this was a savanna-like terrain, with lakes and slow sluggish streams around which the plant-eating animals browsed and the carnivores hunted for prey. Other fossil animals uncovered in these beds were camel-like creatures, deer, tapirs, dogs and various rodents.

From the low point, the road now switchbacks back up through layers of red sediments to the colorful summit of 5,250' Red Pass. This is the high point of the road, an ideal place to stop and enjoy the expansive views. Once you get down into Titus Canyon, that feeling of wide-open space will be lost.

The road descends Red Pass for the next three miles, passing a number of prospect holes, to come to the site of Leadville 15.4 miles in from Highway 374. The Bullfrog excitement brought prospectors through here in 1905. Specimens of lead and copper minerals were found, and claims were filed, but the remoteness of the area and the low-grade ore combined to discourage mining. All was quiet until 1924 when there became renewed interest in the lead deposits. An individual by the name of John Salsberry raised some capital and formed a company known as Western Lead Mines. He bought twelve claims in 1925 and he staked forty more. Salsberry had one crew digging prospect holes in the upper part of Titus Canyon, while another crew was building a road in from Beatty.

In 1926, at the peak of the "Roaring Twenties", an oil man from Los Angeles by the name of Charles Julian wrestled control of Western Lead Mines, and set out to promote his new company's stock. Like some modern day real estate promotions, he induced potential investors to come out to Titus Canyon for a free meal and a tour of the mine. By this time the road started by Salsberry had been completed. For those investors who did not choose the rigors of driving to Death Valley, Julian chartered a fifteen car "special train" using a Southern Pacific locomotive as far as Ludlow, where a Tonopah & Tidewater engine brought the train into Beatty. From there a fleet of autos brought the potential investors on into Leadville. Waiting for them was a band and a grand lunch at which well over a thousand people were served. The scheme worked. A week or two after this promotion, some 330,000 shares of stock in Western Lead Mines had been sold. In late January 1926 that stock had been selling at $1.57 a share. At the end of March Julian's scheme had boosted the price to $3.30. It did not seem to matter that the nearest water was some two and a half miles down the canyon at Klare Spring. Leadville was on the map. In April the townsite of Leadville was laid out with 1,749 lots in 93 blocks. Businesses opened and they advertised in the newly formed newspaper, the *Leadville Chronicle*. On June 25th, the post office opened, and Leadville's prosperity seemed assured.

There were a few problems, however. By this time Julian was under investigation for securities irregularities. And then there was the matter of the lead ore. There wasn't any! The speculative bubble burst and by December 31, 1926, the post office closed its doors in Leadville for the last time. So 1926 was the best of times and the worst of times for Leadville. It was born, matured, and died all in the course of twelve months. In spite of its short life, Leadville was added to the National Register of Historic Places in 1975.

Thanks to National Park Service Protection, little has changed in Leadville since the author took this photo in 1956

Titus Canyon

A half-mile below Leadville the geology suddenly makes a dramatic change. The 30 million-year-old Titus Canyon Formation disappears to be replaced by 550 million-year-old sedimentary rock of Cambrian age. With the change of geology Titus Canyon proper is entered. A Park Service interpretive sign *"Where Rocks Bend"* explains why these layers seem to bend sharply. It is in fact an optical illusion.

Where rocks bend

Klare Spring is reached two and a half miles below Leadville. This is the only water in the canyon. Prehistoric Indians knew the site well. They left their petroglyphs etched in a rock outcrop just up the canyon from the spring. When these primitive rock carvings portray things like bighorn sheep, the object, if not the message, can be easily recognized. Many of the drawings are abstract geometric designs and the meaning of these has been lost in antiquity. Even present-day Native Americans are not sure of their interpretation. Archaeologists have many theories as to what these doodles mean, but in fact, nobody knows for sure.

At a point 1.9 miles below Klare Spring look to the left where the flat surface of the bedding plane in the marble is exposed. On top of the gray limestone rock is a thin layer of hardened brown mud containing fossil ripple marks. These ripples were made in the bottom of a shallow Cambrian sea some 500 million years ago.

Four miles below Klare Spring begin the narrows that so delight tourists. For the next 1.7 miles the canyon walls soar hundreds of feet up, but are barely twenty feet apart in some places. Six miles below Klare Spring, 23.8 miles from Highway 374, the magic of the canyon suddenly ends. The roadway abruptly leaves the canyon and you find yourself overlooking the vast expanse of Death Valley. It is only 2.5 miles down the alluvial fan to the paved road that leads to Scotty's Castle.

The Titus Canyon Narrows

20

Chloride City

Primary Attraction: An historic mining camp of the 1870s, with great views of Death Valley all the way to Mt. Whitney and the Sierra crest.

Time Required: This is pretty much an all day trip out of either Beatty or Stovepipe Wells, particularly if you hike down to the Monarch Mine.

Miles Involved: It is sixteen miles of highway from Beatty to the turnoff, and then another seven miles into Chloride City.

Degree of Difficulty: Of the dirt road portion, about half is Class II, and about half an easy Class III.

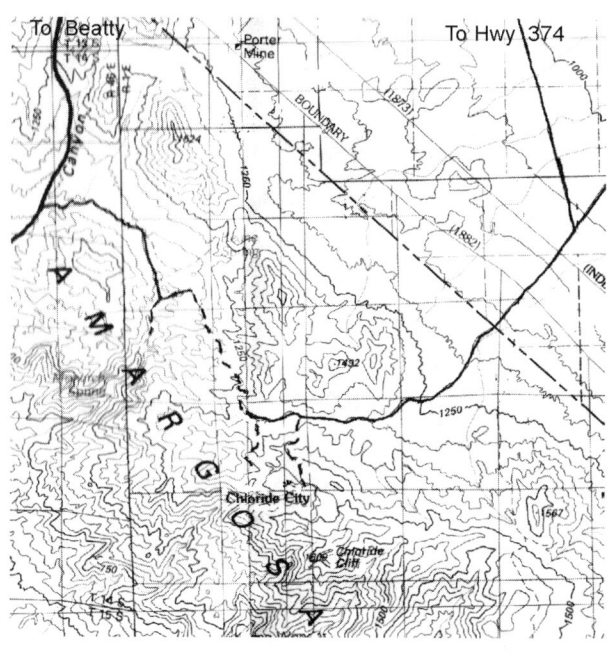

This old mining camp is an easy day trip out of either Stovepipe Wells or Beatty. The best road into Chloride City comes south off Highway 95 near Beatty, but that is out of the way for many people visiting Death Valley. A more convenient way in may be off the Daylight Pass Road northeast of the Stovepipe Wells Resort. The road is no worse than Class III.

Chloride City arose out of silver discoveries in Chloride Cliff in 1873, the earliest of all the Death Valley mines. The mines of this small community struggled for a few years, but by 1880 none were working and everyone had moved on. The Rhyolite excitement of 1904 brought in new capital. The Chloride Cliff Mine was bought by investors in nearby Rhyolite and reopened in 1908. In the following years sufficient ore was produced to warrant the construction of a cyanide mill in 1916. It is questionable whether that investment paid off, because by 1918 the camp was deserted again.

From downtown Beatty take State Highway 374 southwest towards Death Valley. Before leaving town the highway passes the local Death Valley information office where the latest road information can be obtained. At a point three and a half miles outside Beatty, the highway passes the huge Bullfrog Mine operated by the Barrick Corporation until 1999. During the good times, in 1997, Barrick had 289 employees at the Bullfrog Mine. They produced 206,571 ounces of gold and 351,348 ounces of silver. By 1999 those figures had dropped to 52 employees turning out a mere 76,159 ounces of gold and 90,967 ounces of silver. By 2000 the mine was closed.

Just beyond the mine, a side road goes right up the hill to the site of Rhyolite, just a couple of miles to the west. Rhyolite certainly warrants a visit.

Rhyolite's origin goes back to February of 1905 when promoters left out of the Bullfrog boom selected a site a mile away, drew up a plat map, named streets, and subdivided the land into lots. To attract business and settlement, free parcels were offered to merchants; the ploy worked. Within three months the basin contained a sea of white tents, and within a year Rhyolite had eclipsed its slightly older neighbor, Bullfrog, just a mile to the southwest. In 1906 the Las Vegas & Tonopah Railroad extended its tracks to Rhyolite. By 1907 the town of only two years had a population of 6,000. By this time Rhyolite had substantial buildings made of wood and stone, and at least one made of empty bottles (it still stands as a museum). However late in 1907, a financial panic spread across the nation and, with the loss of financial support, many of Rhyolite's mines closed, many to never open again. With this bursting of the bubble of optimism, the citizens of Rhyolite drifted away. By the 1910 census, Rhyolite only had a population of 700; by the 1920 census, nobody was left.

Chloride City

The remains of the bank operated by John S. Cook
and Company dominate Rhyolite's landscape

Nevada Highway 374 crosses the flat expanse of the Amargosa Valley and begins a steady climb into the mountains to the southwest. The state line is crossed at a point 12.7 miles from downtown Beatty. The sign is so tiny that most people miss it. A 4,317' low point in the mountains, Daylight Pass is thirteen miles out of Beatty. Daylight Pass makes a convenient geographical boundary between the Grapevine Mountains to the north and the Funeral Mountains to the south. Note your odometer reading at the pass. Just 2.7 miles beyond the summit look for a desert road going off to the left. The National Park Service has marked it with the customary jeep symbol. This is the turnoff to Chloride City. (If you are coming from the Death Valley side, the turnoff is 3.4 miles above Hell's Gate.)

The well-defined Class II road heads south and east. After two miles a side road to the left goes to Keane Spring. The Park Service has closed the road to vehicle traffic, although it is an easy hike of less than a mile. As small as it is, this spring has been a reliable source of water. During the 1906 Rhyolite Excitement when miners came flocking into these mountains by the thousands, a small village developed around this water hole. Although short-lived, Keane Spring once had a boarding house, livery stable, and of course, a saloon. Even the Porter Brothers, who had a large general store in nearby Rhyolite, opened a branch here. When the "Bank Panic of 1907" dried up venture capitol, Keane Spring did not dry up, but the town did. A few years later a flash flood came down the wash and dispersed what little remained.

The road now begins a gradual descent and within a quarter of a mile you will be in the Monarch Canyon wash. The road goes to the left, but there is an interesting side trip right down into the confining walls of Monarch Canyon. At one time this road went down to the Monarch Mine, discovered in 1905 and worked off and on until World War II. Today you can take a vehicle down the canyon only 0.7 miles where you will encounter the mother of all road washouts. Nevertheless, this wash makes a fine campsite (in good weather) suitable for a 4x4 club outing. From the present day road's end one can hike down the canyon, past the spring a mile or so to the well preserved mine.

Back on the main Chloride Cliff road, within a quarter of a mile, a spring and a water tank are passed on the left. The road now deteriorates to Class III as it cuts across the grain of the landscape. On the hillsides to the right, mines and prospect holes begin to appear. After two miles it returns to Class II. At a point 2.6 miles beyond the water tank, a major road intersection is reached; this is Chloride Junction. The Class I road to the left heads north to Highway 95 and Beatty. For Chloride City you will want to turn to the right. The route has once again deteriorated to Class III.

Within 0.7 miles a ridge top is reached with good views northeast into the Amargosa Valley of Nevada. To the west are some of Chloride City's outlying mines, and beyond on the distant skyline, the crest of the Sierra Nevada Range. At a point 1.1 miles from Chloride Junction, the road forks at a viewpoint overlooking the site of Chloride City. Keep to the left another quarter of a mile and you will be in what was once "downtown".

Chloride City has had a checkered past of boom and bust. It all started in the early 1870s when A.J. Franklin discovered silver ore on what was to become Chloride Cliff.

Chloride City

Chloride City in 1958

In his book *Mines of Death Valley,* Death Valley historian Burr Belden tells about the miners having to go 250 miles to the nearest grocery store in Barstow, California. Ten years later the road blazed in those days was adopted in part by mule trains from both the Eagle Borax Works, as well as the Harmony Borax Works. There were also several skirmishes between the miners and Paiute Indians in this part of the Funeral Range. Because of its remote location, the Franklin Mine could not be operated profitably, and it eventually closed in the late 1870s.

Not much happened here for the next 25 years, even though the silver mines of Panamint City, Lookout, Darwin and Cerro Gordo were going strong. The Rhyolite excitement of 1905 spurred new interest in the district, although the San Francisco earthquake dried up venture capital and with it the mines of Chloride City closed. The bank panic of 1907 depressed the price of silver, keeping the mines idle. By 1908 a few small mines reopened, and in 1916 Chloride City had its first cyanide mill. That operation was closed by 1918, but its foundations still remain. Since then, there have been several renewed efforts to wrestle the mineral wealth from these barren hills.

These are highly metamorphosed rocks, schist, gneiss and quartzite, some of the oldest rocks in Death Valley going back 500 million years to the pre-Precambrian. They have been cut by diorite dikes and with those intrusions came quartz veins, sometimes up to thirty feet thick, containing gold, silver, lead, and even cinnabar, a mercury mineral. Most of the gold and silver ores were low grade, containing one half ounce or less per ton; nevertheless, it was sometimes economically feasible to mine it because the veins were so large. The major mines of the district were the Big Bell, Frisco, Gold Dollar, Chloride Cliff and the Keane Wonder Mines. The latter had production in excess of a million dollars. Because of their dangerous condition, the National Park Service has installed sturdy fencing over the entrance to many of these mines. Only the most foolhardy would try to enter.

Today Chloride City consists of a few wooden shacks of questionable ancestry, mines and tailings piles aplenty, and of course scattered dumps of rusting tin cans. The camp's only grave marks the final resting-place of one James McKay.

After wandering around Chloride City proper, be sure to drive three quarters of a mile to the ridge top beyond the town. The view is grand and glorious. Not only can you look down upon much of Death Valley, including the sand dunes and that great slash in the Panamints caused by Cottonwood Canyon, but if the day is clear, you can clearly see the 14,495 foot summit of Mount Whitney, eighty miles away on the western skyline.

There are sufficient back roads and old mines in the Chloride City area to keep one engaged the whole day. It should prove to be an enjoyable day.

A "Cousin Jack" dugout in Chloride City

21

Echo Pass via Lee's Camp

Primary Attraction: Two Turn of the 20th Century mining camps, interesting geology and some challenging roads.

Time Required: This is an all day outing from Beatty to Echo Pass and return.

Miles Involved: It is 32 miles of highway or good graded road to the start of the Lee's Camp Road, then nearly three miles to the site of Lee, plus another three miles to Echo Pass. From Echo Pass to Furnace Creek Ranch is another fourteen miles.

Degree of Difficulty: It is Class II to the two sites of Lee, and from there Class III with a little IV from there on to Echo Pass. (The worst part of the road is on the western side of the pass, where it is Class V for a short distance.)

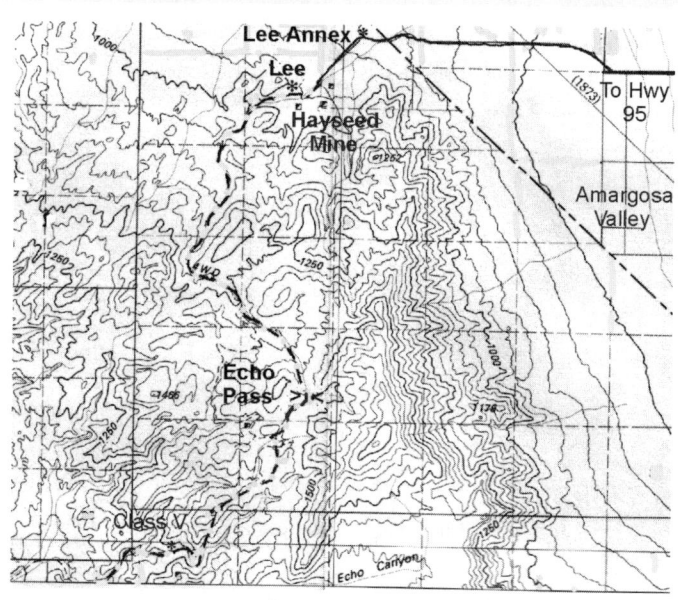

Take U.S. Highway 95 south out of Beatty. After 21.2 miles look for a sign reading *Amargosa Farms* and pointing to a paved road to the right; turn here on Valley View Road. Continue south, passing Big Dune off on the distant right. After 6.6 miles turn right again onto West Frontier Street, a wide graded road; follow this street west. There is hardly any trace left of the old Tonopah & Tidewater Railroad that came through here during the years of 1906 to 1940. There was a relatively large three-room station and a water tank here. The place was called Leeland.

At a point 3.9 miles west of Valley View Road, you will see a Class II desert road going off to the right at an angle. This is the start of your rough road adventure all the way to the summit of Echo Pass. The road works its way westward climbing up the bajada. One wonders whether the desert pavement might offer a smoother, less rough surface than this rocky road. After some 2.3 miles, which seem like ten, the state line is reached. No boundary sign marks its presence, but just beyond is a 75 by 85-foot rectangular rock enclosure with a road going off to the right. This is the site of the Lee Annex, a small community started by L.P. McGarry in 1907, a spin off of the more successful camp just a mile to the southwest. The road going north from here goes to yet a third townsite of Lee, this one clearly in Nevada. Gambling occurred in Lee, Nevada, but any resulting disputes were settled on the California side of the boundary where there was no law enforcement!

Keep to the left heading towards a cove in the mountains. Still Class II, the road actually seems to become a little smoother. Within a mile and a quarter a fork to the left heads for an abandoned tunnel at the base of the mountainside. Keep right and in a few hundred yards you will be driving down Nevada Street in downtown Lee, California. You will know you are there when you see piles of rusting tin cans strewn about. Among them are the low stone walls that were once the foundations of wooden structures.

Lee, California in at its peak 1907
(Nevada Historical Society photo)

Lee's Camp

Legend has it that two Shoshone Indian brothers, Dick and Gus Lee, together with Henry Finley (who was well into his 70s), discovered a gold-bearing quartz vein on the western slope of the Funeral Range as part of the Bullfrog Excitement of 1904. They staked their claims, set up camp near the outcrop, and started a tunnel to tap the vein. Thus the Hayseed and Stateline Mines were born. At first, their small settlement became known as Lee's Camp (that name still appears on USGS topographic maps). In February of 1906 the Lee boys sold their claims to a trio of Tonopah investors. The fact that they already sold those same claims to someone else didn't apparently bother them, for in late March they sold the same claims a third time, always a cash transaction. The Lee brothers then left for parts unknown, leaving the buyers to sue each other for custody. As it turned out, a fourth consortium of owners bought out the interests of the litigants and mining began in January of 1907. At a depth of only 25 feet, the Hayseed Mine tapped into an 18-inch view of gold that had assay values of $8,600 to $123,000 per ton! Unfortunately the vein soon pinched out, but there was the promise of more to come.

At the same time, promoters laid out the townsite of Lee, California to compete with the townsite of Lee, Nevada which was situated three miles to the northeast and had been laid out a few days before. In it's first 30 days, Lee, California boasted of having a rooming house, a restaurant, a general store, and of course, a saloon. By March Lee, California had added a bakery, another restaurant, rooming house and two more saloons. In April the town added a stage station, a barbershop, a meat market, an icehouse, two lumberyards, two more restaurants, three general stores, three feed yards and two more saloons. It was obvious that Lee, California had beaten Lee, Nevada in the race for metropolis of the Funeral Range. By the late summer and early fall of 1907, the population peaked at somewhere between five and six hundred, including twenty women. There was a full range of goods and services available, including a post office and a newspaper, the *Lee Herald*. A telephone line was strung to Leeland, connecting Lee with the outside world, and the railroad people talked of running a spur line into Lee.

The Bank Panic of 1907 began to take its toll as investment funds dried up and mines began to close. Within a year, most of Lee's population and businesses had moved on. The post office closed its doors in 1912, as did Lillard's General Store. Within a few months, the entire town was deserted. Scavengers took the abandoned buildings apart, using the materials elsewhere. As one looks around today, it seems incredible to think that this was once a thriving community of hundreds of people.

Lee, California today

The road continues above Lee, entering a small canyon and deteriorating to Class III in places. At a point 1.6 miles beyond Lee, watch for a wash on the left. Although it may not look like it, this is actually a fork in the trail. The obvious route to the right dead-ends in a half mile at a tunnel. You will want to turn left up this wash.

Within a mile a canyon is entered, and soon the road becomes Class III as it makes its way up the canyon's rocky floor. **Depending on conditions of the moment, there could be some limited Class IV sections in this canyon.**

The country opens up again a couple of miles after turning up the sandy wash. There are side roads going off to the right and left, leading to numerous prospect holes. Finally at a point five miles from Lee's Camp, the rounded summit over the Funeral Mountains is reached. Compared to the rocky canyon below, Echo Pass is anti-climactic.

Once on top you can turn around and return the way you came, or you can proceed on down Echo Wash into Death Valley. **If you elect to go on, be aware that there is a dry waterfall about a mile and a half down the western side. It is at least Class IV going down (my wife says Class V), but the east to west descent is easier than the west to east ascent. Without any doubt, climbing up this dry cascade is a Class V ascent.**

Chapter V

Trails Out of Shoshone

The settlement of Shoshone was given birth by the discovery of copper in Greenwater, thirty miles to the northwest. It has been said that if you wish to see downtown Greenwater, come to Shoshone. That is where all of Greenwater's houses were moved to in 1910, after everyone had abandoned Greenwater in 1907. At the time Shoshone was simply a small siding on the Tonopah & Tidewater Railroad. During your visit to Shoshone, I would highly recommend taking a few minutes to walk through its small museum.

With a population of only one hundred, Shoshone makes a handy base of operations for exploration of the southern end of the Death Valley country. There is a motel, private camping and RV facilities, a general store, restaurant, gas station, and a sometimes open Ranger Station where the latest road conditions may be obtained.

In nearby Tecopa, Inyo County operates a hot spring spa, where weary muscles can be rejuvenated after a hard day of bouncing on the area's jeep trails.

Today about 100 people call Shoshone home

The Shoshone Information Office occupies
an old house moved in from Greenwater

The privately operated Shoshone Museum
contains some interesting exhibits

22

Deadman Pass

Primary Attraction:	This is perhaps the least used of all the backcountry roads in the Death Valley country. It was originally a freight road for wagons taking supplies from the railhead at Death Valley Junction to Greenwater. If you are going into Gold Valley (Excursion #23) or into Greenwater (Excursion #3), Deadman Pass offers an alternate way of getting there.
Time Required:	From Highway 127 to the Greenwater Valley Road should take no longer than an hour.
Distance Involved:	The Deadman Pass Road is slightly less than fourteen miles long.
Degree of Difficulty:	Although it has sandy beginnings, this route is generally no worse than Class II.

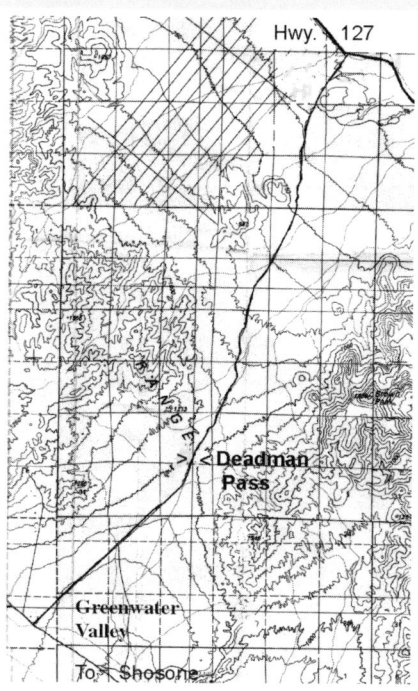

Freight going to the mining camps of Greenwater, Kuntz and Furnace would come off the Tonopah & Tidewater Railroad at Death Valley Junction, to be reloaded on to mule drawn freight wagons. The route of choice was over a pass in the Greenwater Range into the Greenwater Valley and north to the appropriate destination.

The 1939 guidebook to Death Valley that was published as a WPA project says that Deadman Pass was so named during the Greenwater boom days when the body of an unknown man was found there. I have not been able to confirm that with any other source.

From Shoshone take State Route 127 north. Note your odometer reading carefully at the intersection of Highways 178 and 127 just a mile north of town. The unmarked turnoff west to Deadman Pass is 17.4 miles north of this intersection on Highway 127. If you pass the sign along the side of the highway announcing that the elevation is 2,000 feet, you have gone one hundred yards too far north.

Leave the highway here heading west. In the first mile or two there may be sufficient soft sand that you will wish to engage your four-wheel drive. At a point 1.8 miles from the highway, the road forks; stay to the left. As you get up on the bajada, however, the road improves to Class II and remains so all the way to the Greenwater Valley Road.

The broad low divide of Deadman Pass is reached at a point 9.4 miles from the highway. A U.S. Geological Survey marker indicates the elevation is 3,264 feet. From here it is 4.5 miles more to the Greenwater Valley Road.

Deadman Pass Road

23

Gold Valley Solitude

Primary Attraction: An isolated valley, once the site of three competing mining camps. If you are very lucky, bighorn sheep sightings are also possible.

Time Required: This is an all day trip out of either Shoshone or Furnace Creek.

Miles Involved: It is 29 miles one way from downtown Shoshone to downtown Gold Valley. From Furnace Creek Ranch, the one way distance to Gold Valley is 47 miles.

Degree of Difficulty: The route is mostly Class II, with a few Class III sections near the end.

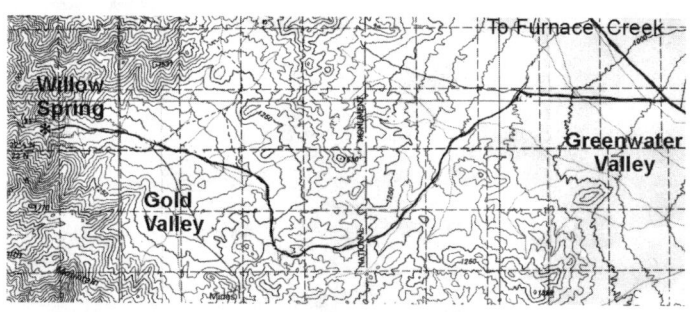

In the first decade of the 20th Century, gold fever once again ran rampant throughout the west, and once again there was a frantic rush to anywhere one's fortune might be made. In 1906 the excitement in the Black Mountains emptied the saloons and boarding houses of Rhyolite, Goldfield, and Tonopah as thousands headed south to the boomtowns of Furnace and Greenwater. The population of Greenwater swelled from 70 to 1000 in just one month. By 1907 more than 2,500 claims had been filed at the Inyo County Courthouse in distant Independence. Some of these claims extended south of Funeral Peak into a basin optimistically named "Gold Valley". Like Greenwater, however, Gold Valley proved to be more sizzle than substance. By 1910 there was nobody left.

During the 1930s, the Automobile Club of Southern California placed a series of baked enamel road signs throughout the back roads of the California desert. They announced the distances to waterholes and other landmarks. When I visited Gold Valley for the first time in 1958, one of those old signs was still in place. In fact, the area was so isolated that not only was the sign still there, but it had not been shot full of bullet holes or otherwise vandalized! That sign is gone today, hopefully in the custody of the National Park Service for some future museum display.

In 1958 the author found this 50 year old Automobile Club of Southern California sign intact

To see Gold Valley as it was in 1910, take State Route 127 north out of Shoshone, immediately turning west on State Route 178. At a point 5.8 miles west of Highway 127, turn right on the graded Greenwater Valley Road. Proceed up this road 10.6 miles, and there on the left you will find a Class II road heading into the Black Mountains. This road goes due west up the bajada for the first 2.5 miles and then comes to a crossroads. The right fork and middle fork are now closed by *Wilderness* designation, so you will have to turn left, soon entering the Black Mountains. The crest of this range is crossed seven miles in from the Greenwater Valley Road, and Gold Valley is below you to the west. After a half mile the road forks. Take either branch, as they both descend into the valley. (The left fork passes some prospect holes and is a half a mile longer than the right fork.)

The stampede to Greenwater in the summer of 1906 brought so many prospectors into the Black Mountains that there wasn't room for everyone. The overflow fanned out in every direction, and some wandered into an isolated valley just south of Smith Mountain. Here they discovered Willow Spring, an oddity in the otherwise dry and barren Black Mountains. Not only was there a spring here, but it had sufficient quantity to feed a year-around stream. Even before the first pound of ore was mined, the Willow Creek Mining District was organized. Chet Leavitt, a strict Mormon recently arrived from the Echo Pass area, proclaimed the area around Willow Spring to be the town of Copper Basin.

Not to be outdone, another newcomer, Ernest Mattinson, started a second competing town nearby which he called Willow Creek. Mattinson lacked the religious convictions of Leavitt, and had a saloon in his town. Within months, everybody in Copper Basin succumbed to the lure of the demon rum and moved to Willow Creek.

For the next ten months there was a lot of looking, but little mining. Traces of copper were everywhere, but none in sufficient quantities to mine. In May of 1907 a newcomer to the district, one Joe Witherell, found not copper, but gold. The timing could not have been better. By this time the bloom was off the copper craze, and the prospectors were only too happy to go for the gold. Hundreds of them started pouring in from all the camps along the western side of the Amargosa River. Two enterprising brothers appropriately named Goldsworthy drew up a plot map, laying out 96 blocks in the City of Gold Valley. Everything was in place, awaiting the day that the first big mines started shipping ore.

At its peak in 1908 Gold Valley had the basic services to provide the needs of several hundred people. Unfortunately there were no mines to support the community. By 1910, Gold Valley was abandoned and but a distant dream. Gold Valley lasted no longer than its chief rival to the east, Greenwater.

Both forks of our road rejoin, and from here it is another 1.5 miles to Willow Spring where the road ends. Only the last half becomes Class III. At the road's end, a half-mile hike down the canyon is a must. Here bedrock in the narrow gorge forces all the subsurface water in the Gold Valley drainage to the surface. Even in the heat of summer there is usually enough water to trickle from one pool to the next. This water supports dozens of species of animals, including Bighorn sheep. Indeed, during the warmer months this is probably the best place in the park to see the Desert Bighorn. Obviously, the National Park Service discourages camping here at this very environmentally sensitive water hole.

The Desert Bighorn *Ovis canadensis nelsoni* appears to be a living remnant of the Pleistocene Ice Age that has been able to successfully adapt and hang on, as the land turned drier and warmer. There are an estimated four hundred to six hundred animals within the park, and naturalists are optimistic that their numbers are slowly growing. Bighorn like solitude and are generally deep in the mountains far from the places that tourists frequent, although Bighorn have been sighted in the rocks a safe distance above Badwater, seemingly watching the crowds below.

There is an ongoing controversy concerning habitat competition between feral burros and the Bighorn sheep. Some say the wild burros foul waterholes and eat forage the sheep would otherwise eat. The conclusion is then made that Bighorn sheep populations have declined because of the feral burros and as the numbers of burros increase, the sheep decrease. In their comprehensive study of the Bighorn sheep made in the late 1950s, Ralph and Florence Welles found no conclusive evidence to support this conclusion. I don't know who is correct, but it is interesting to note that during the late 1980s and early 1990s some 6,000 wild burros were rounded up and removed from the park. Since that time, the Bighorn sheep population seems to be slowly increasing. Is it a coincidence?

The desert bighorn prefer solitude

24

The Ashford Mine

Primary Attraction: This route provides easy hiking access to a Turn of the 20th Century mine.

Time Required: From Shoshone (or Furnace Creek Ranch) to the mouth of Ashford Canyon is only an hour. Add another hour to walk up to the mine.

Miles Involved: It is nearly 33 miles from Shoshone to the Ashford Mill, (45 miles from Furnace Creek Ranch) and then another three miles to the end of the trail.

Degree of Difficulty: The road is Class II from the Ashford Mill to the end of the road.

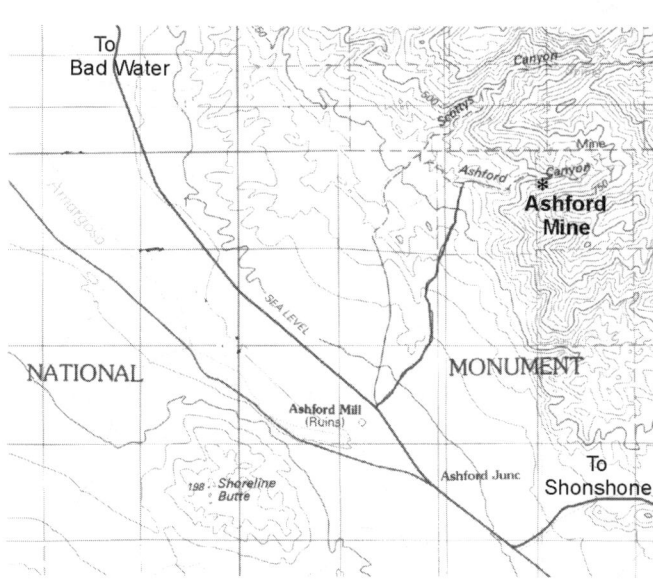

From Shoshone take State Route 127 north 1.7 miles. Turn left on State Route 178 and proceed westward over Salsberry Pass and Jubilee Pass. After 33 miles, the ruins of the Ashford Mill can be seen off to the left. Visit the site if you wish, but there isn't much left to see. This was once the site of a mill that processed ore from the nearby Golden Treasure Mine, often called the Ashford Mine, just five miles to the east. While the mine was located in 1907 at the tail end of the "Greenwater excitement", it wasn't until 1914 that this mill was built. The name "Ashford Mill" is a misnomer, because the Ashford brothers neither built nor operated the facility.

The Ashford Mill ruins in 1956

At the millsite one cannot help but notice Shoreline Butte just to the west. The hill itself is made up of volcanic basalt and fanglomerate of the early Pleistocene Funeral Formation. The rocks themselves are not as interesting as what has happened to them. Late in the Pleistocene, after this hill was already in place, glacial melt-water from the high Sierra flowed out of the Owens Valley into the China Lake Basin, then into the Searles Basin followed by the Panamint Basin, to eventually overflow down Wingate Wash into Death Valley. The result was ancient Lake Manly, a freshwater lake ninety miles long by six to eleven miles wide, with a depth of up to six hundred feet. During that time, wind-whipped waves cut terraces into the shoreline. When the climate warmed up and the glaciers no longer fed Lake Manly, the lake cut new terraces as the water evaporated and the lake began to shrink in size. Ancient Lake Manly is long gone; however, these fossil beaches remain. Geologists call them wave cut terraces. There are at least ten of them here. This same phenomenon can also be seen at Mormon Point south of Badwater and again above Mushroom rock.

On the eastern side of the highway, opposite the road to the mill, a Class I desert road heads towards the colorful south end of the Black Mountains. This is the road that once connected the mine to the mill and it is where you will leave the pavement. After 0.7 miles the road forks; stay to the left (the right fork has been closed). Soon the road deteriorates to Class II. The reddish brown hills on the left are a mixture of Pliocene sediments, mostly conglomerates and other stream deposits. To the right in the Black Mountains, the rust brown rocks are part of a very old, highly faulted complex of Precambrian metamorphic rocks. Levi Noble, a geologist who pioneered geologic study in Death Valley in the 1930s, described the southern end of the Black Mountains as the *"Amargosa chaos"*. The term is very appropriate and has stuck.

Two and a half miles from the highway, one encounters a steep grade with poor traction. However, the road does not truly turn to Class III for another half mile, when you enter the wash. The tracks go up Ashford Canyon a quarter of a mile and abruptly end; however if you want to walk up to the Ashford Mine, simply park in the wash. On the hillside is the remnant of a once paved road, steeply climbing up the ridge to the east. Hike up the road a third of a mile to the ridge top and from here it becomes obvious why this route was chosen by the Ashford brothers when they built this wagon road. Down in the canyon a giant piece of rock has rolled off the mountainside to come to rest in Ashford Canyon like a big chock stone. The former road over this low ridge bypasses this obstacle. Simply walk down the road back into the wash and follow the wash up to the mine. From the end of today's road to the lower workings of the mine, it is an easy hike of about an hour. **Warning: stay out of the underground workings. They are not safe!**

It is unclear when gold was first discovered in this little canyon in the Black Mountains, but it was probably during the Greenwater excitement of 1905. The Gold Key Mining Company had staked claims everywhere, but did not keep up their required annual assessment work. The Ashford brothers, Harold, Henry and Louis, refiled on some claims, whereupon Gold Key promptly sued them. The Ashford boys ultimately prevailed, but by this time it was 1910 and the legal expenses had taken all of their cash. They leased the property for $60,000 to self-styled Hungarian nobleman, Count Kramer. The Count in turn leased the mine to a Los Angeles oilman, Benjamin McCausland, for $105,000. By this time it was 1914. McCausland and his son, Ross, blasted out a road, the remnants of which you see today. They brought in a lot of machinery and installed a modern mill on a bluff on the east bank of the Amargosa River.

They worked the mine at a feverish pace from February to September of 1915. Some fifty men worked around the clock, mining the ore and trucking it five miles down to the mill. They had put about $230,000 into the venture and had cleaned out about $100,000 of the best ore. McCausland defaulted on his lease from Kramer, causing Kramer to leave the Ashford brothers holding the bag. The Ashford's Golden Treasure Mine has never reopened.

If You Should Break Down

What should you do if you are out alone and experience a serious break down while out in the backcountry? Should you stay with the disabled vehicle or go for help? Should you split your group with the strongest member walking out for help, while leaving those less physical able behind? (Back in January of 1850 two young men named Manly and Rogers left the weakened Bennett-Arcan party in Death Valley while they walked 150 miles to get help.) There is no simple answer to that question. The conventional wisdom is to always stay with your vehicle and let someone else find you. But that may not always be the best answer. It depends on your individual circumstances.

Both the National Park Service and the BLM have Backcountry Rangers who occasionally patrol the less frequented dirt roads; however the California desert contains 12 million square miles and your chances of having a ranger stumble upon your predicament are slim. If you are found at all, it is more likely to be by another backcountry traveler like yourself.

Obviously it is always best to travel with companions in a second vehicle. It also pays big dividends to perform preventative maintenance on your vehicle before leaving home. This will minimize at least some of the potential for malfunctions and breakdowns. It is also important to go prepared. If you carry the items listed in Appendix H, a breakdown will be inconvenient, but not life threatening, and you may be able to improvise or affect repairs on the spot.

Nevertheless, bad things do happen to good people. Your ability to cope with the circumstances must be based on rational thought. You must develop a plan. Did you tell anyone where you were going and when you were expected back? Do you have a radio or cell phone to communicate with the outside world? Analyze the pros and cons of staying with your vehicle or walking out for help. Where are you and what are your chances of finding someone else in your general vicinity? If you do set out on foot, do you have the ability to carry sufficient water, food, and some shelter for the time it takes to get to the nearest main road? How far away is help? Where is the nearest road that receives regular traffic? How long will it take to walk there? What are the environmental conditions such as extreme heat and cold? Give the answers careful thought; then develop a plan that has the best chance of success under your particular circumstances.

25
Ibex and Saratoga Springs

Primary Attraction: A wide variety of features including natural springs, old talc mines, and their associated mine camps.

Time Required: Saratoga Spring is a half-day outing out of Shoshone. For a full day's excursion, add Saratoga Spring, the Dumont Dunes, or Sperry Wash.

Miles Involved: It is about 23 miles one way from Shoshone to Ibex Spring. Add another seven miles if you choose to go on down to Saratoga Spring.

Degree of Difficulty: The dirt road portions are mostly Class I and II; only the last two miles into Ibex Spring have some Class III sections.

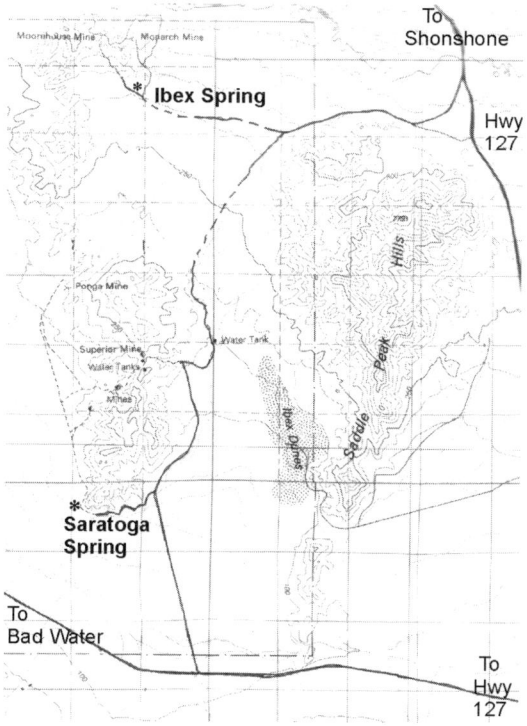

From Shoshone take State Route 127 south in the direction of Baker. Immediately upon leaving town, the highway passes through several miles of soft and easily eroded flat lying sediments. These are old lakebed deposits laid down in the bottom of ancient Lake Tecopa. Geologists estimate Lake Tecopa covered some 85 square miles, and at its maximum could have been four hundred feet deep. Fossils and layers of volcanic ash within the sediments place the age of the lake as much as three million years, meaning it was a body of water well before the beginning of the Plio-Pleistocene Ice Age. Curiously it was probably the Ice Age that ended Lake Tecopa's existence, however. With the added rainfall and melt-water of the Sherwin phase of the early Pleistocene, Lake Tecopa filled to overflowing, breaching its southern shoreline like a bursting dam. A channel quickly eroded causing the lake to drain into what is now Death Valley.

After passing the second left turnoff to Tecopa, you will notice several roads on the right going up to mines in the Ibex Mountains to the west. These are all talc mines, tapping into that great white resource found throughout the Crystal Spring Formation; but more about that later. The largest talc mines on the distant hillside are the Giant, the Eclipse and the Paddy's Pride. The oldest is the Eclipse, which opened in the 1930s. Pfizer operated the Mammoth and Bonny Mines from the 1950s through the mid 1970s.

Ibex Pass is crossed at a point 14.5 miles south of Shoshone. During the steep descent down the south side, distant views of the Dumont Dunes can be had. A good road goes right up to these sand dunes (see Excursion #27). It is one of three dune areas in the California desert where the BLM permits unlimited use by Off Highway Vehicles.

Just before reaching the microwave relay facility, at a point 16.3 miles south of Shoshone look for an unmarked dirt road going off to the right; this is where you leave the pavement. Note your mileage here. The Class I road bypasses the electronic site and heads west. A mile from the highway, the Death Valley National Park is entered, and the road gently descends a sandy wash. In the springtime when conditions are just right, this area comes alive with the yellow brilliance of the desert sunflower sometimes called desert gold, *Geraea canescens*.

At a point 2.8 miles in from the highway, the main road seems to swing south and a side road goes off to the west; turn right here. Although this road was once paved to accommodate heavily laden ore trucks, barely a trace of the old asphalt remains. While the road is mostly Class II, the first Class III pitch comes within a quarter of a mile when you are crossing a wash. It is 2.3 miles from the first fork to the second fork. At a point 5.1 miles in from the highway the next intersection is reached. The road going straight-ahead leads to Ibex Spring and the sprawling remains of the old mine camp around it.

Modern man first set up camp here in 1883 with the erection of a mill to process silver ore from the Ibex Mine. That operation lasted eight years until the ore ran out. The mill shut down, and the camp was abandoned. The Greenwater "excitement" of 1905 brought in a new crop of prospectors and miners and some congregated around Ibex Spring. That boom, too, went bust and with it peace and quiet once more descended upon Ibex Spring. In the 1930s ceramic tile began to become very popular in home construction and the demand for talc, one of tile's major ingredients, rose. The extensive talc deposits in the Ibex Hills were opened up, and once again Ibex Spring became home to those working the nearby mines. The decaying remains of the structures you see today date back to the 1950s when several nearby mines were going strong.

The road past the camp goes up the fan into a canyon where the Ibex, later called the Moorehouse Mine, was located. It operated from 1940 until the 1970s and was the area's biggest producer.

Ibex Spring itself may be a disappointment in that it is overgrown with mesquite, arrow-weed, willow, salt cedar, and other vegetation. Someone has even brought in a few palm trees. As a general principle, the National Park Service would like to eradicate these "exotic species" from our national parks. Here in Death Valley they certainly face a formidable task.

Talc miner's camp at Ibex Spring

At the intersection back a quarter of a mile before reaching Ibex Spring, the road which heads north goes up to the Pleasanton, Mammoth and Rob Roy Mines. In all of these mines, the talc deposits are associated with the Crystal Spring Formation. These are the oldest layers of the larger Pahrump group of very old Precambrian rocks. Millions of years ago, the limestones and dolomites of the Crystal Spring Formation were intruded by a molten rock called diabase. Where this igneous rock came in contact with the sedimentary rock, a zone of metamorphic rock was formed and, with it, talc was formed. These talc zones may be anywhere from a few inches thick up to two hundred feet thick. The talc is often mined through a system of underground tunnels; however, large deposits close to the surface have also been mined by open pit methods.

Pfizer worked the Monarch and Pleasanton Mines in the 1960s. They were purchased in 1972 by Cyprus Industrial Minerals, who worked them for only a year. They have remained closed since, although they still have ore reserves should the price of talc increase significantly. It is interesting to visit these mines, for many still have ore bunkers and loading facilities remaining. **Obviously, it would be foolish to enter any of the underground workings.**

Once you have had your fill of talc mines, and if you still have part of the day left, you might consider going on down the main road to Saratoga Spring. This was the road that went to the left at a point 2.8 miles west of Highway 127. This Class II road heads south, occasionally through some soft sand, but it is usually not a problem. These sandy areas support a large population of the pretty, and at times very fragrant, sand verbena, *Abronia villosa*, a member of the Four-O'Clock family. Its rose-purple flowers have an extended period of bloom from February sometimes into July.

It is 6.1 miles down to the well-marked turnoff to Saratoga Springs, and then another 1.3 miles to the parking area. Saratoga Spring is a very substantial desert water hole, with a reliable year around flow. The several acres of ponds support a unique pupfish, *Cyprindon Nevadensis nevadensis,* found nowhere else in the world. This tiny ice-aged species was trapped when ancient Lake Manly dried up. The surrounding marshes are home to many varieties of amphibians, reptiles, and assorted mammals. The water attracts birds of every description. Some are just passing through, while others stay here all year around.

Unfortunately, Saratoga Springs is also home to a species that is not wanted here. This is hornwort, an annual aquatic plant. Like the tamarisk thickets around Furnace Creek Ranch and the Russian thistle that seems to be everywhere, hornwort is an exotic plant, brought in by someone many years ago. It is Park Service policy to attempt to eradicate these non-native plants.

Saratoga Spring has no doubt been in use by man since the Pleistocene Ice Age; however, most evidence of prehistoric man's occupation only goes back to the period of 1 AD to 1100 AD when the so-called Saratoga Springs Culture existed in Death Valley. Traces of these peoples are found all up and down the valley, but because they were here in relatively large numbers, and because archaeologists first studied them here, they have been conveniently named by their type locality.

The Saratoga Springs people were sophisticated hunters and gatherers, who had replaced the atlatl with the more accurate bow and arrow. Their arrowheads, knives, choppers and scrapers were of fine quality as were their metates and manos. Pottery shards indicate that these people had trading relationships with the Basketmaker and later Pueblo peoples to the east. Shell beads found in Death Valley also show similar contact with Pacific coast tribes to the west. The Saratoga Springs people left rings of stone suggesting they might have been "sleeping circles" or even makeshift houses. They also left curious rock alignments on the desert floor, called geoglyphs. These are very difficult to date, and their purpose still mystifies archaeologists. The conventional wisdom is that they were for religious or mystical purposes, just like the petroglyphs these people pecked into rocks. What happened to these people remains unclear. The Shoshone peoples moved in about 1000 AD and for a while the two cultures existed side by side. Some think the Saratoga people were simply absorbed by the newcomers.

Saratoga Spring

There are remains of two stone cabins at Saratoga Springs. These no doubt go back many years, perhaps more than a century to the 20-mule team borax days. I recall one cold and stormy night here at Saratoga Springs back in the 1950s when I was roaming around this country in my surplus WW II G.I. Weapons Carrier. At that time, one of the stone cabins was still intact, complete with a roof. Rather than sleeping outside in the wind and rain, I threw my sleeping bag on the cabin floor and was quite cozy. I was not alone, however. As soon as I turned the lantern out, the cabin was alive with the scurry of little feet. Being unable to sleep, I decided to attempt to capture my hosts on film. I set up a camera and flash on a tripod in front of a few broken pieces of vanilla cookies. I turned out the lantern again. I did not have to wait long in the dark. Upon hearing a munching sound I depressed the cable release on the camera, and voila! Little did that pack rat know his photograph would be appearing in a guidebook nearly fifty years later.

The author's roomate enjoys a cookie

As dead as the desert may seem in the daytime to the uninitiated, nocturnal life abounds once the sun goes down. One of these nocturnal creatures is the packrat of the genus *Neotoma*. Packrats get their name from the curious behavioral pattern of collecting odd bits and pieces of material, which seemingly have no particular use, to put in their den. When gathering such an item, they often exchange it for another object. The unraveling of a packrat's nest often reveals expended .22 gauge shotgun shells, bits of bright shiny metal, and God only knows what. I have awakened in the morning to find things missing. I once found a Canadian nickel on a rock beside the campfire, which I knew was not there the night before.

Actually packrats' nests, known as middens, can have great scientific value. Scientists have found well preserved nests in caves and rock shelters which have been radiocarbon dated as old as 45,000 years. The packrat selects one spot in his home in which to defecate and urinate, something they do often. During the animal's life, this perch is usually moist. Pollen from nearby plants will adhere to this sticky surface. Thousands of years later some paleobotanist like Dr. Ken Cole comes along, dissects the midden, and extracts the tiny pollen grains. From those, he can identify the dominant plant types, giving us a good look at what vegetation was growing here during the last Ice Age. These middens also reveal ancient insects, and bird and small mammal bones. U.S.G.S. geologist Robert Thompson found a packrat nest in Nevada that was lined with scorpion tails. That must have been one very aggressive packrat with attitude!

From Saratoga Spring it is but four miles south to the graded Harry Wade Road. From here, one can turn right returning to State Route 178 after 25.7 miles. Or by turning left, State Route 127 is just 4.1 miles to the east.

Emergency Communications

It is always advisable to carry some sort of electronic device that will permit you to communicate with the outside world should an automotive breakdown or medical emergency arise. It is even better to have redundant communication systems.

Until satellite telephones become available to everyone, the most reliable radio technology commonly available to anyone is a high frequency (HF) amateur radio transceiver. Depending on the frequency used, you can reliably get out and reach someone, day or night, in any kind of weather. The drawback to such communications is that in order to lawfully operate such a radio, one must pass a series of FCC tests on electronic theory and show a proficiency of Morse Code of 13 words per minute. While thousands of new "hams" pass those tests each year, it takes a lot more study than many are willing to undertake.

After HF amateur radio, perhaps the second most reliable method of radio communication is VHF amateur radio, particularly the popular 2-meter band. Through a series of mountain top repeaters, your transmission is relayed on, and the chances are good that some ham within 100 miles will hear you. The FCC has reduced the licensing requirements to operate such equipment to a basic electronic theory test, without the need to learn and master Morse Code. It is the author's view that every serious backcountry explorer should go through the effort required to obtain the Amateur Radio "Technician" license. VHF transceivers are no larger than a cell phone and there are 2-meter repeaters near Bishop, Independence, Ridgecrest, Beatty and Las Vegas. The drawback is they are line-of-sight and may not get out in enclosed environments such as narrow canyons.

More than a third of the United States population communicates by cellular telephone. That technology works well in urban, suburban, and in some rural areas. If you have a cell phone, by all means consider it a vital component in your toolbox of backcountry communication links. Just keep in mind that in the lonely reaches of the Death Valley country, it may let you down.

Finally there is the old standby, Citizens Band Radio. Designed for short-range communications of 5 to 10 miles, CB radio has provided car to car communications for truckers going up and down the highway for four decades. It has also been popular within jeep club outings, too. After dark when atmospheric conditions change, CB radio signals can extend out many miles. The reliability of being able to communicate by this "skip" is quite low, however, certainly not the thing you would want to base your survival plans on. If you do not wish to go through the effort to obtain a ham "Technician" license, then by all means back your cell phone up with a CB radio.

26

Denning Springs

Primary Attraction:	Interesting geology and a long forgotten mining camp.
Time Required:	This is pretty much an all day excursion out of Shoshone
Miles Involved:	From Shoshone to the southern end of the Harry Wade Road, it is 21.3 miles via State Route 127, then another 13.7 miles on dirt roads to the site of Denning Springs.
Degree of Difficulty:	Seven miles of graded dirt, two miles of Class I, three miles of Class II, with soft sand making the last mile an easy Class III.

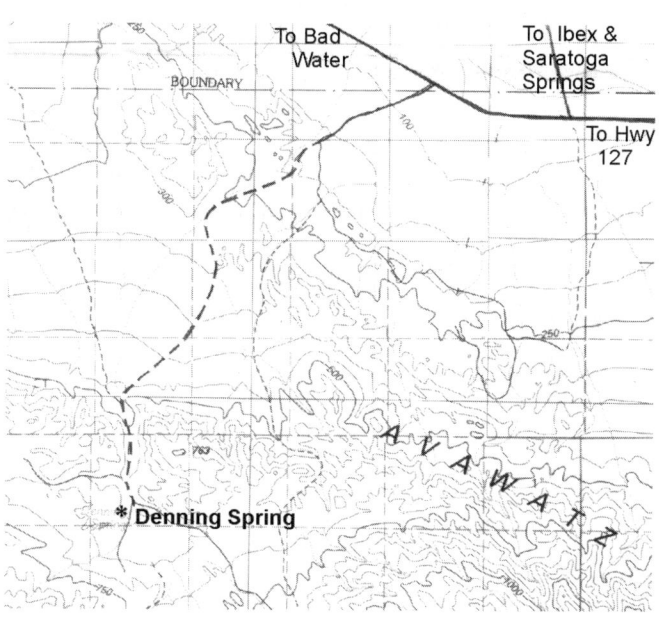

Denning Springs, like its neighbor Crackerjack just down the road, is one of those Turn of the 20th Century boom camps that shone brightly and then faded away to nothing, all in a few years. The camp lasted about five years, which is more than can be said of Greenwater. In his generally comprehensive book, *Ghost Towns and Mining Camps of California,* author Remi Nadeau doesn't mention Denning Springs at all, although he does give Crackerjack three sentences. Noted gold camp historian Erwin G. Gudde doesn't mention either site, probably because they were silver, not gold, camps.

Our back road journey to Denning Springs takes us south out of Shoshone on State Route 127, a distance of 22.3 miles to the south end of the Harry Wade Road. Turn right here and check your odometer.

Take the Harry Wade Road west, passing the side road north to Saratoga Spring after 4.1 miles. After 7.2 miles a sign announces you are in Death Valley National Park. At a point 7.3 miles in from Highway 127, a Class I road goes to the left off the Harry Wade Road; turn left here.

For the next mile and a half the road, still good, climbs the alluvial fan. Soon the wash is entered and the colorful hills close in on both sides. This canyon goes completely through the north end of the Avawatz Mountains. Along the way the road deteriorates from Class I to Class II. Once you are through this passage, the country opens up and yet another alluvial fan is ascended. Cholla and prickly pear cacti are particularly abundant here. In the springtime, phacelia with its showy purple flower is also abundant here.

At a point 12.5 miles in from the highway, a second canyon is entered. You may wish to engage your four-wheel drive here because of the soft sand ahead. It is but another 1.3 miles to the site of Denning Springs.

Denning Springs seems to have gotten its name from Frank Denning, a prospector who wandered the hills of southern Death Valley in the early 1880s, and who eventually found the Ibex Mine a little to the north.

Denning Springs was one of a half a dozen mining camps which sprang up in the Avawatz Mountains in the mini-boom of 1906. Scott Bryan says that Denning Springs had as many as sixty people living here in the 1907-1912 period, but I rather doubt that. Crackerjack pretty much died in the spring of 1908, and it was a larger camp than Denning Springs. Whatever the date of its demise, the site seems to have been intermittently occupied as a millsite until 1937.

Today a few rock walls, pieces of weathered wood, concrete foundations and cleared areas used by tents are all that is left of Denning Springs. Even the water seems to have gone elsewhere.

The road continues beyond the camp, heading south over Avawatz Pass to the site of Crackerjack. Unfortunately, the Fort Irwin boundary is just two miles down the road beyond Denning Springs and that puts Crackerjack off limits.

The mining camp at Denning Spring
was short lived, with little remaining

A Word About Tires

The high road clearance, the added traction of four-wheel drive, and the carrying capacity of most SUVs make them a good general-purpose backcountry vehicle. SUVs are a reasonable compromise between the comfort and luxury of a conventional automobile and the spartan raw power of a farm tractor.

Unfortunately the stock tires your SUV came with do not share that compromise. They are probably "city tires" designed for ease of ride and comfort. They will probably be grossly inadequate to stand up to the rigors of rough roads. If you do much backcountry exploring, your first priority should be making sure that your vehicle has proper footwear.

It is not the size of the tire, or the tread design that should be your major concern, but rather the ability of the tire's tread surface, and sidewalls, to stand up to rocks and other road hazards. In 45 years of four-wheeling in this country and abroad, I quickly learned that a 4-ply passenger car tire is going to let you down, and at the worst possible moment. What is needed is a 6, 8, or even 10-ply truck tire. Shop carefully and talk to other four-wheelers before making your selection.

27

Amargosa Canyon

Primary Attraction:	Large sand dunes, a rare desert river (sometimes), and rock layers of Pliocene swamp sediments containing fossil palm trees where specimens can be lawfully collected.
Time Required:	This is an all day excursion if you like to play in the sand and look for fossils.
Miles Involved:	From Shoshone, it is seventeen miles of paved highway south to the Dumont Dunes Road, then 2.8 miles of graded road to the Dumont Dunes turnoff, followed by another five miles of Class II and III route up Sperry Wash.
Degree of Difficulty:	There is a good graded road into the Dumont Dunes. Beyond, the road up Sperry Wash is mostly Class II, but with its Class III spots, particularly when the Amargosa River has water flowing on the surface.

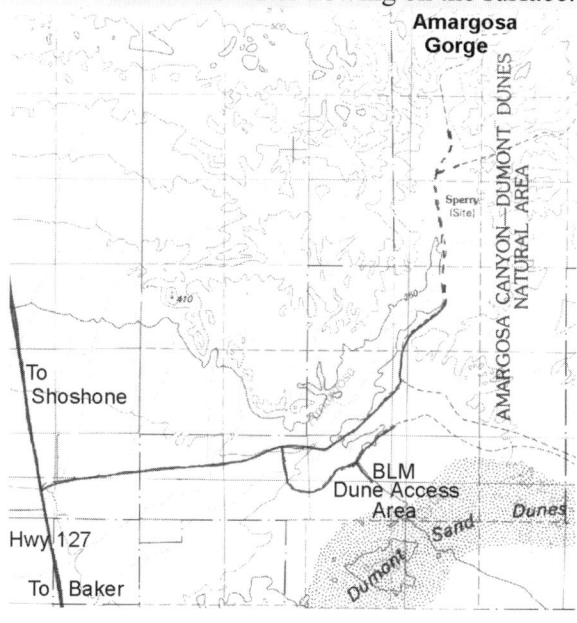

The Sperry Wash area is outside of Death Valley National Park, in lands administered by the Bureau of Land Management where the visitor's activities are less restricted. The Dumont Dunes is classified as an *open use area* in terms of off-road vehicles. In adjoining areas, vehicle use is still prohibited in *Wilderness Areas*, but there are no restrictions on camping and rock hounding.

Take State Route 127 south of Shoshone 17.2 miles, where a sign points the way to the Dumont Dunes access road. Turn left and take this graded road east for 2.8 miles. Here a side road to the right crosses the Amargosa River bed and goes through several BLM camping areas, to end in a mile and a half at the edge of the Dumont Dunes.

The Dumont Dunes were born at the end of the Plio-Pleistocene Ice Age when the sandy beaches left by ancient Lakes Manly and Dumont were blown about by the winds, causing the fine sand to eventually accumulate here. The main dune complex area is about four miles long by a mile wide. The highest dune rises 450 feet above the valley floor. In California only the Eureka Dunes are higher (see Excursion # 28). The total volume of sand here is seven billion cubic feet. Someone figured out that that is enough sand to build a road forty feet wide by six inches thick, that would stretch nearly three times around the earth at the equator!

The Dumont Dunes are somewhat unique because nearly every type of dune formation can be found within these four square miles, including Transverse, Barchan, Longitudinal, Seif, and of course, the ever popular Oscillary dunes. Sand dune types are formed by the pattern of the local winds. Thus it is unusual to have all five types represented in one place. The winds here must be really confused.

The Dumont Dunes are a popular BLM recreation area

The BLM has opened the dunes to unrestricted Off Highway Vehicle use. Many people from Southern California come out here for the weekend, often in big motor homes pulling heavily laden trailers carrying a half dozen different vehicles. Dune buggies, four-wheel drives, motorcycles, and ATVs can ride all over the dunes at will. However, such vehicles must be street legal with a regular license plate, or they must have the California *green sticker*. ATV Operators under the age of fourteen must have an ATV Safety Certificate and must be under the direct supervision of an adult. Those who are age fourteen to seventeen must have the certificate or be under the direct supervision of an adult who does have the certificate. Persons over eighteen must have the certificate only if they are supervising a minor. All operators must wear helmets, and no passengers are allowed on ATVs.

Meanwhile back at the fork 2.8 miles in from the highway, if you keep to the left, you will soon enter the canyon cut by the Amargosa River. This seasonal watercourse derives its name from the Spanish term for bitter waters. The Amargosa is one of the few rivers of the world to end at a point below sea level (Other rivers with that distinction are the River Jordan which empties into the Dead Sea, and the rivers Ural Emba and Kuma which empty into the Caspian Sea.)

The road, such as it is, deteriorates greatly as it crisscrosses the river channel. The watercourse is likely to be dry here in the summer. In the winter the river often has water flowing on the surface. Needless to say, the route is more challenging when the river is flowing because the channel must be crossed several times. **Warning; do not attempt to ford the Amargosa River if you do not know how deep the water is.**

The Amargosa River

At a point seven miles in from State Highway 127, the old right of way of the Tonopah & Tidewater Railroad can be seen descending into the canyon from the mesa top to the east. Eight miles in from the highway was the site of Sperry Station, so named by railroad tycoon Borax Smith after his adopted niece, Grace Sperry. The adobe station buildings have been washed away, and few traces of this way station remain.

The steel rails of the Tonopah & Tidewater were pulled up in 1942-1943. In 1969, many of the ties were still in place but today, even these are largely gone.

The Tonopah & Tidewater was built in 1905-07 and connected Beatty with the Santa Fe tracks at Ludlow, far to the south. Construction began at the Ludlow end on November 19, 1905. By May of 1906 the tracks had been pushed seventy-five miles to this point. The next twelve miles through the Amargosa gorge would be troublesome, and would remain so for the life of the railroad. Laying the roadbed through the canyon involved the digging of massive cuts in some places and filling low spots in other areas. In addition dozens of trestles had to be built, at least three of them more than five hundred feet long.

The Amargosa gorge is no place to be in the summer, particularly if you are performing strenuous work. There were an endless series of labor problems with one contractor going broke, another trying unsuccessfully to use Japanese, and later Mexican, work crews. Work bogged down even with the cooler temperatures of fall. On February 10, 1907, regular train service was scheduled to Sperry Station, but from there to Beatty passengers had to transfer to horse-drawn stages and a less reliable mode of transport, the new-fangled automobile.

Finally in May of 1907, one year after the twelve-mile project started, the tracks reached Tecopa. The railroad's Amargosa gorge problems were not over, however. On August 8, 1908, a cloudburst sent a wall of water raging down the dry Amargosa River channel, reeking havoc with the roadbed in the gorge. (Further north, this same storm caused a derailment that killed an engineer, his fireman, and a hobo.) In 1915 a brake failure led to a train wreck which overturned a locomotive and several freight cars. In January of 1916, heavy rains again damaged trestles in the Amargosa gorge.

While the Tonopah & Tidewater was a vital link between the people and mines in the country east of Death Valley, it was only profitable for five of its thirty three years. Service was discontinued in 1940, with the rails pulled out in 1943.

Not too many years ago, there was a paved county road going through this part of the canyon. It turned up Sperry Wash to come out on Tecopa Pass on the road between Tecopa and Goodsprings. That has all washed out. When *Wilderness* areas were made in these hills, a non-wilderness corridor was left in the wash, should that road ever be re-established.

Finally at a point 7.2 miles in from the highway, there is a washed out railroad trestle, and here, further travel is blocked by the BLM. This is where things get interesting, however; if you don't mind a little walk, you can hike up the old railroad grade through the Amargosa gorge all the way to Tecopa. This is a very scenic passage with high palisades towering over the canyon bottom. There is water in here all year around and the path leads through several meadow areas that teem with a wide variety of animal life. If you can arrange for someone to pick you up in Tecopa, I would highly recommend the five-mile hike through the gorge. It is a two to three hour hike, but level and easy walking for the most part. I first made the trek in mid-May and found the gorge to be very warm, so warm that we took a swim halfway through. The next time was the day following Thanksgiving and the weather was perfect.

John C. Fremont's second California Expedition of 1844 came through the Amargosa Gorge enroute back to the Great Salt Lake. Fremont was not the first man of European extraction to camp here as the canyon was just off the Old Spanish Trail connecting Las Vegas with Los Angeles. Further, the presence of water has attracted man to this area for perhaps as long as 10,000 years. Traces of old Indian trails can still be seen on the mesas on either side of the gorge. Clusters of so called *sleeping circles*, circular areas five to six feet across cleared of stones, have also been found along some of these ancient trails. Bedrock mortars have been found along the river. I found one exceptional example near Acme Siding that has a depression sixteen inches deep. Of particular interest which archaeologists have yet to explain are *geoglyphs*, rock alignments laid out on the desert floor, seemingly best visible from the air. One in this area consists of 28 conical piles of gravel in three groups, in an alignment 489 feet long. This curious feature could date back as far as 6,000 BC.

Another hike that I would recommend is upper Sperry Wash. Leave your vehicle at the ruins of the washed-out trestle where Sperry Wash enters the Amargosa Canyon. Walk eastward going up Sperry Wash. The hills on either side of the canyon are Pliocene sediments laid down under swampy conditions two million years ago. In these sediments can be found the fossilized remains of several kinds of trees, including palms, large ferns, and cycads. Cycads are palm-like trees which started in Permian times, were very abundant in the Triassic and Jurassic when dinosaurs were roaming about. Cycads survive to this day.

In 1998 paleontologists from the Los Angeles County Museum discovered the fossil remains of an entirely new type of camel here. While camels were quite common in the Pliocene, this one was unique in that it resembled a goat more than a camel. It was apparently well adapted to climbing up rocky slopes.

At one time a graded dirt road went up Sperry Wash to rejoin the pavement near the Noonday Mine. A corridor was left in the wilderness to accommodate this road; however, what Congress giveth, nature and the BLM taketh away. The road washed out and the BLM simply closed the corridor administratively.

In the late 1950s and 60s, the hills on either side of Sperry Wash were a favorite haunt of rock hounds who came in here for red and yellow agate. Not only have fine specimens of red and white palm fiber been found, so have black agatized roots and limb sections, and pink and tan cycad pieces. Indeed, entire petrified logs have been found. However, since the road washed out and the adjoining *Wilderness* areas were established in 1994, few people venture in here anymore. Each rainstorm uncovers new fossilized material just waiting to be found. The area is still open to collectors who are willing to walk in here.

Sperry Wash has another item of historical interest. On a large boulder, the inscription "*Aqui Año 170*" has been found. It appears to be quite old and some theorize it was left by an early traveler who came through here on his way to one of the missions on the California coast. Still others think it dates to the 1830 – 1850 era of the so-called "Old Spanish Trail". This was a route established by organized bands of horse thieves moving herds between New Mexico and Southern California. The trail passed through Tecopa just a few miles to the north.

If you enjoy camping in quiet solitude, pass by the Dumont Dunes, and pitch your tent in the Amargosa Canyon. Walk the canyon bottoms and the mesas above. Not only is the area rich in animal life, but there is something of interest here for almost everyone.

An old railroad trestle in the Amargosa gorge

Note: There are environmental organizations out there that are looking for any excuse to force the BLM to close the lower Amargosa Canyon to vehicles. Drive responsibly and do not provide that reason!

Got Gas?

Many backroad explorers feel more comfortable if they are carrying an extra five or ten gallons of gasoline. Keep in mind that gasoline carried in any container, other than the vehicle's fuel tank, poses a somewhat greater fire hazard. Extra gasoline should never under any circumstances be carried in plastic containers, and even the GI "Jerry Cans" of heavy metal are notorious for their leaking gaskets.

If you must carry extra gasoline, observe these Do's and Don'ts:

- Do secure the gas container so that it cannot tip over or bounce around. Utilize an appropriate external mounting bracket.
- Don't carry any gas can inside the passenger space of a vehicle. Not only is it an extreme fire hazard, but it is sure to leak, creating noxious fumes.
- Do carry an ABC fire extinguisher of adequate size.
- Don't fill the container while it is attached to the vehicle. Avoid static electricity by setting it on the ground when filling it.
- Do put the extra fuel inside your car's gas tank as soon as you can.
- Don't forget to bring a pouring spout, preferably with a screen filter to catch the larger rust particles that might be in the gas can.

Unless you are driving a real gas hog, the need to carry extra fuel in the Death Valley country should not be necessary, providing you top off your tank before heading into the backcountry. Gasoline can be obtained at Furnace Creek Ranch, Stovepipe Wells, Scotty's Castle, Goldfield, Beatty, Shoshone, Big Pine, Lone Pine, Olancha, Trona, and even Panamint Springs. By leaving any of these places with a full fuel tank, you should be able to get to the most remote corner of the park and back again.

Chapter VI

Trails Out Of Big Pine

For the outdoorsman Big Pine, California is synonymous with hunting and fishing in the High Sierra or possibly mountaineering in the Palisades. Thus it seems like a strange place to make a gateway to Death Valley National Park. However, with the passage of the 1994 California Desert Protection Act, which created Death Valley National Park and greatly expanded its boundaries to the west, Big Pine has indeed now become the jumping-off place for hundreds of square miles in the northwest corner of the park. Most of this parkland is roadless *Wilderness*, but it remains closer to Big Pine than anyplace else. Since this isolated portion of the park receives relatively few visitors, the National Park Service has not yet established an information office in Big Pine, as they have in Beatty and Shoshone. For up to date road information, check with the Interagency Visitors Center in Lone Pine.

In addition to the backcountry excursions described herein, there are lots of additional opportunities for backroad exploring in the White and Inyo Mountains east of Big Pine. (Those routes are described in *Inyo-Mono SUV Trails*.)

Since 1994, Big Pine has become a gateway to
Death Valley National Park

Big Pine's roots go back to 1869. Once the Owens Valley Indian Wars were over, small farming communities began to develop up and down the valley, and

Big Pine was one of them. The community got a big boost in 1877-78, when an irrigation ditch system better distributed the waters of the Owens River, and farms flourished. That all came to an end in 1924 as the City of Los Angeles acquired the water rights and the ditches dried up. Big Pine became relegated to being a bedroom community of its larger cousin, Bishop, just fourteen miles to the north.

Nevertheless, 1200 people still call Big Pine home. It has a market, two sporting goods stores, four places to eat and four motels. It also has a couple of service stations. Your fuel tanks should be topped off before heading east. Take advantage of these services for there will be none where you are going.

28

Steel Pass from the Eureka Valley

Primary Attraction:	"Singing" sand dunes and lonely landscapes.
Time Required:	From Big Pine to the summit of Steel Pass and return, this outing will take the better part of a day.
Miles Involved:	It is 48 miles from Big Pine to the Eureka Dunes, and from there another fifteen miles to the summit of Steel Pass. If you elect to cross over into the Saline Valley and return from there, the round trip distance back to Big Pine is another seventy miles. **Do not underestimate your fuel consumption. Top off your tank before leaving Big Pine. There are no services anywhere along the way.**
Degree of Difficulty:	The access roads to the Eureka Dunes are Class I or better. Beyond the dunes, it is a Class II road to the lower narrows in Dedeckera Canyon. Here there are four rock ledges to be climbed, Class IV, III, III, and IV in that order. Once over these obstacles, it is all Class II to the summit except for one more short, but steep, hillside which has a short Class III pitch.

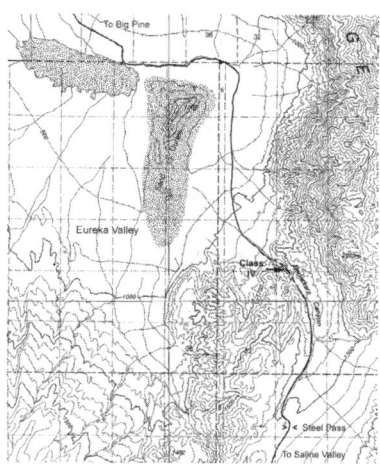

One of the most lonely jeep trails that you are likely to find in the Death Valley area is the cross-country route between the Eureka Valley and the Saline Valley. It is not shown on many maps, and hence people may not realize such a road even exists. **This is a route you should not be attempted unless you have another vehicle with you.** The route can be done in either direction; however, it might be a little easier going from south to north.

From the north end of Big Pine, take State Route 168 eastward as if you were going into the White Mountains. Note your odometer reading as you leave Highway 395. The Owens River is crossed, followed by the site of Zurich Siding on the old roadbed of the narrow gauge Carson & Colorado Railroad that went through here between 1883 and 1960. Soon a paved road to the left goes north to the "big ears" of the Cal Tech radio astronomy parabolic dishes pointed skyward. Here deep within the Owens Valley, sheltered by the High Sierra on one side and the Inyo Mountains on the other side, is a listening post for radio waves coming from deep space.

At a point 2.3 miles from Highway 395 there is an intersection, with paved roads on each fork. The left fork is State Route 168; go to the right. Soon the road climbs into the Inyo Mountains passing through a narrows known as Devil's Gate. At a point 13.6 miles from Highway 395 a dirt side road goes right to Papoose Flat in the heart of the Inyo Mountains. Continue eastward on the paved road another 1.9 miles to where the graded dirt Saline Valley Road turns off to the right (see Excursion #29). To go into the Eureka Valley, keep left on the paved road.

At a point 16.3 miles from Highway 395, the crest of the Inyo Mountains is crossed and the road begins its descent into the Eureka Valley. The paved road stays just outside of the national park boundary as it goes through Little Cowhorn Valley, crosses Joshua Flat and drops down into the Eureka Valley. Once on the valley floor, the paved road makes a sharp turn to the right, and at 31.8 miles from Big Pine the pavement ends. The next seven miles are graded gravel.

At one time it was possible to take a Class III road north from the big bend, into Fish Lake Valley by way of colorful Horse Thief Canyon, where petroglyphs can be found. Another Class III route left at this curve to go northwest into Soldier Pass Canyon. Both of those routes were closed on October 31, 1994, with the passage of the California Desert Protection Act, and with it, the creation of the Piper Mountain Wilderness area.

The graded dirt road heads southeast through a narrow BLM corridor that has national park land on either side. At a point 38.1 miles from Highway 395, a graded road goes off to the left. This, too, occupies a narrow corridor between the Piper Mountain Wilderness on the left and the Sylvania Wilderness on the right. This is the present day route into Fish Lake Valley, where it connects with State Routes 168 and 266.

At a point 0.6 miles beyond this intersection, 38.7 miles from Highway 395, a side road to the right goes south to the Eureka Valley Sand Dunes. This is the way to Steel Pass. If you continue straight ahead you will pass the sulfur mining camp of Crater and eventually enter the north end of Death Valley. From this intersection it is 38.4 miles to the nearest gas pump at Scotty's Castle.

We turn right and immediately enter Death Valley National Park. An intersection is reached at a point 9.2 miles from the Eureka Valley Road. Straight-ahead 0.4 miles, the National Park Service has a small campground at the edge of the dunes. It consists of an outhouse and two picnic tables. No camping fees are currently being charged. Users are expected to carry out their own trash. (In the years ahead, this primitive campground may be relocated nearby to a less environmentally sensitive location.)

The Eureka Dunes, a National Landmark

For the route to Steel Pass, turn left at this intersection. It goes eastward along the north base of the dunes and then turns south again to skirt the eastern end of the dune field. The large natural sand pile is 680 feet high, 3.3 miles long and 1.5 miles wide, making it the highest dune in California. In 1984 the U.S. Department of the Interior designated these sand dunes as a Natural Landmark when the Bureau of Land Management administered the area. The area was put into Death Valley National Park with the passage of the 1994 California Desert Protection Act. Driving and camping on the dunes is prohibited. You can walk out upon the dunes, however, which is something I would recommend. **Please don't disturb the vegetation**.

This dune is one of only two sand dunes in California that are known to *bark* or *boom* when conditions are just right. (Other such dunes that exhibit this strange phenomenon are the Kelso dunes in the Devil's Playground south of Baker, and three localities in Nevada.) The *booming* or *roaring* sound can be generated when conditions are just right, by starting sand avalanches off the top of the dune. In order to achieve the effect, the sand grains must be (1) very dry and in very low humidity, (2) well sorted, and (3) of medium size.

These dunes have been forming here since the end of the Pleistocene glaciation. The sand contains five species of beetles that have evolved here independently of beetles elsewhere. They are now unique, found nowhere else in the world. This situation is similar to the evolution of the desert pupfish and minnows in Death Valley, and the Inyo black toad of Deep Springs Valley.

Also present are three rare and endangered plants: the Eureka Dune Grass, *Swallenia alexandrae,* the Eureka Evening Primrose, *Oenothera avita eurekensis,* and the Nevada Oryctes, *Oryctes nevandensis,* plus one rare plant, the Shining Locoweed, or Shining milk-vetch, *Astragalus lentiginosus micans.* **Please do not disturb any insects or plants while you are walking upon the sand.**

From the first intersection near the campground, a Class I road heads eastward and eventually circles around the eastern side of the dunes. Ahead and to the east are colorful layers of brown strata in the Last Chance Range. These are old marine sediments of Cambrian and Ordovician age. Those layers with the conspicuous horizontal stripes are the Bonanza King Formation. Below it is the Carrara Formation; above it is the Nopah Formation. The oldest is 560 million years old, the youngest 500 million years.

Although the road crosses areas of powdery fine silt that turn into bottomless mud in wet weather, and traverses some sections of soft sand, the trail remains mostly Class I for nearly five miles beyond the campground. Then fourteen miles in from the Eureka Valley Road, the trail deteriorates to Class II. It is another two miles to Dedeckera Canyon.

Dedeckera Canyon was named after a plant discovered by the very accomplished amateur botanist Mary DeDecker of Independence. The shrub July Gold, *Dedeckera eurekensis,* is considered to be a rare plant by the California Native Plant Society. It is only found on north facing limestone slopes between 3,500 and 7,000 feet in the White, Inyo, and Panamint Mountains, including this locality.

Your backcountry adventure begins upon entering Dedeckera Canyon. You are in the canyon no more than a quarter of a mile when the lower narrows are reached. Here you will encounter four sections of bare bedrock ledges that you must climb up and over. These obstacles are less than fifty yards apart. Fortunately, each is only ten to fifteen feet long. At one time someone had poured some concrete here to make the going easier, but that has mostly washed out. The first ledge is Class IV, followed by two at Class III and the last Class IV again. (The first rock ledge is rather narrow, and my wife, Loris, considers it to be Class V. I rate all four ledges as only Class III for those coming down the canyon.) Short wheelbase four-wheel drive vehicles with high clearance and without running boards should have no serious problems. **Drivers of wide or long wheelbase vehicles should get out and first scout the way on foot.** Once these obstacles have been overcome, the road ahead is mostly Class II.

The Dedeckera Canyon narrows.

The upper narrows are a quarter of a mile above the lower narrows, but they present no problems for vehicles. The upper narrows are a good place to look at the very old Cambrian marine sediments of the Nopah Formation. Dedeckera Canyon was eroded out of the crushed rocks in a fault zone.

Because of the sensitive botanic habitat, the National Park Service would prefer that visitors do not camp in Dedeckera Canyon. As this publication goes to press the matter is under review, and there is the possibility that camping may be formally banned in certain areas.

Once you pass through the upper narrows, the canyon is left behind and the country soon opens up. Should you pass this way in the winter, the hillsides will appear to be rusty brown from the dry stems of the Wild-Buckwheat, *Eriogonum fasciculatum* var. *polifolium*. The springtime is another matter. The many wildflowers found here range from the lowly carpet phlox to the tall stately Prince's Plume, *Stanleya pinnata*.

The Class II road skirts around the western edge of a large Joshua tree-covered flat and heads for a gap in lava covered mesas. This lava, dark basalt, poured out of the earth during Pliocene times, covering many hundreds of square miles. The volcanism was not a one-time event, but occurred over a long period of time. Sometimes it was ash, not lava that was ejected from the volcanic vents. The road passes such a layer of white ash at a point three miles above the upper narrows.

A layer of white volcanic ash is sandwiched
between two layers of basalt lava

A mile beyond the outcrop of ash, a short but steep hill is encountered. Engage your four-wheel drive and put your transmission in low range. The Class III ascent should cause no serious problem if the road is dry. Once on top it is only 1.5 miles across the broad flat to Steel Pass, seemingly named for a steel post that once stood here. The elevation is about 4,500 feet. A two-pound coffee can holds a register in which people passing through can leave their names and comments.

Prior to the 1994 inclusion of this area into Death Valley National Park, Steel Pass saw relatively few backcountry travelers. When I first came this way in the 1960s, I doubt if the route over the pass saw more than a dozen vehicles a year. The summit register now suggests that figure has increased substantially. **This is still very lonely country, however; it is no place to face a vehicle breakdown. For this reason a party of at least two vehicles is recommended.**

At one time, a side road left went several miles into the Last Chance Range to some mining claims. The CDPA designated this area as *Wilderness* and the National Park Service has now closed that side road.

The road ahead on the Saline Valley side of the pass (see Excursion #30) also passes through a *Wilderness* area, but this time a small narrow corridor of non-wilderness was left to accommodate this jeep trail. Having failed to convince Congress to eliminate the corridor, some environmental activists are trying to get the National Park Service to close the road administratively.

From Steel Pass it is twelve miles to Lower Warm Springs in the Saline Valley. The first two miles below Steel Pass are Class III as the route twists and winds its way through the boulder-filled alluvium. Beyond the two-mile point, the remaining ten miles to Lower Warm Springs is all a slow, but generally easy Class II.

This road off of Steel Pass was forever closed by the CDPA

This is very lonely country

29

The Saline Valley Road

Primary Attraction:	Hot springs, sand dunes, gold mines, salt marshes, bird watching, old borax works and salt trams are all things to see along the Saline Valley Road.
Time Required:	To properly see the sights of the Saline Valley, a minimum of two days should be allowed.
Miles Involved:	From Highway 395 in Big Pine to State Route 190, it is one hundred miles. **No services of any kind are available along the way. Be sure your gas tank is topped off before leaving Big Pine.**
Degree of Difficulty:	Although it has a washboard surface for many miles, the main Saline Valley Road is a wide graded strip that cannot even be considered Class I in difficulty. However, there are many side-roads going off the Saline Valley Road which lead to interesting features. These side roads range in difficulty from Class II to Class IV.

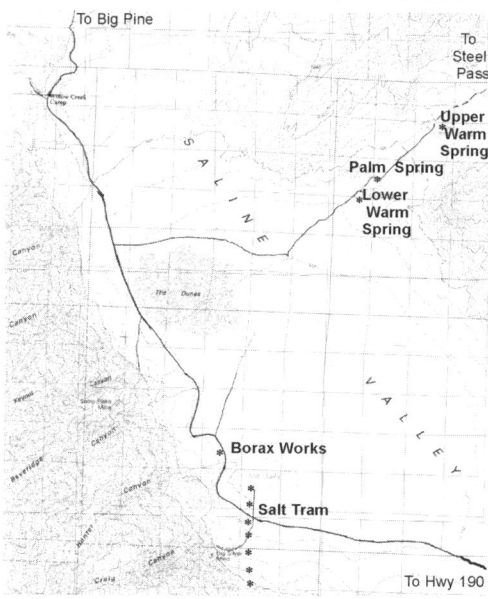

The Saline Valley was added to the newly created Death Valley National Park with the passage of the California Desert Protection Act late in 1994. Saline Valley is an enormous region of more than four hundred square miles. This vast area is rich in archaeological and historical resources, has some interesting geologic features, and contains some very important wildlife habitat. Running through this enclosed basin is a rough road occasionally maintained by the County of Inyo. Along this thin strand of graded dirt, access can be made to old gold mines, salt mines, borax works, sand dunes, hot springs, well-watered canyons, and salt marshes. The Saline Valley Road has a little something for everyone.

Your back road odyssey begins on Highway 395 at the north edge of Big Pine. Here there is a U.S. Forest Service display describing the ancient Bristlecone pines of the White Mountains. There is also a county campground. Take State Route 168 eastward; note your odometer reading as you leave Highway 395.

The Owens River is crossed after 1.5 miles, followed by the site of Zurich siding on the old roadbed of the narrow gauge Carson & Colorado Railroad which went through here between 1883 and 1960. Soon a paved road to the left goes north to the "big ears" the Cal Tech radio astronomy parabolic dishes pointed skyward. Here deep within the Owens Valley, sheltered by the High Sierra on one side, and the Inyo Mountains on the other side, is a listening post for radio waves coming from deep space.

At a point 2.3 miles from Highway 395 there is an intersection, with paved roads on each fork. The left fork is State Route 168. It is the main access route into the White Mountains; stay to the right. Soon the road climbs into the Inyo Mountains passing through a narrows known as Devil's Gate. At a point 13.6 miles from Highway 395 a dirt side-road goes right to Papoose Flat in the heart of the Inyo Mountains (see *Inyo-Mono SUV Trails*). Continue eastward on the paved road another 1.8 miles to where the graded dirt Saline Valley Road turns off to the right. This is 15.4 miles from Highway 395. Those wishing to go into the Eureka Valley (see Excursion #28) should keep to the left on the paved road.

To go into the Saline Valley, turn to the right on the graded county road. A sign announces it is 67 miles to the Hunter Mountain Road, 84 miles to State Highway 190. **Be forewarned: there are no services of any kind for the next one hundred miles.** A second sign announces the road is not plowed in the winter. The elevation here is 7,500 feet, the high point of the entire route.

Keep in mind that if you do visit the Saline Valley during the winter months, there is the possibility that a storm could bury this road in deep snow at any time. The road at the south end of the valley goes over a 6,200-foot high point that could also be closed by snow. Unwary drivers of conventional vehicles have found themselves stranded in the Saline Valley with no way out. Persons with four-wheel drive vehicles do have two additional options; they can exit over the Class III Steel Pass route that has a high point of 4,500 feet (see Excursion #30). A second option would be to go up the Class IV Lippencott Grade to the Racetrack (see Excursion #33). The high point on that route is 3,900 feet.

The graded Saline Valley Road begins a gradual descent as it heads to the southeast. At a point 1.3 miles from the pavement, the road forks; stay to the right. In a quarter of a mile, both forks come together again.

The county road stays just outside the Death Valley National Park boundary as it skirts around the south end of Cowhorn Valley, and remains so for the next four miles as it continues its gradual descent. Unfortunately, the road surface feels like one is driving over an old fashioned washboard. Then, a little more than six miles from the pavement, the graded road begins a series of steep switchbacks down into Marble Canyon, just a half mile below. Here one enters Death Valley National Park.

Placer gold was discovered in the sandy gravel of Marble Canyon as early as 1882. Dry washers operated here regularly from 1894 until 1906, and again during the depression years of the 1930s. It was found that the richest gravels were on top of the bedrock, some one hundred plus feet down. The shafts and mine headframes you see today date from this later era. The lode source of this gold may be close, but it has never been found.

The county road turns left and heads down Marble Canyon. After a quarter of a mile, a Class III side road climbs steeply up a draw to the south side to the Opal Mine. If you want to visit this old mine, there is an easier way to get there. Stay on the county road going down Marble Canyon.

After descending Marble Canyon for 1.4 miles, the county road suddenly makes a right turn and climbs out of the defile via Opal Canyon. A side road to the left continues down Marble Canyon, crosses Jackass Flats, and after seven miles eventually ends at an unnamed playa.

The county road leaves Marble Canyon by way of Opal Canyon. A half a mile up from the bottom of Marble Canyon, a Class II and III side road to the right goes to the Opal and Silver Spur Mines. They were minor silver and lead producers around the Turn of the 20th Century.

The county road continues to head south, gradually gaining altitude. At Whippoorwill Flat, the pinyon-juniper forest is entered, and for the next several miles there are some nice campsites along the road. Prior to October 31, 1994, one could camp here and have a cheery campfire. Camping is still permitted, but now that this is part of the National Park, campfires are prohibited.

Today the pinyon and juniper forest in the greater Death Valley area extend from 5,800 feet on up to 9,000 feet or more. This has not always been the case, however. By examining 10,000-20,000 year old packrat middens in Death Valley, paleobotanists Phillip Wells and Deborah Woodcock, together with Geffrey Spaulding working in the Eureka Valley, found that at the end of the Pleistocene Ice Age, the juniper trees, *Juniperus osteosperm,* were growing much lower, perhaps down to 1,000 feet. They also found widespread evidence of the Whipple yucca, *Yucca whipplei,* which no longer grows anywhere in the Death Valley area. These finds substantiate the long held views that those times were cooler, and somewhat wetter, but still a semi-arid environment. Interestingly, no pollen of the Pinyon pine was found. Scientists working throughout the Great Basin Region have a wealth of evidence suggesting these trees moved in during the mid-Holocene, 3,000-4,000 years after the Pleistocene ice had retreated.

It is curious to note that many of the juniper trees here are infested with mistletoe, *Phoradendron juniperinum,* a true plant parasite. However, the pinyon trees growing just a few feet away have no mistletoe growing on them.

After reaching a high point of about 7,300 feet, which some call North Pass, the county road begins its sometimes-steep descent of Whippoorwill Canyon. Soon the pinyon and juniper forest is left behind, and with that are the first distant views of the salt flats at the bottom of the Saline Valley, still nearly 25 miles away. The county road crosses the upper Waucoba Wash drainage, goes over a notch in a ridge, and begins its long straight descent into the Saline Valley.

At a point nearly seventeen miles in from the pavement, a Class II side road right heads up the alluvial fan to the base of the Inyo Mountains. If you keep to the left 1.6 miles in from the Saline Valley Road, you will find the remains of the Blue Monster and Lucky Boy Mines. If you continue straight ahead, the road will deteriorate to Class III as you enter lower Lead Canyon, so named by miners who found that commodity here. If you bear to the right upon entering Lead Canyon, you will find the Bunker Hill Mine. All of these mines sought lead and silver.

A Class I side road 22 miles in from the pavement goes right a short distance to the private property surrounding Willow Creek Camp. The camp has served as the offices, shops, and living quarters for a number of nearby talc mines including the White Eagle and Gray Eagle Mines. Those mines have operated on and off for many years; but even when they are closed, the camp remains occupied.

For the next five miles, the county road continues its gradual descent, heading for the distant sand dunes. At a point 32 miles in from the pavement and 48 miles from Big Pine, an unmarked Class I side road goes off to the left. This is the dusty road to Lower Warm Springs, one of the premier attractions in the

Saline Valley. (For a description of this road to Lower Warm Springs, and points beyond, see Excursion # 30.)

The main Saline Valley road forks 1.5 miles south of the Warm Springs turnoff. You may take either fork, as they soon rejoin. The branch to the left has one hundred yards or so of flour-like dust, but it gets you much closer to the sand dunes. Go left if you wish to visit the dunes.

The Saline Valley Sand Dunes

The main county road goes to the right. After a quarter of a mile a Class II side road heads up the alluvial fan towards the Snow Flake Talc Mine, perched on the hillside high above Beveridge Canyon. This road becomes a rocky Class III after only a mile.

In this canyon is the site of Beveridge, one of the most remote ghost towns in the west. I have spent about a week camping and exploring this old camp; once after a long eight-hour backpack over 10, 668' New York Butte, and once after a forty minute helicopter ride from the Lone Pine Airport. I can tell you without any reservation, the helicopter was easier! The site of Beveridge can also be reached by climbing up from the Snow Flake Talc Mine. The route from the Saline Valley is more strenuous than the Burgess Mine route (see *Inyo-Mono SUV Trails*) which goes over the top of the Inyos to descend to the camp. The Snow Flake Talc Mine route involves a dry trail-less climb of some 3,000 feet in the most rugged country in the Death Valley region.

Continuing south on the Saline Valley Road beyond the Snow Flake Talc Mine turnoff, the "sand dune cutoff" comes in from the left after a mile. Here you can look to the right and see the Snow Flake Talc Mine road switch-backing 1500 feet up the mountainside. After another 1.5 miles, another miner's camp, with its enormous junk pile, lies hidden behind the mesquite thicket on the left. A side road to the right goes up to the mouth of Beveridge Canyon, where the year around stream disappears into the alluvial fan.

At a point 4.4 miles south of the Warm Springs turnoff, a large salt cedar tree marks the beginning of private property on both sides of the county road. A half-mile ahead, Artesian Road goes off to the left. This Class II road was once a very dusty alternative route to Lower Warm Springs. Most of that road has now been closed by *Wilderness* designation, but that was no great loss. The road now stops at an artesian well two miles to the northeast.

A tenth of a mile south of Artesian Road, the crusty white ruins of the Conn and Trudo Borax Works can be seen on either side of the county road. Borax was found here long before similar deposits in Death Valley were exploited. Partners Conn and Trudo began extracting the borate minerals here in 1875. This was six years before Aaron Winters recognized the white substance in Death Valley, seven years before Isadore Daunet started the Eagle Borax Works, and nine years before Coleman and Smith started the Harmony Borax Works in 1884 and the Amargosa Borax Works in the following year. Conn and Trudo operated here continuously until 1907, hauling their product out by wagon via San Lucas Canyon, a route that has subsequently become hopelessly washed out.

Remains of the Conn and Trudo Borax Works

Saline Valley Road

Continuing south on the county road, after 0.6 miles a fence on the left marks the beginning of the wildlife refuge established by the BLM and the State Department of Fish and Game in the days prior to the Saline Valley Salt Marsh being added to Death Valley National Park. Continue on down the county road another 0.4 miles and you will find a short side road entering the fenced-off refuge. The salt marsh is an excellent place to observe wildlife, particularly the birds, some of which live here all year around. Many more species simply stop and rest on their annual migration routes.

The abundance of wildlife did not escape the notice of prehistoric man either. Many archaeological sites have been found throughout the Saline Valley. Most were winter camps occupied only seasonally by small bands. However, the vast number of sites found suggests a very long period of use, perhaps 2,000 years. Even in historic times small bands of Shoshone have occupied the Saline Valley.

At a point 8.4 miles from the Warm Springs turnoff, just beyond the end of the wildlife fence, roads leave the county road on the right and the left. To the right, a Class II road goes up the alluvial fan to the still privately owned Essex Mine, later called the Big Silver Mine. On the other side of the county road, a pair of tracks follows the old salt tram towers 0.7 miles down to the water's edge. The last fifty yards of this road can get very muddy, so park well back from the water.

During World War I salt of remarkable purity was extracted from the brine in the bottom of the Saline Valley. Test shafts sunk into the old lake bed revealed that the salt deposits were at least thirty feet thick. This tramline was used to hoist the product some 7500 feet up Daisy Canyon and out of the Saline Valley, to the 8,900' crest of the Inyo Mountains, and then down 5200 feet to a railroad terminal at the eastern edge of Owens Lake near Swansea. The tramline was thirteen miles long and a masterpiece of engineering. In 1974 it was added to the National Register of Historic Places. What you see here are the last few towers at the eastern end. Many of the towers between the salt lake and the bottom of Daisy Canyon are gone. For the very ambitious, however, the old mule trail used in construction of the tram can still be followed up Daisy Canyon, where many of the towers still survive. For those less eager for exercise, the summit station can also be visited by a breathtaking Class III road along the Inyo Crest (described in *Inyo-Mono SUV Trails*).

Towers of the old salt tram

For the next seventeen miles the Saline Valley Road heads east along the valley floor, and then gradually turns south again as it climbs the bajada. At a point eleven miles beyond the salt tram a four foot high rock cairn on the left marks the turnoff to the Lippencott Grade (see Excursion # 33). This Class IV road will take you to the Racetrack playa and, from there, on to the Hunter Mountain Road or the road to Ubehebe Craters. In the last forty years the Lippencott Grade road has been closed by washouts more than it has been open, so it is best to check with the Rangers before attempting it. Nevertheless, it does make a potential escape route from the Saline Valley should both ends of the county road be buried in deep snow.

The Saline Valley and the nearby Lee Flat area are still home to a population of feral burros, in spite of the best efforts of the BLM and the National Park Service to eliminate them. Four miles beyond the Lippencott Grade turnoff, a small area to the left is fenced off. This is a burro exclosure erected by the BLM some years back to study the effects wild burros were having on the desert forage. As you can see, the plants outside the fence look pretty much the same as those protected on the inside. The empirical evidence at this exlosure pretty much supports the findings of National Park Service researchers Ralph and Florence Welles. In the period from 1954 to 1961 the Welles tried to determine if the feral burros were having an adverse impact on the bighorn sheep populations. They observed healthy bands of each species living side by side in mutual habitat, and concluded the perceived burro impact was highly over-rated. Nevertheless, two decades after the Welles' study, the feral burro population had doubled. By the 1980s the wild burro population reached the point that they could no longer be ignored by the BLM and the NPS. Further, the National Park Service is philosophically dedicated to the removal of all exotic species within the park. Resource managers won't be happy until the last of the three hundred remaining burros are rounded up or shot. The only drawback to the *final solution of the burro problem* is that it costs the government $1,500.00 for each and every burro disposed of. Full funding of the endeavor has been a problem, but the project moves forward, and soon Death Valley National Park will be burro-free.

Six miles beyond the Lippencott Grade turnoff, the county road enters Grapevine Canyon, and the geology changes dramatically. Gone are the Paleozoic marine sediments seen previously all along the eastern face of the Inyo Range. Here we find quartz monzonite, a silica-rich form of granite. This igneous rock, of early Cretaceous Age, is probably closely related to similar igneous rocks introduced in the Sierra Nevada about that same period of time.

Geology also played a key element in the formation of Grapevine Canyon. It was a series of faults that pushed the eastern flank of the Inyo Mountains upward in relation to the floor of the Saline Valley. That fault system turns at the base of Daisy Canyon and heads to the southeast, heading directly for the Panamint Valley sand dunes. Grapevine Canyon was eroded out of the broken and sheared off rocks along this fault zone. This same zone of broken rock also allows subsurface water to seep to the surface creating a series of springs. In the springtime, particularly in wet years, there is a small stream that runs the entire course of the canyon. This water not only supports a thick jungle of grapevines, from which the canyon gets its name, but it also supports a wide variety of birds, reptiles, and mammals. As you drive along the road, you are likely to flush out dove, quail, and chukars. These birds all rely on that life-giving trickle of water. There are precious few good places to camp in the Grapevine Canyon; but if you do, remember Park Service policy requires that you do not camp within two hundred yards of any water source.

The road up Grapevine Canyon is a bit steep in places, but the road is good and most vehicles should have little problem. Near the top of this 4½ mile long canyon, an old corral reminds us that this was, and still is, cattle country. Grazing was not permitted in the old Death Valley Monument; however, the

BLM did have a few grazing allotments in lands outside the monument. When the new and greatly expanded Death Valley National Park was created on October 31, 1994, three pre-existing BLM grazing allotments where included in the park expansion. These cattlemen were able to retain their grazing permits within the new park. Thus it is that you may see cattle in Grapevine Canyon.

At a point 30.3 miles from the Lower Warm Springs turnoff and 78.4 miles from Big Pine, the top of Grapevine Canyon is reached, and with that we come to the Hunter Mountain Road at an elevation just a few feet short of 6,000 feet. Some call this South Pass. The Hunter Mountain Road is also graded and is often in better condition than the Saline Valley Road. By turning left, one can cross Hunter Mountain and eventually descend to Ubehebe Craters and the floor of Death Valley. By this route it is 52 ½ miles to the nearest gas pump at Scotty's Castle.

To go to State Route 190 you will want to turn right. Proceed a tenth of a mile, then stop, get out, and look over the edge; it is a grand view. Below is Mill Canyon and beyond are the Panamint Valley sand dunes. Still further out, the entire length of Panamint Valley stretches to the south

The road soon enters the pinyon and juniper forest and within a mile of the South Pass climbs to a high point of 6,250 feet. From here, the rest of the way is all downhill.

During a June 1998 scouting trip, after an unusually wet El Niño winter, the roadsides in this area were alive with a wide variety of wildflowers. In places the hillsides were covered with a yellow carpet of Fremont xeraside. There was also the tall stately Prince's Plume of yellow, the tiny gilia and everything in between. The orange mallow was common, as was the ubiquitous Indian paintbrush, some with a very crimson coloration. Mohave aster, with its purple petals surrounding a yellow core, was common. In this particular year, even the Blue sage put on its best flowering face for us. But the wildflower that most attracted our attention was the pure white Desert Mariposa lily, *Calochortus kennedyi*. Never anywhere had we seen this unique species in such profusion. A few miles later we would see them colored bright orange.

Five miles from South Pass, the road begins to cross Lee Flat with its enormous Joshua tree forest. Joshua trees, *Yucca brevifolia,* are closely related to other types of yuccas. Joshua trees are considered to be "indicator plants" of the Mohave Desert. They are widespread throughout the higher elevations in the Southern California deserts, as well as Southern Nevada, and small portions of NW Arizona and SW Utah. They were supposedly so named by the Mormon pioneers entering Utah, who thought they resembled Joshua lifting his arms to heaven.

Pay close attention to the road ahead. This is open range where the cattle can roam freely. Not everything out there with four legs is a cow. We have seen feral burros grazing among the cows. Perhaps they were trying to escape the notice of National Park Service personnel.

Lee Flat

Seven miles from South Pass the first traces of asphalt begin to appear on the roadway. In another mile the park boundary is reached. A mile and a half beyond the entrance sign, a side road to the left goes 1.2 miles over to the Lee Mines, the Wonder Mine and the Silver Reid Mine.

These low hills are composed of the Tin Mountain limestone of Mississippian age, and the slightly younger Lost Burro Formation of Devonian age. At some point in geologic time, hot solutions from deep within the earth forced their way upward into cracks and along layers in these sediments. Upon cooling, the minerals in the solutions were left behind. Those solutions contained concentrated amounts of calcite, quartz, barite, and, of great interest to the prospectors, silver, gold, lead, and zinc.

One of the first mines to tap into these orebodies was the Emigrant Mine, later called the Lee Mine. It was found in the 1870s, probably shortly after the big finds in Darwin in 1874. In his 1884 report to the U.S. Director of the Mint, geologist H.C. Burchard said this of the Emigrant Mine:

> *Emigrant Mine with a shaft 100 feet in depth and lateral drifts which show a vein 4 feet wide, with a rich streak of gold and silver on both walls. Assay $200 per ton. The ore is sacked and shipped to San Francisco.*

Obviously, it would take pretty rich ore to be transported all the way to San Francisco for processing. A few years later, a mill was set up about seven miles to the northeast in what would become known as Mill Canyon. Still later, a mill was set up next to the mine; its stone foundations can still be seen today. When I first visited this mine in December of 1958, the old mill was in ruins; however a leasee was operating the mine, with the ore going to Darwin for processing. From present day appearances, it does not seem that the mine has been worked in recent years. **There are still open shafts and holes, however, so watch your step and do not attempt to enter any of the underground workings.**

A little more than a mile beyond the turnoff to the Lee Mines and eleven miles from South Pass, a side road to the right crosses the western edge of Lee Flat. It then descends into San Lucas Canyon before climbing again to a 8,200 foot high point at the old mining camp of Cerro Gordo.

For State Route 190, stay to the left on the now mostly paved road. The highway is but six miles to the south. Once at Highway 190, you may find yourself low on fuel. You have two options: you can turn left, descend into Panamint Valley and proceed to Trona, or go over Towne's Pass to Stovepipe Wells. By going this way, the nearest gas pump is 12.7 miles at Panamint Springs Resort or 38 miles at Stovepipe Wells. By turning right, the nearest gas pump is 32 miles at Olancha or 35 miles in Lone Pine.

30

Steel Pass from the Saline Valley

Primary Attraction:	Natural hot springs, suitable for bathing. You can also experience the true desert wilderness from the comfort of your car.
Time Required:	The traverse of Steel Pass into the Eureka Valley is an all day outing.
Miles Involved:	From Lower Warm Springs to the summit of Steel Pass is only fifteen miles. However, the distance from Big Pine to Lower Warm Springs, then over Steel Pass into the Eureka Valley and back to Big Pine again is 124 miles. **Do not underestimate your fuel consumption! Top off your tank before leaving Big Pine.**
Degree of Difficulty:	The Saline Valley Road to the Warm Springs turnoff is graded dirt, and while it has a washboard surface in places, it is a maintained road. The seven miles from the Saline Valley Road to Lower Warm Springs is all Class I. From there on, the next thirteen miles are Class II, with the last 2.3 miles to the summit being generally Class III. For those wishing to go on over the pass into the Eureka Valley, the route is mostly Class II, with only one short section of Class III descending a series of four rock ledges in lower Dedeckera Canyon.

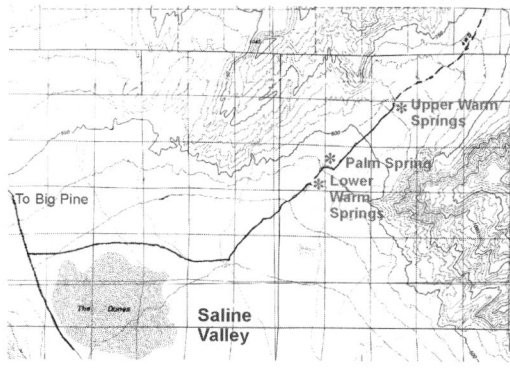

One of the most lonely jeep trails that you are likely to find in the Death Valley area is the cross-country route between the Saline Valley and the Eureka Valley. It is not shown on many maps and hence people may not realize such a route even exists. **This is a route you should not attempt unless you have another vehicle with you.** The route can be done from either direction, with the Saline to Eureka Valley direction being a little easier on your vehicle.

Our backroad outing to Steel Pass begins at the turnoff to Lower Warm Springs from the Saline Valley Road. This is 48 miles in from Big Pine, the last 32 miles of which are graded dirt.

Although not maintained by Inyo County, as is the Saline Valley Road, the Lower Warm Springs road is nevertheless Class I, making it passable to all vehicles, including motor homes and those pulling travel trailers. It heads due east passing the northern margin of the Saline Valley sand dunes that cover about six square miles. These northern-most dunes don't shift much with the wind because clusters of mesquite have stabilized them. An early morning stroll across the sand will reveal a wide variety of animal tracks left the previous night.

A cluster of mesquite and palm trees is reached after seven miles. A National Park Service sign says *Saline Warm Springs - Clothing Optional Use Area.* The main road stays to the left, but other turnoffs to the right go to campsites nestled amid the mesquite thickets.

The many acres of travertine terraces here suggest the warm springs have shifted around a bit during the last 10,000 years; however they seemingly have always attracted man. Artifacts found on the elevated desert pavement nearby show that native Americans camped here, at least during the winter months. In historic times, the springs attracted workers from nearby borate, silver and salt mines, and as early as the 1920s, even a few tourists. In the late 1940s and early 1950s, articles about the warm springs appeared in the pages of *Desert Magazine* and the secrets of the Saline Valley began to get out. More and more people were finding their way in there. Citizens built improvements, piping the warm waters to concrete-lined pools where one could soak a weary body in relative comfort. *Al fresco* bathing has been a long-standing tradition at the warm springs, a practice that continues to this day. While the pools are technically a "clothing optional area", in practice many of the bathers are wearing only a big smile.

In the 1960s Lower Warm Springs was the home of a hippie colony of considerable size. In spite of their professed commitment to love and peace, these folks sometimes displayed hostility to "outsiders" and casual visitors. The Bureau of Land Management had so many complaints, they had to step in and assume more authority and control over the site. The BLM made it a more family friendly public spa, and permitted a permanent volunteer caretaker to look after things. Besides keeping the pool clean, he has planted palm trees, constructed steel fire pits, and installed two outhouses (one of which has a solar-voltaic powered electric light!) The National Park Service generally did not change things when the area was included in Death Valley National Park late in 1994. Indeed, the caretaker was provided with a radio transceiver for emergency use. All that may soon change, however.

In 1998 the National Park Service began the four-year process of formulating a new *General Management Plan* for Death Valley National Park. One of the things that will attract scrutiny is the recreational use at the Saline Valley warm springs. One of the two rough dirt airstrips has been closed for safety reasons, and the fate of the other one is in doubt. In recent years, camping has been permitted anywhere, at no charge, for periods of up to thirty days. That, too, may change. The Park Service is considering the construction of walk-in campsites from a central parking area. With that, the charging of nightly camping fees seems sure to follow. Two of the attractive features at Lower Warm Springs are the dozens of palm trees planted in the last forty years and several hundred square feet of meticulously maintained green grass. The Park Service takes a dim view of "exotic species" running rampant in our National Parks, so there is reason to suspect this introduced flora, such as the grass and palm trees, might some day be torn out. One of the cold water springs contains a dozen or so koi fish someone has planted. Their future seems in doubt.

Fearing that the National Park Service had plans to tear out the soaking tubs, too, a group of users got together and formed an organization to keep a wary eye on the warm springs. They are the "Saline Preservation Association" (SPA). At the moment, the Park Service appears to be unwilling to anger the public and has no plans to restore the area to its pristine prehistoric condition. However, the construction of any new tubs will not be permitted.

The things that are not likely to change are the waters themselves. My field notes indicate that on December 14, 1969, I measured the water temperature at Lower Warm Springs at 112°F, with the bathing pool being 106°F. Twenty-nine years later, on December 19, 1998, I found the source spring to be 114°F, with the nearest pool 110°F, and the pool by the grass 106°F.

The road continues past the north side of Lower Warm Springs and heads in a northeast direction. The potholes increase in size causing the road to deteriorate to Class II. Palm Spring is slightly more than a half a mile away. Its cluster of tall palm trees stands out like a green beacon in a sea of brown. Campsites around Palm Spring are plentiful, although they do not have many of the amenities of those around Lower Warm Springs. Missing are the mesquite thickets which provide both shade and privacy.

The source pool at Palm Spring has the hottest water of the three warm spring areas. It was measured at 123°F one cold December morning. The source feeds two widely separated bathing pools through buried pipes. The bath waters measured a more tolerable 108° and 106° respectively.

Palm Spring

The road passes beyond Palm Spring, still heading northeast across the creosote-covered alluvium. On the distant hillsides to the left and right, the peace symbols laid out in stone are Vietnam War protest remnants dating from the early 1970s. With the adoption of the new Management Plan, I would hope that the National Park Service would remove these modern geoglyphs and restore the hillsides to their natural condition.

A mile and a half above Palm Spring, a cluster of mesquite trees on the left mark the location of yet another spring in this chain. On the mesa tops in this area, archaeologists have found the remnants of old Indian villages. It seems that ancient man was just as fond of soaking up the hot mineral waters as today's generations.

Judging from the many acres of travertine deposits and their thickness, hot springs have existed in this corner of the Saline Valley for thousands of years, possibly since the end of the Pleistocene Ice Age. One such travertine terrace is reached 1.8 miles beyond Palm Spring. The road briefly turns to Class III as it scrambles up the side of these water-borne mineral deposits.

As you make your way north, notice the Saline Range to your left. Most of these mountains are covered by three million-year-old basalt lava of Pliocene Age. But ahead and to the left, you can see the banded layers of the five hundred million-year-old sedimentary rocks that form the core of these mountains. These are very old marine sediments of the Wood Canyon Formation, the Zabriskie Quartzite, the Carrara Formation, the Bonanza King Formation, and the Nopah Formation. All are of Cambrian age, a time when life on earth was limited to a few primitive organisms living in the sea.

Three miles above Lower Warm Springs is Upper Warm Spring. In historic times this spring escaped man made "improvements" such as soaking tubs and palm trees; it has always retained its natural condition. In the days before this area became part of Death Valley National Park, the BLM constructed a six-foot chain link fence surrounding a half-acre around the spring. The object was to keep wild burros from fouling the waterhole; it seems to have worked. Upper Warm Spring looks pretty much today as it did thirty years ago. And the 99°F-water temperature seems to have changed little, too.

A mile and a half above Upper Warm Spring, the road leaves the bajada and enters the wash. The wheel tracks are not so distinct now, although the route remains Class II. On the bajada on either side of the wash are a variety of cacti, including prickly pear, cholla, and the round cottontop barrel cactus. The wash is a narrow open corridor between *Wilderness* areas on either side. For the curious hiker, however, there are petroglyphs and other signs of early Indian evidence in these lava fields. **Remember the defacement and collecting of artifacts is a serious violation of Federal law.**

As barren as they may seem, the great lava fields of the Saline Range must have supported game animals in earlier times. Prehistoric Indians have left their petroglyphs in several places, seemingly magical symbols to ensure good hunting. At one such site, the author found a large basalt boulder, with a rounded depression, clearly a mortar in which seeds, pinyon pine nuts, and other commodities were ground to a powder. At another site, random obsidian flakes behind a lava squeeze suggest ancient man used the site as a hunting blind, overlooking what was possibly a game trail.

Four miles above Upper Warm Spring the road passes the toe of a lava flow coming out of the Saline Range. When this basalt poured eastward out of a crack in the earth's surface, it was a hot viscous, slow-moving mass. Geologists use a Hawaiian term "aa" to describe this type of lava flow. The fluid fast-moving type of flow is called "pahoehoe". Geologist B. Clark Burchfel of Rice University, who studied these mountains, found both types of lava flows.

A basalt lava flow near Marble Bath

The 1913 Ballarat quadrangle and 1957 *Dry Mountain* 15-minute topographic maps show a feature named "Marble Bath" some distance above Lower Warm Springs. I have searched for, but never found Marble Bath, and I have not talked to anyone who has. Indeed, I was never sure just what it was that I was looking for. The late Wendell Moyer, who knew the Saline Valley as well as anyone, shared my search and subsequent frustration. Dr. Moyer had a great sense of humor, however, and he took positive measures to respond to the Mystery of Marble Bath. He hauled an old bath tub to the place on the map, and filled the bottom with hundreds of children's blue playing marbles which he had ordered from Dow Corning on the East Coast. Thus, anyone looking for Marble Bath could find the landmark. Unfortunately, the National Park Service did not share his humor and removed it.

Ten miles above Upper Warm Spring, the wash is left and once again the road winds its way up the alluvial fan. In the process the road deteriorates to Class III. The route remains this way for a little more than two miles. Suddenly, however, a low ridge is climbed, and on top the land falls away to the north. Anti-climatic as it seems, this is 4,500-foot Steel Pass, so named for a steel post once imbedded here. A two-pound coffee can holds a register in which people passing through can leave their names and comments.

Prior to the 1994 inclusion of this area into Death Valley National Park, Steel Pass saw relatively few backcountry travelers. When I first came this way in the 1960s, I doubt if the route over the pass saw more than a dozen vehicles a year. The summit register now suggests that figure has increased substantially. This is still very lonely country, however; it is no place to face a vehicle breakdown. I know I was out here alone once, when I broke a rear axle near Marble Bath. I was eighty miles from my home in Bishop and completely on my own. Fortunately I was able to able to limp back on the drive train to my front axle.

From the summit of Steel Pass, it is fourteen miles down to the nearest graded road at the Eureka Dunes, and fifty miles beyond them to Big Pine (see Excursion #28).

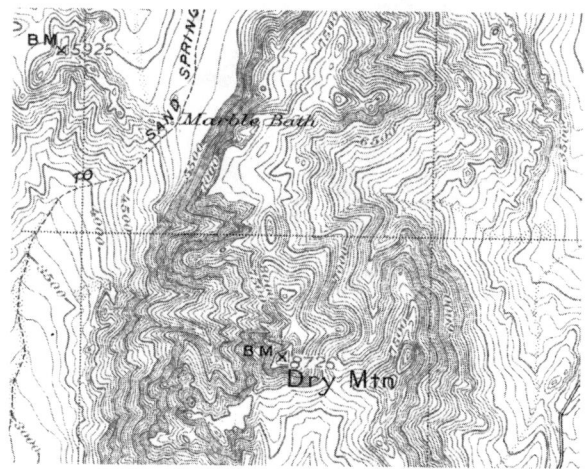

Marble Bath is shown on the 1913 topographic map

The back country of Death Valley is littered with the rusting remains of many vehicles. The National Park Service does not want any more.
Do your preventative maintenance before you leave home!

Chapter VII

Trails Out of Panamint Springs

Panamint Springs is situated on State Highway 190, on an alluvial fan coming out of Darwin Wash. From its lofty perch five hundred feet above the north Panamint Dry Lake, it commands a grand view of the northern part of the Panamint Range. There is no spring here as the name would imply. Water is piped out of Darwin Canyon just to the west.

The Panamint Springs Resort and RV Park offers the basics to a traveler: a restaurant with very good food and patio dining, a bar, motel rooms, RV sites with full hook-ups, tent campsites, showers, limited groceries, propane and unleaded gasoline. The facility is open all year.

Panamint Springs is an island of green in a sea of brown

These guys grazing near Lake Hill seem to have escaped the Park Service roundup

31

The Big Four Mine

Primary Attraction: An abandoned mine, and a very challenging trail.

Time Required: This is a half-day excursion out of Panamint Springs Resort.

Miles Involved: The mine is only seven miles off State Route 190, and less than twelve miles from the Panamint Springs Resort.

Degree of Difficulty: Everything from Class I to Class V (with very little in-between!) **The outing all the way to the Big Four Mine is not for the inexperienced or the faint of heart**. While heavily laden ore trucks once plied this road, it was in a time long ago. Never more.

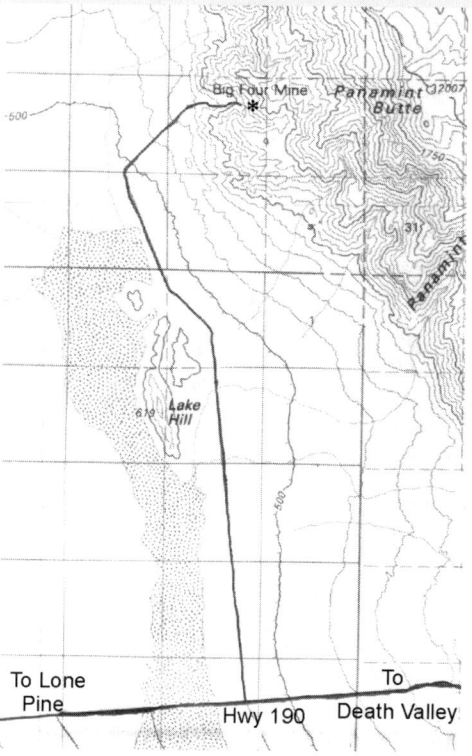

From the Panamint Springs Resort, take State Route 190 eastward down into Panamint Valley and across the north Panamint Dry Lake. At a point 4.5 miles from Panamint Springs (two miles east of the Panamint Valley Road) look for a wide graded dirt road heading north; turn left here.

The graded road is deceptively good for the first few miles as it approaches Lake Hill, prominent on the valley floor just to the left of the road. There is an interesting theory as to how this small mountain came to be here in Panamint Valley. U.S.G.S. geologists Wayne Hall and Hal Stephens looked at the rocks on Lake Hill and found them to be largely Ely Springs dolomite with a little Eureka quartzite. These rocks of late Ordovician age sat on top of young Quaternary alluvium and were totally out of place, isolated from other rocks of the same age. In looking around to determine where they came from and how they got here, Hall and Stephens found identical rocks near the crest of the Panamint Range some 3½ miles to the east. They postulated that during the extensive faulting during the late Pliocene, an enormous piece of the mountain broke off and slowly slid nearly 5,000 feet down the mountainside to come to rest on the floor of the valley; thus, the origin of Lake Hill. While that theory may sound a bit far fetched, I can offer nothing better.

Lake Hill dominates the northern end of Panamint Valley

During the Pleistocene Ice Age, Lake Hill was an island, not just once, but several times. When the ancestral Owens River filled China Lake, the overflow went through Poison Canyon to create Lake Searles. When that basin filled to its natural capacity, the overflow went around the southern end of the Slate Range to fill Panamint Valley. The resulting lake, at its maximum, was some 56 miles long, up to ten miles wide, and as deep as 900 feet in places. When the shoreline reached a point 1,910 feet above sea level, the water then flowed down Wingate Wash to create ancient Lake Manly in what today is Death Valley. The summit of Lake Hill is 2,030 feet above sea level. Thus when Lake Panamint was full, (during the Tahoe stage of the Wisconsin period) only the highest 1,020 feet of Lake Hill were above the surface of the water.

One should keep in mind, however, that the water levels in Lake Panamint fluctuated greatly throughout the Pleistocene. Wave cut shorelines have been observed anywhere from 1,045 feet above sea level all the way up to 1,977 feet. You may well ask, "How could the water get as high as 1,977 feet above sea level when it spilled out of Panamint Valley at 1910 feet?" The answer is that the Panamint Mountains continue to be pushed upward, and what may have been 1,910 feet in the Pleistocene is now 1,977 feet.

But enough of this geologic trivia; Lake Hill is worthy of a climb if you don't mind a five hundred foot ascent, walking all the way over rough rock. The climb to the summit can be done in an hour. Take your binoculars. To the southeast you can pick out a Holocene fault cutting across the alluvial fan. The western side of the fault has been raised with the resulting displacement having disrupted the drainage patterns on the alluvial fan.

If you are ever fortunate enough to fly low over Panamint Valley in a light aircraft, you might spot some prehistoric rock alignments known as geoglyphs. Although not as spectacular as the prehistoric intaglios found on the desert pavement near Blythe, or those of Nazca in Peru, the Panamint Valley geoglyphs are nevertheless a unique prehistoric resource that archaeologists have yet to adequately explain.

And speaking of archaeology, the northern end of Panamint Valley likely had more people living in it 9,000 years ago, or even 5,000 years ago, than live there today, even on holiday weekends during the peak of the winter tourist season. When anthropologist E.W. Nelson came through here in 1891, he found one hundred Indians living at the northern end of Panamint Valley, mostly living at Warm Sulfur Springs and in the Panamint Dunes. Even as this ancient lake was drying up for the last time, early man inhabited its swampy shores. We know this because excavations have uncovered crude Pinto Culture points going back 9,000 years.

Usually when we think of *archaeological digs,* our minds conjure up a series of strings laid out in a grid pattern of one meter by one meter, with the archaeologist carefully picking away with a trowel, a dental explorer, and a very fine camel's hair brush. Back in the 1960s, before Lake Hill was off limits to vehicles, I encountered a tractor digging trenches near the south base of the hill. When I asked the operator what he was looking for, I learned that a noted archaeologist was trying to reach the bottom of the alluvium which had washed down off Panamint Butte in the last several thousand years. Buried somewhere down there was the same layer of soil upon which these ancient occupants dwelled. She was looking for evidence of their times. That tractor destroyed my concept of meticulous excavations.

It is unlikely that you will find any "Clovis points" at Lake Hill, but keep in mind that the collecting of arrowheads, regardless of age, is prohibited in our National Parks. Remember, too, that Lake Hill, like the Panamint Dunes, is now classified as *Wilderness*. Vehicles must stay on the established roadway.

The roadway to Lake Hill is a good Class I, and a reasonably good Class II for a ways beyond. At a point 5.6 miles north of State Route 190, the roadway makes a distinct turn to the right. This is the closest point to the sand of the Panamint Dunes. A desert track once led over to them, but that route was closed by the BLM and with the expansion of Death Valley National Park in 1994, that vehicle ban has been maintained. If you want to visit the dunes, it is a four-mile walk one way.

At this bend in the road, the route begins to climb the alluvial fan, and as it does so the road deteriorates. The road remains a rough Class II for the next three-quarters of a mile, but as you pass between two mounds of basalt lava, the road becomes Class III. Within another quarter of a mile, it deteriorates further, to Class IV in places as it goes up the rocky wash.

Soon the canyon is entered. On the right is 280 million year old limestone of the Keeler Formation of Pennsylvanian and Permian age. On top of that is the only slightly younger Owens Valley Formation, also of Permian age. One minute your wheels are trying to gain a foothold on the white limestone on the south side of the canyon, and a few minutes later, the wash has taken you to the brown Cambrian metamorphosed sediments of the Nopah Formation on the north side of the canyon. It is here that the road seemingly ends. In fact, it does not, but you must cross the gravel pile to the right, and drop down into the rocky stream channel a few feet on the other side. **Scout the route ahead of foot before proceeding. This challenging maneuver is of Class V difficulty, and should not be under-estimated.** It can be done, but it is easier to walk the last half-mile to the ruins of the Big Four Mine.

The Big Four Mine, also known as the War Eagle, was a lead mine with claims first filed in 1907. Not much happened until 1940, however, with the first ore being shipped out by truck in 1942. Between late 1944 and late 1952, records show that 470 tons were mined, containing 16.6 percent lead, 12.5 percent zinc, and 2.6 ounces of silver per ton. The mine is high on the left side of the canyon and worked in three levels. A series of ore shoots and an aerial cableway brought buckets of ore to the canyon bottom. Some of the bunkers remain; some have collapsed. A road to the middle level has been obliterated by a torrent of basalt lava washed down from the ridge top. **You can hike to the upper workings, but the slope consists of steep loose rocks and is treacherous. As always, do not enter any of the underground workings.** If you want to see the ore they were mining, there is a small pile on the canyon bottom near the old mine camp.

Ore bunker at the Big Four Mine

The Darwin general store in 1908
(Photo courtesy County of Inyo, Eastern California Museum)

32

Back Door to Darwin

Primary Attraction:	Interesting geology, old mines, and a rare desert riparian habitat.
Time Required:	This is a half-day excursion out of Panamint Springs Resort. Better yet, take all day and hike to Darwin Falls, and explore some of the side roads that lead to old mines on Zinc Hill.
Miles Involved:	This is a loop trip of 37 miles from Panamint Springs and return.
Degree of Difficulty:	There is a little Class I, but the road is mostly Class II, with a touch of Class III in a few places.

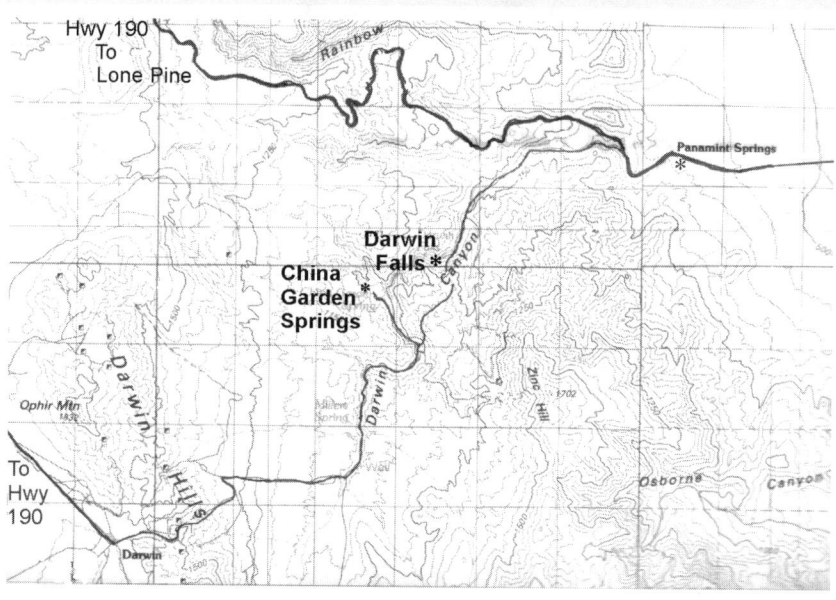

The century old mining camp of Darwin can be visited by a perfectly good six-mile long paved road off State Route 190. But if you wanted to get about on paved roads, you would not have bought this book. So, I am going to take you to Darwin by the less traveled back door.

From the Panamint Springs Resort, head west on State Route 190 in the direction of Lone Pine. After exactly one mile, turn left onto the graded dirt road going up Darwin Wash. At one time this road was asphalt, but today that surface is but a distant memory. While technically it cannot be considered any worse than Class I, the washboard surface is enough to rattle your teeth loose.

The road stays within the confines of the canyon bottom for the first few miles, passing through some interesting though complex geology. At first the rocks on either side are a granite-like Quartz monzonite. Soon, however, they turn into a highly metamorphosed basement complex of older rocks, capped by a much younger volcanic series. At a point 2.4 miles in from the highway, the BLM closed the last mile of road to Darwin Falls to help protect the wildlife, which depend on this rare desert stream. You must walk this last mile from the small parking area (no overnight camping). It is a very pleasant walk with a gain in elevation of only a couple of hundred feet. At the end of the trail is lovely Darwin Falls, the first of nine such falls in the next half mile of canyon.

Darwin Falls

Beyond this first fall, the route is generally trailless. The canyon has a couple of narrows where some rock scrambling is needed to get over the waterfalls.

With the change in Death Valley from a monument to a park in 1994, together with its considerable expansion, the Saline Valley, the Eureka Valley and much of the Panamint Valley have been added to the Death Valley National Park. A bend in the park boundary was made to include Darwin Falls. The National Park Service has pretty much taken over where the BLM left off. Under BLM management, Darwin falls was an *Area of Critical Environmental Concern*, and so it remains under National Park Service stewardship. The area does not get as many visitors as Badwater or Golden Canyon, but the number of people walking into the falls is considerable.

While the road no longer goes all the way to Darwin Falls, it does not end either. From the parking area, a Class II road ascends a side canyon onto the western flank of Zinc Hill, a 5,000 foot ridge on this northern end of the Argus Range. The road is all uphill for the next three miles and while four-wheel drive may not be absolutely necessary, many will feel more comfortable with its added traction.

At a point 1.6 miles above the Darwin Falls parking lot, the road passes an ore bunker. A Class III road turns to the left here to climb even higher on Zinc Hill to the mines above. Another such jeep trail is a quarter of a mile up the main road. With names like Empress, Wynog, and Darwin Zinc, the mines of this mountain have, over a 75-year period, produced much lead, zinc, copper and silver. A number of mines were accessible only by mule trail, the remnants of which can still be occasionally seen. An enjoyable day can be spent exploring the routes to these mines by suitable backcountry vehicle and on foot. **As always, stay out of the old mine workings. The shoring is bad and to enter is foolhardy.**

At a point 2.8 miles above the Darwin Falls parking area, a summit is reached and the road begins to drop back down into Darwin Wash on the other side. The route now returns to Class II in its descent. In another 1.1 miles the road swings to the left, but a fork to the right goes down the canyon a mile to China Garden Spring. This was the site of an old ore mill, now largely in ruins. There is a nice spring here in the shade of big cottonwood trees, with a pond containing, of all things, brightly colored koi fish. One wonders how long the National Park Service will permit this exotic species to inhabit this pool.

During Darwin's heyday, Chinese lived here growing vegetables, which they sold to the hungry miners in Darwin; hence its name. It is possible to hike down the canyon to Darwin Falls, although there is no trail and some rock scrambling is necessary to bypass several of the waterfalls. If you have any thoughts of doing this, you need to have Michel Digonnet's book, *Hiking Death Valley*.

Layers of 300 million-year-old marine
sediments near China Garden Spring

Back on the main Darwin road, the Class II road continues on up the canyon. Notice on the left how the layers of sedimentary rock have squeezed, twisted, and contorted. At a point 2.2 miles above the side-road to China Garden Spring, Miller Spring is reached. There was once a mill here that processed ore from the surrounding mines. The site remains in private hands. A tenth of a mile beyond, the deteriorating, but still paved road to Darwin is encountered. From here it is only four miles to downtown Darwin.

Darwin gets its name from Dr. Darwin French, whose expedition came through this general area in 1860 while searching for the illusive "Lost Gunsight Mine" of Death Valley fame. In their quest for fabulous wealth, the French group somehow overlooked the silver-bearing veins all around Mount Ophir.

Those minerals remained overlooked until October or November of 1874. Word of the strike soon got out, and men poured out of nearby Cerro Gordo and Panamint City to get in on the ground floor. By 1875 the town of Darwin was established. Within a year there were some twenty mines operating in the vicinity, feeding two smelters, and the population grew to seven hundred people.

By 1876, Darwin had a population of one thousand rowdy miners who supported the town's fifteen saloons. At that time, the Cuervo smelter was turning out twenty tons per day; the Defiance smelter, sixty tons per day; and the New Coso smelter, an astounding one hundred tons per day! To fire these hungry furnaces, pinyon wood had to be packed in on long mule trains from the Argus and Panamint Ranges. Other mules were hitched to freight wagons to carry the heavy ingots of silver, lead, and zinc for many miles south to the railroad in Mojave. An estimated 29 million dollars worth of precious metals came from the mines of Darwin between 1875 and 1952. This does not include another seven to eight million more from other nearby mines just to the north and east.

In 1938 geologist V.C. Kelley wrote that Darwin reached its peak in 1880, with a population of 5,000 people. Historian Remi Nadeau says Darwin reached its zenith in 1876 just before the new discoveries at Mammoth City and Bodie siphoned off some of Darwin's population. Whatever the date, as the most easily worked orebodies were depleted, mines began to close. Nevertheless, one mine or another seemed to be working more or less continuously to the start of World War II. That conflict spurred its own type of activity as tungsten was found and mined, beginning in 1941. The town got another economic shot in the arm in 1945 when the Anacoda Company acquired the consolidated Darwin Mines and reopened many old workings.

To this day, Darwin refuses to die. The post office established in 1875 is still open, nearly 125 years later. Today Darwin has a population of less than one hundred people. Unfortunately when those people want to put groceries in their pantry, or put gas in their cars, they have to drive 35 miles to Lone Pine. **Note: The buildings in Darwin are all privately owned. Look around the town if you wish, but please stay on the street and do not trespass on private property.**

From Darwin, there is a paved county road that goes north five miles to meet State Route 190. From here it is a return trip of seventeen miles back to the Panamint Springs Resort.

If you are interested in learning more of Darwin's past, try to find a copy of the 1996 book, *Darwin, California*. The author is full time attorney and part time Darwin resident and historian, Robert Palazzo.

Excursion #33 includes the infamous Lippencott Grade

33

Around Hunter Mountain

Primary Attraction:	High mountain scenery, old mines, and if you are very lucky, you might see stones that mysteriously seem to move by themselves.
Time Required:	This is a full day's outing, when the days are long. It would be better to camp along the way and make the circuit in two days.
Distance Involved:	It is 53 miles from Panamint Springs to Teakettle Junction via Hunter Mountain and Hidden Valley. The return trip from Teakettle Junction back to Panamint Springs via the infamous Lippencott Grade is another 55 miles. **There are no services of any kind along the way. Top off your fuel tank before you start.**
Degree of Difficulty:	Most of this route is Class I and II. **The road below the Lippencott Mine can range anywhere from Class III at best, to completely impassable, depending on conditions of the moment. Further, conditions can change instantly. Always check with the rangers before attempting the Lippencott Grade.** The Hunter Mountain Road can be closed by snow in the winter. If you want to see the skating stones on the racetrack when snow closes the Hunter Mountain road, you should come up the Lippencott Grade from the Saline Valley, or come in by way of Ubehebe Crater.

This backroad loop exposes the visitor to another aspect of Death Valley National Park that most tourists never see. The topography and scenery range from the pinyon and juniper slopes of Hunter Mountain to the austere beauty of the Racetrack Playa to the Joshua tree covered landscape of Lee Flat. **Top off your gas tank before leaving Panamint Springs. You have 108 miles of back roads ahead with no services of any kind.**

Trails Out of Panamint Springs

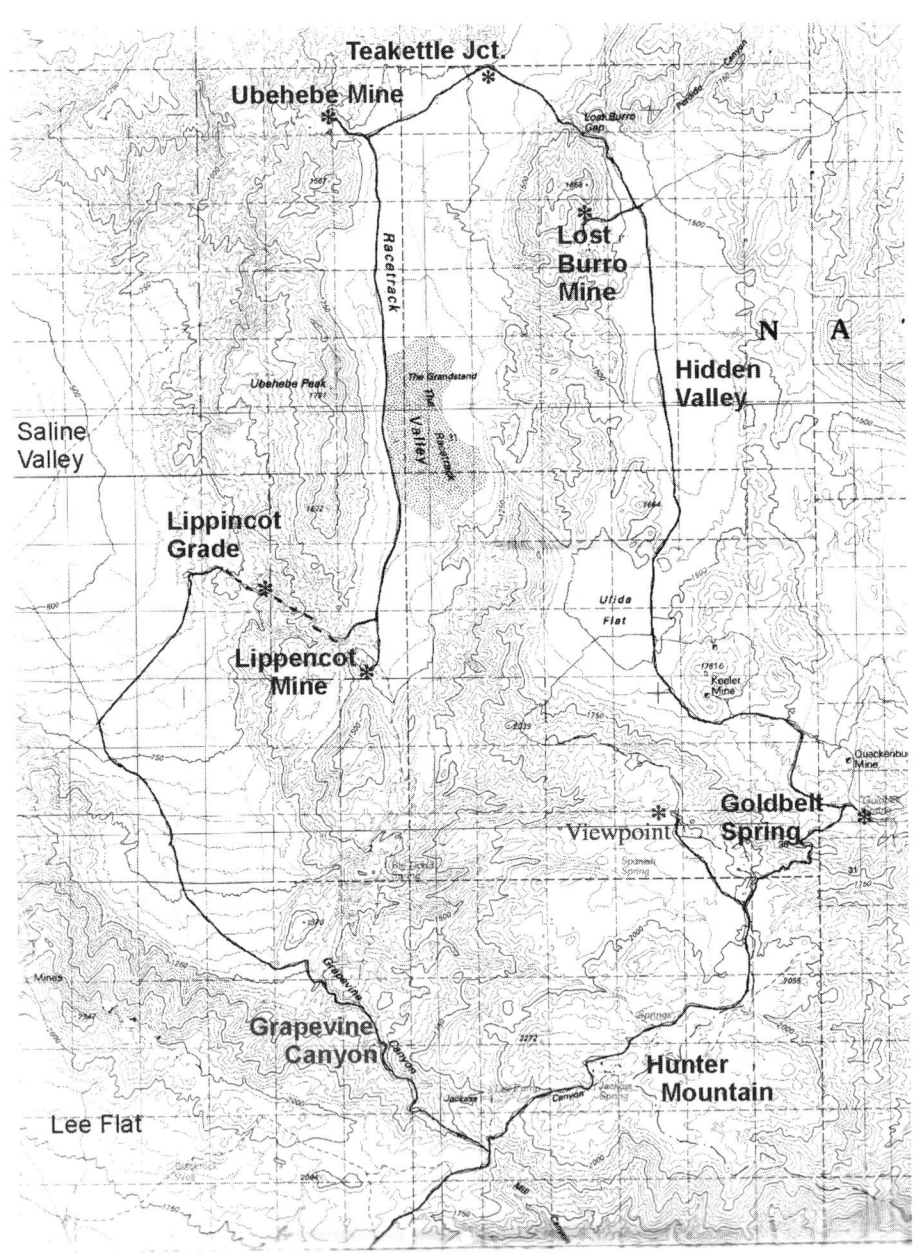

We begin our backroad adventure at Panamint Springs, at an elevation of 1,900 feet, where we head west on State Route 190. After crossing the mouth of Darwin Wash, the State Highway climbs the spectacular grade which circles the edge of Rainbow Canyon. These are relatively young Pliocene volcanic rocks, which rest unconformably upon much older Paleozoic limestones. The marine sediments can only be seen in a few road cuts near the top of the grade.

At a point 12.7 miles from Panamint Springs, a long ago paved road turns off to the right; this is the Saline Valley Road. A sign warns it is 85 miles to Big Pine, with no services along the way. Turn north here, noting your mileage as you leave the highway. The county road heads north across the southern end of Santa Rosa Flat. The elevation here is 5,000 feet, so we have already climbed 3,100 feet.

After four miles the road swings to the east, and then north again crossing a low limestone ridge. On the other side of the ridge, 5.8 miles from Highway 190, a Class II side road to the right heads for the low hills a mile to the east. This was the site of the Lee, the Wonder, the Silver Reid, and other mines. This is an interesting side trip of slightly over a mile.

These low hills are composed of the Tin Mountain limestone of Mississippian age, and the slightly younger Lost Burro Formation of Devonian age. At some point in geologic time, hot solutions from deep within the earth forced their way upward into cracks and along layers in these sediments. Upon cooling, the minerals in the solutions were left behind. Those solutions contained concentrated amounts of calcite, quartz, barite, and of interest to the prospectors, silver, gold, lead, and zinc.

One of the first mines to tap into these orebodies was the Emigrant Mine (later called the Lee Mine). It was found in the 1870s, probably shortly after the big finds in Darwin in 1874. In his 1884 report to the U.S. Director of the Mint, geologist H.C. Burchard said this of the Emigrant Mine:

> *Emigrant mine with a shaft 100 feet in depth and lateral drifts which show a vein 4 feet wide, with a rich streak of gold and silver on both walls. Assay $200 per ton. The ore is sacked and shipped to San Francisco.*

Obviously, it would take pretty rich ore to be transported all the way to San Francisco for processing. A few years later, a mill was set up about seven miles to the northeast in what would become known as Mill Canyon. Still later, a mill was set up next to the mine; its stone foundations remain. When I first visited this mine in December of 1958, the old mill was in ruins; however, a leasee was operating the mine, with the ore going to Darwin for processing. From present day appearances, it does not seem that the mine has been worked in recent years. **There are still open shafts and holes, however, so watch your step and do not attempt to enter any of the underground workings.**

The Lee Mines in 1958

The Lee Mines in 1998

Returning to the Saline Valley Road, turn right to resume your loop around Hunter Mountain. At a point eight miles north of Highway 190, a major unmarked intersection is reached. The left fork crosses the west edge of Lee Flat to descend into San Lucas Canyon before climbing again to an 8,200-foot high point at the old mining camp of Cerro Gordo. For this excursion, you will want to keep to the right here on the Saline Valley Road.

Soon a second low limestone ridge is crossed and beyond a sign announces you are entering Death Valley National Park. The road now crosses Lee Flat with its enormous Joshua tree forest. Joshua trees, *Yucca brevifoli,* are closely related to other types of yuccas and are quite widespread in the Mohave Desert. Indeed, they are found throughout the higher elevation deserts of Southern California and Southern Nevada and adjoining small areas of Arizona and Utah. They were supposedly so named by Mormon pioneers entering Utah, who thought they resembled Joshua lifting his arms to heaven.

This area has been used for cattle grazing for well over one hundred years. Grazing was not permitted in the old Death Valley Monument; however, the BLM did have a few grazing allotments in lands outside the monument. When the new and greatly expanded national park was created on October 31, 1994, three pre-existing BLM grazing allotments where included in the park expansion. Those cattlemen were able to retain their grazing permits within the new park. Thus it is that you may see cattle on and near Hunter Mountain. Pay close attention to the road ahead. This is open range where the cattle can roam freely. Not everything out there with four legs is a cow. We have seen feral burros grazing among the cows. Perhaps they were trying to escape the wrath of National Park Service personnel who are committed to eliminating them from the park.

Once across the flat, the road begins to gently climb into the lava-covered hills to the east. During a June 1998 scouting trip, after an unusually wet El Niño winter, the roadsides were alive with a variety of wildflowers. In places the hillsides were covered with a yellow carpet of Fremont xeraside. There was also the tall stately Prince's Plume of yellow, the tiny gilia and everything in between. The orange mallow was common, as was the ubiquitous Indian paintbrush, some with a very crimson coloration. Mojave aster with its purple petals surrounding a yellow core was common. Even the Blue sage put on its best flowering face for us. But the wildflower that most attracted our attention was the bright orange of the Desert Mariposa lily. Never anywhere had we seen this unique species in such profusion. Just five miles up the road we would see them pure white.

As the road climbs, the Joshua trees give way to juniper and pinyon trees. At a point fifteen miles in from the highway, persons riding on the right side of the car will have fleeting glimpses down into Mill Canyon and to the Panamint

Valley Dunes beyond. Indeed, from some turns of the roadway you can look south down the entire length of Panamint Valley. The elevation of the road here is nearly 6,000 feet. The elevation of the Panamint sand dunes below is about 2,500 feet.

At a point 15.6 miles in from the highway, a second major intersection is reached. Like the last one, this one is unmarked. The left fork makes a 4,000 foot descent of Grapevine Canyon into the Saline Valley. Again keep right on the road which now hovers somewhere between Class I and II. We will return via the left fork near the end of our journey.

At this intersection we leave the Pliocene volcanic rocks. For the next eleven miles we will be in granite-like rocks called quartz monzonite. They have been potassium-argon dated at 134 million years, putting them into the Cretaceous Period. These rocks are closely related in composition and age to the granitic rocks of the Sierra Nevada.

If you come through here in the springtime, and are very lucky as I once was, you might see the variety of Mariposa lily that has pure white petals. Also watch for Ceanothus, a large shrub with fragrant white flowers found only in the park's higher elevations. It is a favorite browse for deer (yes Virginia, there are deer here on Hunter Mountain).

A quarter of a mile beyond the intersection there is a small sandy basin to the left, where the dune primrose seems to thrive at a much greater elevation than is its normal habitat. If you look closely, you may barely make out an old overgrown wagon road contouring around the western side of the hill. By walking along this old trail a half mile to the ridge top, and then following the rusting 1½ inch pipe down to the bottom of the canyon, you will find century old Lee Pump overgrown with wild rose and grapevine. Only the top of the boiler protrudes above the thick jungle of vegetation. At one time this steam powered pump lifted water from Jackass Creek out of the steep canyon, where gravity sent it seven miles down hill to the Lee Mines.

At a point 17.3 miles in from the highway, our dirt road dips down into the canyon and tiny Jackass Creek is crossed. This desert watercourse originates at a spring of the same name just up the canyon. During the winter months, this rare desert stream will flow several miles down into Grapevine Canyon to join another stream that flows nearly to the Saline Valley. The Hunter Mountain Road can also be very icy here in the winter. **Use great caution when ice covers the roadway.**

At 18.6 miles from the highway, the road reaches its high point on Hunter Mountain at an elevation of 7,000 feet. There are some nice campsites among the pinyon pines. At 22.3 miles look for a cattle guard in a drift fence to the right. By going through this gap in the fence, and continuing south for nearly a mile, you will find an old log cabin, which some think goes back to the early 1870s. History does not suggest it is quite that old.

William Lyle Hunter was a Confederate officer who came west in 1865 to start a new life. Hunter ran mule trains in and out of Cerro Gordo in the early 1870s, hauling ore and supplies. He established a ranch on Lee Flat to support his fifty mules. He married in 1875, and eventually had four sons and a daughter. When the mines closed he moved to the Owens Valley to ranch and eventually became the Inyo County Clerk. His next to youngest son was Bev, who took to grazing cattle and collecting wild horses. In Lester Reed's book *Old Timers of Southeastern California,* Bev Hunter says this cabin was his, which would suggest that it was built around the turn of the 20th Century.

Log cabin off the Hunter Mountain road

Back on the main road, the route deteriorates to Class II as it leaves the pinyon forest and begins its steep descent of 2,000 feet to the Goldbelt Spring area. On the way down, good views can be had of the sand dunes near Stovepipe Wells, some twenty miles away to the northeast as the crow flies. At a point 26 miles from the highway, a side road right goes 1.2 miles to Goldbelt Spring.

Some writers have described Goldbelt Spring as if it were an honest to goodness mining camp in the mold of Greenwater or Ballarat. That may be a bit misleading. Goldbelt Spring is one of those desert water holes where sourdough prospectors have camped for well over a century, as they searched for, and sometimes found, mineral wealth in the nearby hills. At times, those who stopped here simply pitched a tent. Others seeking a more substantial shelter fashioned a cabin out of whatever building materials they could find. The residents of Goldbelt Spring were a long way from their source of supplies, and they seldom stayed for extended periods of time. A crowded day at Goldbelt Spring during the Greenwater excitement of 1906 might have meant six people were living here, and certainly no more than a few dozen at its peak.

Today's ruins at Goldbelt Spring seem to be remnants of a later era when talc miners set up camp here in the 1930s and 40s. Unfortunately the last four wooden structures have all collapsed and the single "cousin jack" dugout is about to suffer the same fate.

I would recommend a scenic and enjoyable all day hike from Goldbelt Spring, down Marble Canyon to Cottonwood Canyon. The trick is to have someone pick you up at the bottom end. The distance is a long fourteen miles, but it is all down hill. While there are springs along the way, carry plenty of water. Keep your eyes open for petroglyphs on the canyon walls. They are there, but easily missed.

Back track the 1.2 miles back to the Hunter Mountain Road and turn right. The main road now is pretty much Class I, as it makes its way down the bajada. The road heads west, then north, then west again, before entering Ulida Flat to head north once again. Along the way, several roads turn off to the right leading to talc mines.

At a point eleven miles from the Goldbelt Spring turnoff, an unmarked crossroads is reached. The Class II road to the right goes up to the tiny seep called Rest Spring and beyond to the White Top Mountain area where one can look down into Death Valley (see Excursion #15).

The left fork, an easy Class II, goes 1.2 miles to the Lost Burro Mine. Here, a gold bearing vein one to four feet wide was found at the contact point where the Cretaceous granitic rocks forced their way up through the Tin Mountain limestone. The first claims were staked in 1907. Between then and 1912, the mine is said to have produced $85,000 in gold. Between 1935 and 1942 when gold mines were shut down by Presidential Order, the official output was reported at 255 ounces, worth a mere $5,281.00. However geologist Jim McAllister looked at the size of the workings in the early 1950s and estimated the output was more like 2,800 ounces worth something in excess of $100,000. Could the operators have been under reporting their income?

The mill built in 1917 has been salvaged for use elsewhere; however, the timber frame remains. There is a weather-tight cabin at the mine that can be used as an emergency shelter in a storm, if you don't mind sharing your quarters with the mice and packrats.

Around Hunter Mountain

The Lost Burro Mine

The main road continues north, where it slips through a little canyon known as Lost Burro Gap before entering the Racetrack Valley. While this canyon is only a mile long, the steeply dipping limestone rocks here represent one hundred million years of the earth's history. First is the Hidden Valley dolomite of Silurian age. Mid-way through the canyon is the Lost Burro Formation of Devonian age, and finally at the lower end is the Tin Mountain limestone of Mississippian age. All three of these formations contain fossils of the primitive animals that lived in the sea at that time, but they are tough to find.

At a point fifteen miles from Goldbelt Spring, 40.2 miles from Highway 190 (without any side-trips), yet another important intersection is reached. This is Teakettle Junction, so named for the variety of teakettles which over the years people have placed to adorn the sign. The right fork, a graded road, heads towards Ubehebe Crater some twenty miles to the north. To complete our loop, we will want to turn left, taking us in a generally southerly direction.

At a point 2.2 miles south of Teakettle Junction, a short Class I side road right goes over to the Copper Bell and Ubehebe Mines. If you elect to make this short side trip, the Copper Bell is to the left, the Ubehebe to the right.

The same William Hunter who ran mule trains out of Cerro Gordo, together with a partner, John Porter, found copper minerals here in 1875. But because the site was so remote and the copper content marginal, they were unable to profitably mine it. After Hunter's death in 1902, the two mines changed hands. In 1906, during the Bullfrog and Greenwater excitement, two imaginative mining promoters, A.D. Whittier and Jack Salsberry, became involved. The Ubehebe Mining Company was formed and shares at $1.00 par value were offered for 15 cents. Salsberry, a man of unbridled enthusiasm, claimed he had fifty million tons of 10% copper ore in sight. The estimated value was at least a billion dollars. He talked of building a smelter and railroad. Two miles northwest of the Racetrack playa, Salsberry laid out the townsite of Salina City, later renamed Latimer, to flatter a major investor. Historian Richard Lingenfelter says Latimer never had more than twenty tents at its peak. (I have never been able to find the site.) Needless to say, the grandiose dreams and schemes of stock promotions never lived up to their promise.

Nevertheless, the Ubehebe Mine did turn into a bonafide mine, although it was lead, zinc, and even a little silver, not copper, that were the important commodities produced. Mining began in 1916, peaked in 1928, and continued off and on into the early 1950s. When I first visited the mine in 1958 the tramline to the upper mines was down, but all of the structures were still in good condition. The underground workings looked like the last day the miners left them. Such is not the case today. **Stay out of the tunnels and shafts!**

Continue south another three miles on the graded road and you will reach the northern end of the Racetrack playa, a dry lakebed that isn't always dry. It is during those infrequent wet spells, usually in the winter, that wind-blown rocks and other solid objects move about on the playa surface leaving a track in the mud to mark their route of movement. The National Park Service has a sign that nicely explains the process. While this phenomenon has been observed elsewhere in the western United States, including the Bonnie Claire playa east of Scotty's Castle, the best examples of skating stones have been recorded here. Geologist Paula Messina, who wrote her Ph.D. dissertation on this phenomenon, has tried in vain to be present when these stones moved. Alas, nothing moved an inch while she was watching. She did find that, in general, most of the objects moved with direction of the prevailing winds, a north to northeast direction. But once in the middle of the playa, the tracks left by the objects were often very convoluted.

It should be noted that driving on the playa surface is no longer permitted. You may certainly walk out there, but please leave your car on the road.

These boulders really do move!

From the Racetrack, the Class I road continues south. At a point 9.5 miles south from Teakettle Junction, there is an intersection where a road turns off to the right. This is the upper end of the infamous Lippencott Grade, which makes a steep descent into the Saline Valley to the west. Before starting down, however, you may wish to continue on south another 1.4 miles to the site of the Lippencott Lead Mine.

Straight ahead, a Class I road continues 0.2 miles to a Park Service campground whose only improvement is a toilet. Beyond here the road deteriorates to Class III, and continues on another mile to the Lippencott Mine.

The Lippencott Mine's earliest days are obscure, but probably go back to the years just before World War I. It was not until World War II, however, that the demand for lead prompted an extensive exploration of the orebody. During that period, lead from this mine was shipped to Santa Ana, California, where it was made into automotive batteries. After the war zinc, and to a lesser degree silver, became important byproducts. **Warning: Stay out of the tunnels and underground workings.**

To complete our loop, we must turn right at the intersection 9.5 miles south of Teakettle Junction. Forty years ago, the road into Panamint City was not considered particularly difficult, but the Lippencott Grade out of the Saline Valley was an extreme challenge. Boy, how times have changed! The Park Service has run a blade over the Lippencott Grade as a convenience to the backcountry ranger who patrols this area. **Be forewarned, however; it doesn't take much to wash out the Lippencott Grade. It can be opened one week and closed the next. Save yourself some grief and always ask the rangers about its present status. Unless you obtain recent information to the contrary, consider the route down to be Class IV, and the route up Class V. When in doubt, scout the road ahead on foot before attempting to drive it.**

From top to bottom, the Lippencott Grade is 4.5 miles long. In that distance, the change in elevation is 2,000 feet. It is still easier to go down the road than up it, but today those differences should not deter you if you want to make the ascent.

At a point 16.5 miles from Teakettle Junction, the main Saline Valley Road is reached. This is a good graded road receiving occasional maintenance by the Inyo County Road Department. There are lots of interesting features in the Saline Valley.

By turning right you can see the old salt tram, rest your weary bones in hot springs, or possibly take the jeep trail over Steel Pass to come out in the Eureka Valley (see Excursions #30 and 28). By staying on the county road you can also eventually come out onto Highway 395 at Big Pine (see Excursion 29). To return to Panamint Springs, you must turn left here. At 2,200 feet, this is very near the low point on this circle tour. It is a climb of nearly 4,000 feet up Grapevine Canyon to rejoin the Hunter Mountain Road where we kept to the right so very long ago.

Once on the Saline Valley Road, it is six miles to the lower end of the canyon. In the springtime, particularly in wet years, there is a small stream that runs the entire course of the canyon. This water not only supports a thick jungle of grapevines, from which the canyon gets its name, but it also supports a wide variety of birds, reptiles, and mammals. As you drive along the road, you are likely to flush out dove, quail, and chukars. Remember that this is within the park, and camping within 100 feet of flowing water is prohibited.

At the top of Grapevine Canyon, 27 miles from Teakettle Junction, we rejoin the road we came in on. By turning right we retrace our route 15.6 miles back to Highway 190, and from there it is another 12.7 miles back to the Panamint Springs Resort.

34

Osborne Canyon

Primary Attraction: Interesting geology and an abandoned mine are the main features of this excursion. Osborne Canyon, Lookout Mountain, and Snow Canyon can be combined for several days worth of four-wheeling outside of the national park where the restrictions of what you can and cannot do are less onerous.

Time Required: Osborne Canyon is a half-day outing from Panamint Springs.

Distance Involved: The off highway portion is nine miles one way.

Degree of Difficulty: The first four miles of dirt road are Class I or better. The remaining five miles are generally Class II or III, with a few short sections of Class IV.

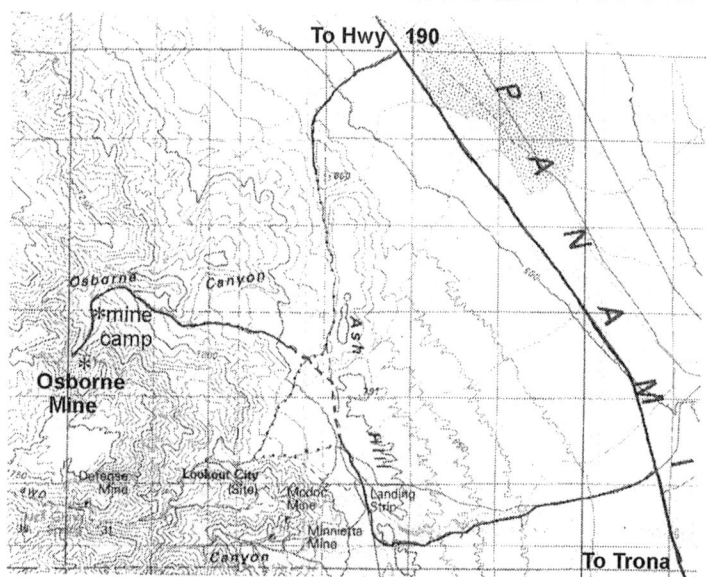

There are three ways to reach the entrance to Osborne Canyon, all of which are washed out and a bit confusing. I shall describe the easiest route.

From Panamint Springs, go east on State Highway 190 for 2.6 miles, then turn right onto the paved road to Trona. Go another 7.5 miles to a graded dirt road on the right. (If you are coming from the direction of Trona, this turnoff is 6.5 miles beyond the Wildrose Canyon Road.) A sign reading *"Minnietta Mine"* marks the turnoff. Note your odometer reading here as you leave the pavement.

After three miles or so, this graded road deteriorates slightly to Class I. At a point 3.6 miles in from the highway, you will reach the Nadeau Shotgun Road coming in from the left. Veteran desert freight hauler Remi Nadeau built this road in 1876. It was called the "Shotgun Road" because it cut straight across the bajadas of the Argus Range as if it had been fired from a shotgun (see Excursion #43).

Stay to the right following Nadeau's old road. After 0.3 miles a side road goes left to the Minnietta Mine. The Minnietta Mine is a worthy side trip (see Excursion # 43), but to find Osborne Canyon you will want to continue straight ahead.

A tenth of a mile farther the road forks; either fork will take you to Osborne Canyon. My recommendation is to stay right, continuing north along the western base of Ash Hill. This fork is washed out in places, but generally no worse than Class III. At one time this was a reasonably good road, but El Niño storms over the past fifty years have brought down a lot of new alluvium, making the boulder strewn route much more difficult.

If you pass this way in the springtime, Ash Hill, to your right, often puts on a vivid display of purple phacelia. That plant seems to thrive on the soils derived from this olivine basalt rock. Later, in the summer, cottontop cactus clusters on the left display their colorful flowers.

At a point six miles in from the pavement, yet another intersection is reached. It can easily be recognized by the presence of a tractor-loading ramp. The left fork heads south up a boulder strewn wash to rejoin the Stone Canyon Road into Lookout after 1.5 miles (see Excursion # 35). The right fork heads west up the wash into Osborne Canyon. As you start up this road, the elevation is 2,400 feet. In the next three and a half miles, the rough Class II road climbs nearly 2,000 feet.

As you begin to make your way up the road, the rocks at either side of the canyon are varieties of impure limestone, part of the Keeler Canyon Formation. Suddenly however, the rocks change from Paleozoic marine sediments to well-weathered igneous rocks of Jurassic age. While looking like granite to the layman, these younger rocks are technically a leucocratic quartz monzonite. They are a part of the Jurassic pluton that forms the igneous core of the Argus Range, and may be related to similar rocks in the Sierra Nevada.

The canyon forks three miles up Osborne Canyon from the tractor-loading ramp. The road swings to the left following the south fork. In a tenth of a mile, a couple of stone buildings are clustered on a bench to the left above the wash. This is the Surprise Mine Camp. The mine itself is another half mile up the canyon.

The Surprise Mine Camp

A quarter of a mile beyond the Surprise Mine Camp, the quartz monzonite ends as the Carboniferous marine sediments once again reappear. First there is the Lee Flat limestone on both sides of the wash. Then, on the left, comes an exposure of the Perdido Formation, followed by the Tin Mountain limestone. Notice how the once flat lying layers have been tilted upwards, twisted and contorted by the forces of metamorphism. Just beyond this interesting outcrop, the road ends at a lonely ore bunker.

These layered rocks have been metamorphosed by heat and pressure

J.L. Osborne located the mining claims of the Surprise Mine in 1942. Osborne and his partner Slater tapped into several chimney-like orebodies of lead and silver minerals imbedded in the layers of steeply dipping and faulted Tin Mountain limestone. The principal minerals mined were galena (lead sulfide), cerrusite (lead carbonate), anglesite (lead sulfate), and pyromorphite (lead chlorophosphate). Silver and zinc minerals are also often associated with lead, and this was the case here, too, although here it was the lead that paid the bills.

Of the several tunnels, the main adit goes into the hillside 160 feet. Off it is a stope from which 210 tons of ore were extracted in 1942. The main period of operation, however, was in the years 1947-1951 when A.L. Foss worked the mine. There was no mill on the property. The ore was shipped by dump truck 55 miles to Keeler, from where it was transported by rail to the smelter.

The total production is thought to be around seven hundred tons. The mine seems to have last been worked in 1953, although the present owners still keep their claims valid. **Please respect the owners' property.**

When I first visited the site in June of 1958, the 1300' tramline connecting the mines high on the hillside with the lower bin still swayed in the wind. That cable is still there, but it now lies on the ground. From the road's end, it is a short, but steep hike up the hillside to the mines. **Caution: the underground workings are not safe. Do not enter!**

An aerial tramway once brought buckets of ore down from
the Surprise Mine to the bunker in the canyon bottom

35

Lonely Lookout

Primary Attraction:	A forgotten and historic old mining camp perched high on a mountaintop in the Argus Range. This entire excursion is outside of the national park.
Time Required:	If you like to stop and look around, this is an all day outing.
Miles Involved:	From Panamint Springs to Lookout it is 18.5 miles.
Degree of Difficulty:	The dirt road portions range from graded gravel to a little Class IV at the Stone Canyon narrows. The Class III sections total 2 miles.

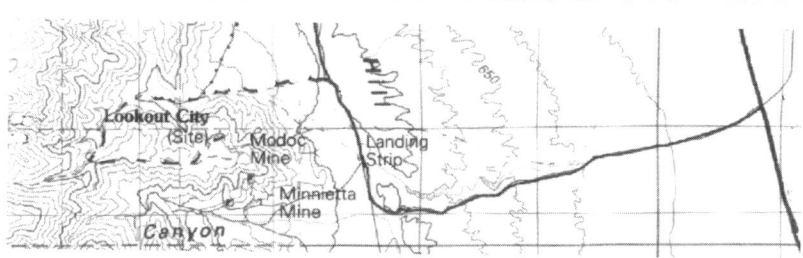

You don't need to be a ghost town buff to have heard of such old mining towns as Calico, Bodie, and Randsburg. These places are easily accessible in the family car and are popular destinations for weekend trips. For every one of these well-known places, there are dozens of other camps forgotten by everyone except a few western historians. Lookout is one such camp, practically unknown to everyone and seldom visited, except by a hardy few in backcountry vehicles.

To reach Lookout from Panamint Springs, go east on State 190 for 2.6 miles, then turn right onto the paved road to Trona. Go another 7.5 miles to a graded dirt road on the right. (If you are coming from the direction of Trona, this turn-off is 6.5 miles beyond the Wildrose Canyon Road.) A sign reading *"Minnietta Mine"* marks the turnoff. Note your odometer reading here as you leave the pavement. After following this graded road for three miles or so, it deteriorates to Class I. At a point 3.6 miles in from the highway, you will reach the Nadeau Shotgun Road coming in from the left. Veteran desert freight hauler Remi Nadeau built this road in 1876.

Stay to the right following Nadeau's old road. After 0.3 miles a road goes left to the Minnietta Mine. The Minnietta Mine is a worthy side-trip (see Excursion #43), but to go to Lookout you will want to continue straight ahead.

A tenth of a mile farther the roads fork; either fork will take you to Lookout. The left fork is the most direct route, but it has one tricky Class III portion. The right fork makes a circuitous loop to the north and is a moderately challenging Class III. This route bypassed the Modoc Mine, a property that was once fenced off. If you pass this way in the springtime, this might be the preferred route as the western side of Ash Hill on the right often puts on a vivid display of purple phacelia. In the summer, the abundant cottontop cactus clusters also display their colorful flowers. If you do choose this route, stay to the left at the tractor-loading ramp 1.9 miles to the north.

By turning left at the third road junction, you will find the most direct route to Lookout. In 0.4 miles you will come to concrete foundations marking the last remnants of the once very substantial Modoc Mine Camp. The mostly Class III road continues on, skirting the northern base of Lookout Mountain. A mile more and you will see a tunnel and ore bunker on the left. To the right, a road comes from the north. This is the northern loop route described previously. By coming through the Modoc Mine, you have made a shortcut saving two rough miles.

The road soon enters Stone Canyon. As you proceed up the road, it deteriorates to Class III. In another 1.6 miles, the canyon narrows with white marble exposed on both sides. Here is a short Class IV pitch, but once on top, the road improves to Class II for the next quarter of a mile. If you are looking for a sheltered campsite, look along here.

Slightly more than a mile in from the mouth of Stone Canyon, the canyon forks. The right fork goes over to the Defense Mine and dead-ends. Keep to the left here, starting up the switchbacks. Loose boulders have rolled down off the slope above onto the roadway. You will have to carefully pick your way around these, as some are too big to move. Drivers of long and wide vehicles could have a little trouble here. It is but 0.4 miles of easy Class III to the top of the ridge where there is a three-way intersection.

The right fork is the original stage road built in 1877. It continues up the canyon and goes to Darwin; however, the Navy has installed a locked gate that prevents through travel. This road crosses part of the China Lake Naval Weapons Center where unauthorized travel is prohibited. The middle branch dead-ends at a mine. To go to Lookout, take the left fork. It doubles back to the top of the ridge and approaches Lookout from the west. A bulldozer has been brought across this section in recent years and the rest of the way is a very pretty Class II. There are nice views of Telescope Peak and the entire Panamint Range.

There is one last fork 0.9 miles beyond the three-way fork; stay left. Lookout is but a quarter of a mile farther.

The road to Lookout

In May of 1875 silver was discovered on the eastern slope of the Argus Range overlooking Panamint Valley. Because of the fine view, the newly formed mining district was called the Lookout District. A town of the same name sprang up near the diggings on top of a barren and windswept ridge. At first the ore proved to be so rich in silver that it could be sacked and carried by mules across Panamint Valley to Panamint City, then a thriving community of one thousand people. New prospects on Lookout Mountain developed into viable mines, and in less than a year the production of this spunky little camp attracted the attention of San Francisco mining speculators, including Senator George Hearst. The Senator and his associates bought the Modoc and other promising mines. The boom in Lookout began.

In 1876 when Nadeau's mule teams started hauling in supplies, among the first cargo were two large ore reduction furnaces which would permit silver to be smelted at the mines. By the fall of 1877 these two furnaces were turning out more than three hundred silver-lead bars every day from ore averaging $200 per ton. As happened elsewhere, the bullion was cast faster than it could be hauled away. Large stockpiles of ingots built up. By 1877, the insatiable appetite of the furnaces had consumed everything nearby that would burn. At that point, a road was built across Panamint Valley to the pinyon-covered slopes of Wildrose Canyon, where ten kilns were constructed of stone to supply the furnaces of

Lookout with charcoal. At the same time, another road was built to the west across the Argus Range. By May of 1877 a tri-weekly stage connected Lookout with Darwin and Panamint City. By this time Lookout boasted of some thirty to forty houses, with three saloons, two general stores, and a livery stable.

Lookout City around 1877

The Modoc furnaces on Lookout Mountain
(Photos courtesy County of Inyo, Eastern California Museum)

The camp remained active through the 1870s, but gradually the more accessible orebodies were exhausted, and the miners began to drift away to more promising camps. The mountaintop metropolis faded into history, although the mines of Lookout Mountain have experienced several short lived revivals. Although the richest ore is worked out, even now each major increase in the price of silver brings renewed activity in the Minnietta, Carbonate, Defense, and Queen of Sheba mines.

Lonely Lookout

The elements, vandals, and bottle hunters have all taken their toll on the windswept site of Lookout. Nevertheless, the stone walls of about forty buildings remain in various stages of ruin. Judging from the number of broken champagne bottles, life in Lookout must have been mighty tolerable in spite of its isolation. The foundation of a wagon scale once used to weigh ore shipments can still be seen on the north side of Main Street. At the eastern end of town, an ancient boiler lay rusting in the sun for many years. Today Lookout's only inhabitant is a cactus wren, who each spring builds her nest in the protected shelter of a doorless safe.

It seems a paradox that the Wildrose Charcoal Kilns, only one small chapter in the Lookout story, are visited by tens of thousands of tourists each year. Yet the town and its mines that built them, just a few miles away, are seldom heard of, much less visited.

Camp at Lookout if you wish, but please do not utilize the remains of the buildings for firewood. In the forty years since I first visited the site, I have noticed a lot of deterioration. Help save what is left for the next visitor to enjoy.

Lookout today

36

Snow Canyon

Primary Attraction:	Two old gold and silver mines, and all the challenging trails a four-wheeler could want. This outing makes a great weekend destination for any four-wheel drive club.
Time Required:	The two old mine camps in the bottom of Snow Canyon are a little more than an hour out of Panamint Springs. To visit the mines high on the mountainside, figure all day.
Miles Involved:	From Panamint Springs to the Golden Lady Mine Camp is 18 miles.
Degree of Difficulty:	It is a Class I or better road to the mouth of the canyon, then Class III to the two mine camps. Climbing the ridge to the mines is mostly Class III and IV, with a few Class V ruts to overcome.

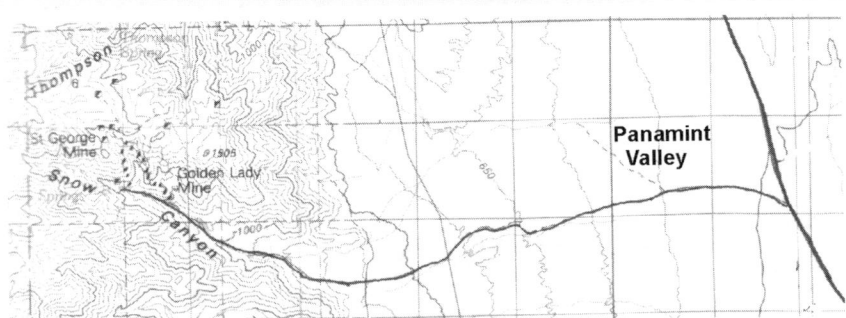

To reach Snow Canyon from Panamint Springs, go east on State 190 for 2.6 miles, then turn right onto the paved road to Trona. Go another 7.5 miles to the graded Minnietta Road on the right. Note your odometer reading, but continue south on the highway. At a point 3.2 miles south of the Minnietta Road, look for an unmarked Class I road to the right. (If you are coming from the direction of Trona, this turn-off is also 3.2 miles beyond the Wildrose Canyon Road.)

The desert road, mostly Class I and II in spots, heads westward gradually climbing the bajada formed by alluvium coming out of Thompson, Snow, and Wood Canyons in the Argus Range. At a point 3.7 miles from the pavement, the old Nadeau Shotgun Road (see Excursion # 43) is crossed. By turning to the right, you can return to the Minnietta Road just three miles to the north (see Excursion # 35). For Snow Canyon simply cross the Nadeau Road and continue westward.

After another mile, yet a second crossroads is reached. Here, however, the BLM has posted the roads to the left and right as closed. The lands on either side of the Snow Canyon Road are now part of the *Argus Range Wilderness*, another creation of the California Desert Protection Act of 1994. (Prior to 1994, one could take the left fork into Wood Canyon.)

At a point 5.5 miles from the paved highway, our desert road drops down into the wash coming out of Snow Canyon. The ascent on the other side is Class III. Soon the road improves to Class II again and remains that way for 0.6 miles, when it again crosses the wash and briefly becomes Class III. At a point 6.9 miles in from the pavement, extensive stone walls on the right mark the beginning of the Golden Lady Mine Camp. A tenth of a mile beyond, a fork to the right climbs to the millsite, and up to the mines high on the north wall of Snow Canyon. It was near this intersection that the mine had its living quarters. There are rock walls of a half dozen structures, plus two corral enclosures made from the same rock. If you wander through the bushes just east of the intersection, the circular stone ruins of the mine's first arrastra can be found.

The Class II road climbs steeply to the right a tenth of a mile to the mine's millsite. There is plenty of flat ground here for a large group to camp. Little remains of the mill, save for some stone foundations and crumbling red brick indicating the site of small reduction furnaces. Above the millsite, a steep and badly rutted Class IV road climbs the mountainside one thousand feet or more to the various workings of what was once the Golden Lady Mine. **Use extreme caution if you use this road.**

The rocks in the bottom of Snow Canyon are the same Cretaceous granite that makes up much of the Argus Range. But the rocks where the ore was mined, high on the canyon's north wall, are the same Carboniferous limestone formations as those containing the Modoc, Minnietta, and other mines of Lookout Mountain.

History does not easily recall exactly when the Golden Lady Mine was discovered. It was in those heady days of the early 1870s when Panamint and Lookout were booming. In spite of its name, more silver than gold was produced.

From the Golden Lady Mine Camp the Snow Canyon road, now Class III, continues up the canyon 0.4 miles where it comes to the somewhat younger St. George Mine camp. Here, too, is ample flat ground where a small group might make camp. None of the buildings are left at the camp, except for the powder magazine half dug into the hillside. **It is unsafe to enter!**

Beyond the mine camp, the Class III road continues up the canyon a quarter of a mile to a fork. The right fork heads steeply up a side canyon to the north to ascend to the mines high above. The left fork circles around to the millsite and the bunkers, which once collected the ore brought down the mountainside by aerial tramline.

The St. George Mine was originally known as the Merry Christmas Mine because the first of its two systems of quartz veins was discovered in December. The quartz, when crushed to a fine sand, revealed free gold. Other associated metals included a variety of sulfide minerals, iron pyrite, chalcopyrite and arsenopyrite. Green malachite, a common copper mineral, can also be found along the road between the mill and the mine where it has spilled off heavily-laden ore wagons. Like its neighbor the Golden Lady, the St. George Mine produced more silver than gold.

A small seasonal stream reaches as far down the canyon as the St. George millsite in wet years. During these periods dove and quail are very abundant here in Snow Canyon. Although they are seldom seen, the night air is alive with the sounds of the hoot owl. More conspicuous are the small bands of feral burro which also inhabit the canyon.

The road ends at the millsite, and here the *Argus Range Wilderness* begins. For those so inclined, one can hike up the canyon for a mile or more before the going gets really steep.

Millsite of the St. George Mine

Chapter VIII

Trails Out of Ballarat

The ghost town of Ballarat may seem to be a strange hub to use as a base for outings because it has little in the way of services. Nevertheless, it is centrally located in Panamint Valley, and all of the west side canyons of the Panamints are ready accessible from Ballarat.

The year was 1893. The excitement of Panamint City had already died down when Charles Anthony and John Lamphier began to stake claims in Pleasant Canyon. They generated little attention until three years later when Henry Ratcliff found a promising lode in the summer of '96. At the same time, James Cooper staked some claims farther up the canyon. The word got out, and once again dusty prospectors appeared from nowhere, and headed up the western canyons of the high Panamints.

In less than a year, the Ratcliff Mine was going strong, and it became obvious that a town was needed to house the two hundred miners. There simply wasn't enough room in Pleasant Canyon, so a few of the mine buildings were moved down to the alkali flats at the mouth of the canyon. An eighty-acre townsite was laid out, and the land was subdivided into lots. Thus was born the town of Ballarat, named after a world-famous Australian gold camp. Ratcliff's employees lived in Ballarat and commuted the six miles to work each day by wagon. By June of 1897, there was sufficient need to establish a post office at Ballarat.

The Ratcliff Mine operated successfully from 1897 to 1903, producing nearly a half a million dollars in gold. It was by far the largest and most productive mine in Pleasant Canyon. After the Ratcliff ceased operation in 1905, the World Beater Mine opened just a half mile up the canyon. Ballarat had a renewed lease on life. As all mines eventually do, the diggings in Pleasant Canyon also shut down. The big rush to Skidoo came in 1906, and the miners moved north a few miles. But the long supply route from Mojave still ran through Panamint Valley, and Ballarat's existence was prolonged a little longer. Finally in 1917, Ballarat's last saloon closed its doors for good.

Ballarat's most famous person in recent years was Charles Ferge, known best as "Seldom Seen Slim". He came to Ballarat in 1913 and never left. Although he liked to project the image of a recluse, he enjoyed pulling the odd tourist's leg. I can recall that when I was a kid, Slim would come into Ted Lang's service station in Argus, showing large square iron pyrite crystals to city slickers enroute to the first Death Valley 49ers' encampment. Slim passed it off as gold, but even I, at age 11, knew better. Slim died in 1968 and is buried in Ballarat's Boot Hill. So interesting and well known was he that his funeral was featured on national television.

Left to right: seldom seen Slim, Walter Sorensen,
Chris Wicht, and Fred Grey taken on Thanksgiving Day, 1935
(Photo courtesy County of Inyo, Eastern California Museum)

The buildings of Ballarat were made of two materials: wood or sun dried adobe bricks. After Ballarat's decline, the wooden buildings were dismantled for use elsewhere, leaving only the adobe structures. As infrequent as it is here, a century of rain has taken its toll, and every year there seems to be a little less left of old Ballarat. In recent years, there has been a small General Store in Ballarat (no gasoline) and a small waterless campground where a very nominal fee is charged.

Ballarat's adobe walls are slowly melting away

37

Jail Canyon

Primary Attraction:	An old miner's camp in a remote canyon.
Time Required:	This is a half-day round trip out of Ballarat or Panamint Springs Resort.
Miles Involved:	It is thirteen miles from Ballarat to the end of the road at the Jail Canyon miner's camp, or 25 miles from Panamint Springs.
Degree of Difficulty:	Once off the Indian Ranch Road, it is mostly Class II, with only a few Class III sections across the wash.

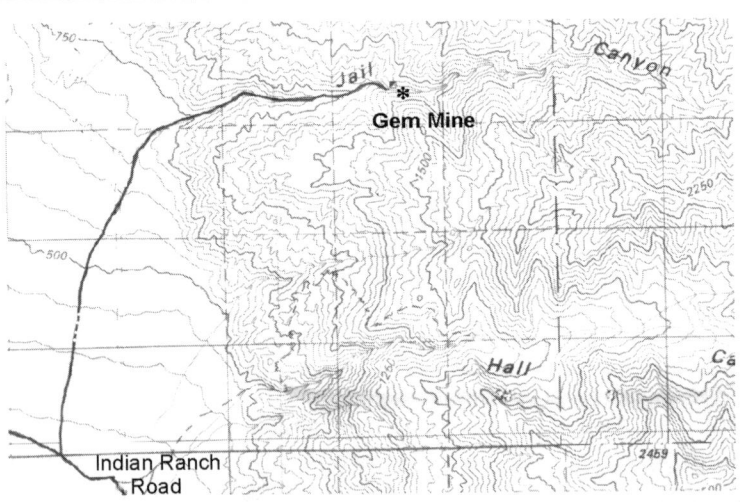

One of the most spectacular four-wheel drive routes in the entire Death Valley region was the route from Jail Canyon over the ridge into Hall Canyon on the western slope of the Panamints. Unfortunately, *Wilderness* designation has closed that road, and today one can go only as far as the abandoned miner's camp in Jail Canyon.

From downtown Ballarat, go north on the graded county Indian Ranch Road. At a point 7.7 miles north of Ballarat, look to the right for an unmarked road that heads north and starts to climb the alluvial fan; turn right here. Ahead you will see white-looking sand and gravel which washed out of Jail Canyon during a flash flood. This material cut across the jeep trail in several places, but the route has been re-established. At a point two miles up from the Indian Ranch Road, Death Valley National Park is entered. A mile beyond that, a Class III track once turned off to the left to go into Tuber Canyon and the site of the O.B. Joyful Mine. That side road has now been closed by *Wilderness* designation with the passage of the CDPA.

Jail Canyon is entered at a point 2.7 miles above the Indian Ranch Road. A few short Class III portions will be encountered in the next mile or so. You will also encounter a giant boulder, the size of a house, in the bottom of the wash. Was this boulder washed down the canyon by a flash flood, or did it roll off the hillside above? What do you think?

This house size boulder rolled down to the
canyon bottom from the ridge to the left

Finally, 5.4 miles from the Indian Ranch Road, an old miner's camp is reached. This is the site of the Corona Mine, which prior to 1949 was known as the New Discovery Mine and before that, the Gem Mine. Bedrock has forced underground water flowing down from the very summit of Telescope Peak to rise to the surface here. There are a couple of structures left, leaning badly, but still standing. Also here are the ever-present piles of rusting cans, vehicles, and machinery so typical at these old mines.

The geology here is of very old Precambrian metamorphic rocks that were later intruded by Cretaceous granite. Hot mineral solutions making quartz veins occurred at the contact of the two rock types. These quartz veins contain gold, silver, lead and zinc. It was these veins that were discovered by one Jack Curran in 1899. He called his find the Gem Mine. Curran had no money to build a mill, but Charles Weaver, a Ballarat merchant, did. Curran gave a half interest to Weaver for his three-stamp mill. With the building of a waterwheel at the spring, Weaver's mill did the trick. Soon they were making monthly shipments of bullion.

After 1900 the history of the Gem Mine becomes somewhat obscure. The waterwheel and original mill were destroyed by a flash flood in 1901. When Geologist R. J. Samson visited Jail Canyon in 1931, the Gem Mine was still being worked. When I first came in through here in 1957, I found a man named Troster living here. He said he had owned the claims for many years, but he was doing no serious mining.

Look up to the precipitous south wall of Jail Canyon. At one time the steepest jeep trail in the Death Valley region (it climbed 1,000 feet in one half mile) switch-backed up the canyon wall. It went on over the ridge into some prospects in Hall Canyon. It was a thrilling ride with some of the hairpin turns so sharp, even short-wheelbase vehicles had to back up and maneuver around them. Alas however, this masterpiece of engineering was closed with the expansion of the park in 1994. You can still hike the road, of course, but the effect is not the same. The trail starts in a wash 0.2 miles below the Corona Mine Camp.

Jail Canyon is not the sort of place you would want to drive all the way from Los Angeles just to see. But, after you have explored the other canyons on the western slope of the Panamints, this one should go on your list, too.

This cabin at the Gem Mine Camp is on its last legs

Surprise Canyon Road Now Closed
See page 232 for details

38

Panamint City, Paradise Lost

Primary Attraction:	An interesting canyon, an old ghost town and smelter, and the most "challenging" route in all of the Death Valley country.
Time Required:	From Ballarat to Chris Wicht's Camp, takes only 30 minutes; to go on to Panamint City, one to two days more are needed, if you make it at all!
Miles Involved:	From Ballarat to Chris Wicht's Camp is only six miles. From Chris Wicht's Camp on to Panamint City is another seven miles.
Degree of Difficulty:	The first six miles are mostly Class I as far as Chris Wicht's Camp. The last five miles into Panamint City are mostly Class II. In between is a half-mile of the most difficult vehicle route imaginable. A flash flood has washed away all the sand and rocks, leaving a series of rock waterfalls. The first is Class VI and several others are Class V. **This outing is not for the timid or inexperienced four-wheeler. Do not attempt this route without a winch and plenty of help. The degree of difficulty in getting a vehicle up to Panamint City under the present circumstances cannot be overstated. Most vehicles that successfully make it to Panamint City, come back with some body damage!**

The thirteen miles from Ballarat to Panamint City are probably packed with more history and stories than any other place in the Death Valley area. The first time I made this journey, I was in a new 1955 Dodge station wagon. We had a little trouble getting up the canyon because the car was heavily laden with camping gear, but we did make it all the way to Panamint City. Thanks to El Niño rains, that road ceased to exist after a single summer thunderstorm. The road into Panamint City may again return to its Class II or Class III days, but some serious tractor work will have to be done first.

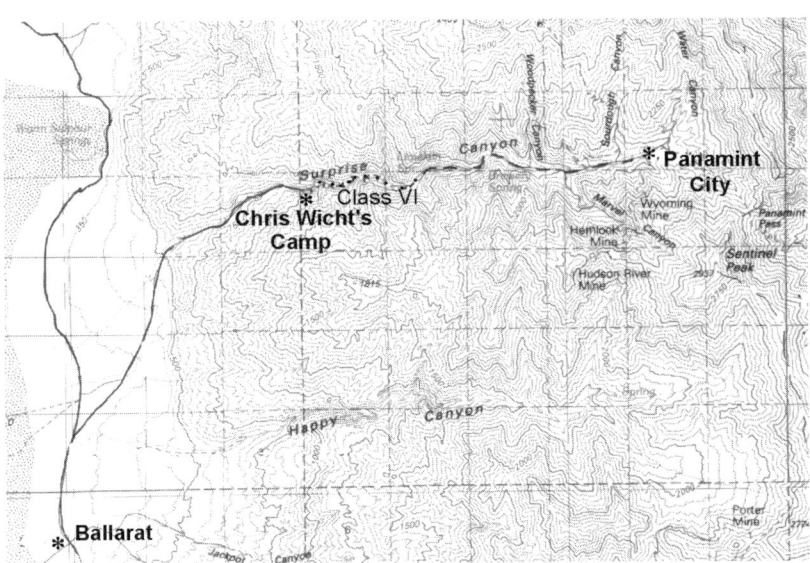

From Ballarat go north on the graded Indian Ranch Road. After 1.5 miles you will see low crumbling walls of the old stage station about a quarter of a mile off the road to the west. It was here that tri-weekly stages from Darwin and Lookout would stop to rest and change horses for the arduous ascent of Surprise Canyon.

At a point 1.9 miles north of Ballarat, a good side-road heads east towards the Panamints. A metal post reads *Surprise Canyon*. Turn right here, but stay on the road. There is a BLM *Wilderness* area on either side of the road. This route climbs the alluvial fan and after 1.4 miles enters the mouth of Surprise Canyon. Immediately after entering the canyon, the walls close in and the road gets steeper. I have seen this road anywhere from Class II to Class V, depending on local weather conditions. At the moment it is Class I, but one storm could change that instantly.

In less than two miles, some cottonwood trees and old buildings on the right mark the site of Chris Wicht's Camp. In 1998 a sign announced it was Novack Camp, but that is nonsense. To me it will always be Chris Wicht's Camp. I can recall swimming in the pond here as a youngster. At that time the camp was deserted, although half a dozen buildings remained, some in reasonably good condition.

This was once the home of Chris Wicht, a one time Ballarat bartender. Tired of digging borax in Death Valley, Chris came to Ballarat in 1902, at a time when the town was booming. He opened a saloon that proved to be the most popular "watering spot" in Panamint Valley for some fifteen years. While tending bar, Chris was at times both shot and stabbed, but he always managed to recover. It was finally the bottle that killed Chris, but it took eighty years to do it. He is buried in the Argus Cemetery, just south of Trona.

Chris Wicht's grave in Argus CA

The road once went right past the entrance to Chris Wicht's Camp and from there, dropped down into the streambed. **This route has washed away. Do not attempt it.** To proceed upstream, you have to first backtrack 0.2 miles down the canyon, get in the streambed there, and then follow the stream back up the canyon. The first 0.8 miles beyond Chris Wicht's is mostly Class III, with one short Class IV pitch. At the 0.8-mile mark, however, you encounter a series of "waterfalls" in the narrows. This is the place where all the gravel was washed out, leaving a series of two six-foot waterfalls to overcome. The ability to proceed on seems impossible, but it has been done. Members of the Bakersfield Trail Blazers 4 x 4 Club have hand carried tons of rocks to the base of the various falls, but careful winching is still necessary to get up (and down) the canyon.

If you wish to proceed, here are some tips:
  Go prepared. Bring a couple of long 2 x 12 planks and plenty of short pieces of lumber to use as cribbing to support the planks.
  Go short and light. Use a bobtail rig like a CJ-5, or an old style Toyota Land Cruiser, with the top, doors, windshield, and all other excess weight removed. Do keep the roll bar and winch.
  Go with plenty of help. Getting a vehicle up Surprise Canyon is labor intensive.
  Go at the right time of year, such as in the late fall when there is the least amount of water.

The road up Surprise Canyon washed out in the 1980s
leaving a few hundred yards of very difficult Class V and VI road

Limestone Spring is 1.7 miles above Chris Wicht's. If you can make it that far, the worse is over. It is mostly Class II beyond. Panamint City is 3.5 miles above Limestone Spring.

As you enter Panamint City, the brick chimney of the smelter built in 1874 is the dominant feature on the skyline. If it were not for the chimney and the remains of a scant half dozen other structures, the visitor today would never believe that this quiet peaceful valley once contained a rough and rowdy camp of some two thousand people.

It all started in January of 1873 when a veteran prospector named Richard Jacobs battled the bone-chilling cold to discover a large silver lode near the head of what is now called Surprise Canyon. By the fall of '74, prospectors seeking "the big bonanza" were pouring in, and roads had been blazed into the Panamints from all directions. By December, Panamint City had a mile-long Main Street and a population of two thousand.

Alas, Panamint City was not to become another Cripple Creek. Her orebodies were no Comstock Lode. The rock here was hard, and the quartz veins elusive. The "Bank Panic" of '75 played havoc with mining stocks. Another blow was dealt to the camp on July 24, 1876, when a disastrous flash flood came roaring down Surprise Canyon, taking much of the town with it. Still some mines survived the worst that nature could hand out. But then on May 1, 1877, the bottom dropped out of the stock market when it was revealed that the mines of Virginia City had played out. Economics had succeeded where nature had failed. Down Surprise Canyon came the miners, the storekeepers, and the ladies from Maiden Lane. Decades later, in 1925, and again in 1947, attempts were made to reopen some mines, but the silver lode once again proved to be as elusive as ever.

The old smelter at Panamint City as it appeared in 1921
(Nevada Historical Society Photo)

The first time I visited Panamint City, in the 1950s, the road was passable for ordinary pickups, and indeed, Panamint City had two permanent residents. They were Orpha Hart and "Shotgun Mary" Thompson, two elderly no nonsense sisters, who were known to run strangers off with a gun. They seemed to enjoy the notoriety of their cantankerous reputation, although more than once an Inyo County Sheriff Deputy had to go up there and attempt to adjust their outlook towards strangers. Nevertheless, I always found their bark was worse than their bite, particularly when you approached them carrying a gift in a brown paper bag.

Today's visitor to Panamint City will find the big mill a photogenic subject, as are those few weather-beaten structures that still survive. High above the townsite, a tramline to the Wyoming Mine still swings in the breeze. A burro trail climbs Frenchman's Canyon to Panamint Pass and down to Hungry Bill's Ranch on the Death Valley side.

For the history buff, a day in Surprise Canyon is a must. If you don't have the time and resources required for the drive in, and very few of us do, then walk! The seven-mile hike in, involving 3,600 feet of gain, makes a long day, but one well worth the effort. If you can arrange a car shuttle, the hike up to Panamint City, over the crest of the Panamints via Panamint Pass, and descending to the Johnson Canyon trailhead (see Excursion #6) makes one of the most outstanding backpacking outings in Death Valley National Park.

The smelter in 1965

Last Minute Update: The road up Surprise Canyon is now closed! Just days before this book went to press, the BLM agreed, in a Consent Decree, to block vehicle access to Surprise Canyon to all except the owners of private property within the canyon. What led to this road closure was a lawsuit brought against the BLM by three environmental groups: The Center For Biologic Diversity, the Sierra Club, and Public Employees For Environmental Responsibility. While the lawsuit mainly involved other issues in the California desert, the Surprise Canyon road closure was a last minute addition. On March 20, 2001, Judge William Alsup, a Federal Court Judge in San Francisco signed the Order in which the BLM would initiate an immediate road closure, followed by the installation of a locked gate at the canyon's entrance. One of the troubling aspects of this litigation is the rational for closing Surprise Canyon, habitat preservation, can be applied to all of the roaded canyons in the Panamint Range. What roads will be closed next?

39

Rogers Pass via Pleasant Canyon

Primary Attraction:	Old mines galore, with plenty of high Panamint backcountry and scenery.
Time Required:	The loop trip up Pleasant Canyon, over the ridge into Middle Park, and then back to Ballarat by South Park Canyon can be done in a single day. There is so much country to see here, however, that taking two days would be even better.
Miles Involved:	It is only twelve miles from Ballarat to Rogers Pass. Add another twenty miles to return to Ballarat via South Park Canyon.
Degree of Difficulty:	The entire route is usually no more difficult than Class III. **Winter snows can bury the roads above Stone Corral anytime between December and March.**

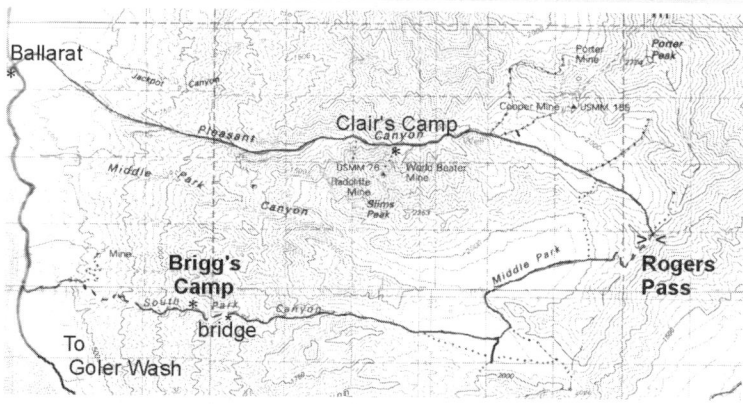

Like Surprise Canyon just to the north, the Pleasant Canyon road takes you high onto the pinyon-covered slopes of the Panamint Range. Unlike Surprise Canyon, however, you can climb one canyon, cross over a ridge, descend into an isolated valley, cross another pass, and descend by yet another canyon to make a complete loop. Like many of these outings, the condition of the route can vary greatly from one month to the next. Between December and March, it is a good bet that deep snow will make the high elevation portions of this loop impassable.

Our journey back through time, and into the high Panamints, starts in Ballarat. A sign in downtown Ballarat points eastward to the Pleasant Canyon Road. If you are in doubt, ask at the General Store. Follow the graded dirt road northeast out of town (not to be confused with the Indian Ranch Road, which starts northwest out of Ballarat). If you are on the correct road it will soon turn eastward. In 0.5 miles, a Class II road turns off to the left. This road goes into Jackpot Canyon and soon ends at a spring. Keep right on the main road and soon you will be in Pleasant Canyon.

At a point 2.5 miles from Ballarat, bedrock in the canyon bottom forces subsurface water to the surface. For the next mile up the canyon, this stream will be your constant companion. Indeed, sometimes the streambed is the road. On occasion, water and mud can produce Class III sections in the roadway, but often the route is no worse than Class II.

The streambed is lined with cattails and Desert Willow, *Chilopsis lineras*, the latter of which sometimes attempts to overgrow the roadway. The Paiute Indians made good use of both of these plants. The slender willow twigs were used for baskets and sometimes for medicinal purposes. The cattails were used as an absorbent in babies' diapers.

Four miles from Ballarat, a 1750' long aerial cableway goes up the steep south wall of the canyon to the Anthony Mine. One of the canyon's oldest mines, it was found in 1893 by Charles Anthony. In its century long history, it was originally known as the Anthony Mine, later the Knob Mine, and most recently the Gold Bug. Over the years, the mine's quartz veins have produced both gold and lead.

Another half mile up the canyon, a similar aerial cableway goes up the north canyon wall to yet another mine. It is interesting to note in this area that while the barrel cactus appears in great numbers, they are all growing on the steep canyon wall, and none are growing on the south side of the canyon. They obviously prefer the dry, well-drained soils, and warm sunny exposures of the canyon's northern slope. The more moist and shady south wall of the canyon is preferred by the creosote bush.

At a point six miles from Ballarat, Clair's Camp is reached. This was the camp and millsite for the Ratcliff Mine, which is perched high up on the canyon's south wall. Again, it was an aerial cableway that lowered the ore five hundred vertical feet to the canyon bottom where it could be crushed and milled. This was the mine found by Henry Ratcliff in 1897, and the one that turned out to be the richest in Pleasant Canyon. During the five-year period between 1898 and 1903, it produced 15,000 tons of ore, which by some estimates were worth up to a million dollars.

W. D. Clair bought the mine in 1912, but nothing much happened until 1927, when the mine was reopened. It operated until 1942, when President Roosevelt's Executive Order closed all the nation's gold mines. It was during this later period that 20,000 tons of the old tailings were put through a cyanide mill, recovering about $5.00 per ton in gold that had been missed the first time. The mine reopened again in 1949. This time gold was not the principal metal sought, but rather galena (lead) and scheelite (tungsten).

I came up Pleasant Canyon for the first time in the mid 1950s. By that time Clair had long ago died, but his family had a caretaker living here. A locked gate blocked further travel up the canyon. Fortunately, the gate could be opened with the offering of a few tin cans: one containing Prince Albert and a couple more of Lucky Lager. The caretaker is now gone. The gate is still there, but it is unlocked. It has been many years since Clair's Camp has seen any maintenance, much less heard the steady pounding ore mill.

One can prowl through the deteriorating buildings, but do be watchful for nails protruding upward from pieces of wood. The mine's main kitchen and mess hall building was made of earthen walls. Here, too, the lack of upkeep has taken its toll. Stay well away from the redwood water tank; it is leaning badly and looks like it could fall over at anytime. The remnants of two boilers can be seen at the mill. The steam from them powered a steam engine, which drove a wide belt that turned the ore crusher. In its one hundred-year history, the mill here has utilized several types of devices to crush the ore. The last mill used was a 4' x 6' Marcy ball mill. It is still there, although badly vandalized. Prior to that, a twenty-stamp mill was utilized. Some of its remains lie on the junk pile.

Clair's Camp

After passing Clair's Camp, the canyon opens up a bit. Soon another aerial cableway goes up the south side of the canyon. This, too, brought ore down from the Ratcliff Mine.

A mile above Clair's Camp on the left side of the road was a miner's camp, burned a few years ago to cover the murder of its caretaker. On the right, a short steep side road climbs up the hillside a half mile to another millsite, that of the World Beater Mine, another important producer in this canyon. When I wrote the first edition of *Death Valley Jeep Trails* in 1968, I took a picture of two friends standing here beside the enormous ten-stamp mill. Unfortunately, nothing remains of the mill today, except for its stone foundations. The mill was being dismantled in preparation for a move to Tonopah when a worker's cutting torch accidentally set it on fire. The actual tunnels and shafts of the World Beater Mine are high on the slopes above. It was an aerial cableway that brought the ore down to the mill.

A 1968 photo of the ten-stamp mill at the World Beater Mine before it burned

Passing the lonely wooden structure at the World Beater Mine camp, the road soon enters the pinyon juniper forest. By this time you have risen some 4,500 feet since leaving the mud flats at Ballarat. The shrub with the yellowish-green stems is ephedra, commonly called Mormon tea. You can produce a passable cup of tea by boiling a handful of stems in water. The Indians are said to have drunk this solution to cure intestinal ailments. Some say it is an acquired taste. I must add sugar to counter the bitter taste left by its high tannic acid content. Try it if you wish, but do pick it here. The park boundary is just ahead, where the taking of any plant material is prohibited.

Two miles above Clair's Camp, a water trough is passed on the left, and just ahead is Stone Corral, the new park boundary. An old stone corral was built at the site of a reliable spring, and hence its name. This corral was used as a reference point when some of the earliest mining claims were staked. It is thought to have been built by Paiute Indians who came here in the fall to collect pinyon nuts. At one time, water was piped from this spring all the way down to the World Beater Mine camp.

On the left, a Class III side road leaves the main road here. It climbs nearly 1,300 feet in a little more than a mile to pass through a 7,145' gap in the ridge and go to the site of the Porter Mine, found by Henry "Harry" Clay Porter. Harry was 36 years old when he left the coal fields of Pennsylvania to come to California. He turned to prospecting in 1899. In 1902 he and his partner Wade Richardson set out on a two year search for the "Lost Mexican Mine", and they may have actually found it. They sold their find, which they called the "Mountain Boy", for $10,000 and went their separate ways. With his grubstake renewed, Harry continued to prospect in the Panamints. In 1908 he found a quartz vein showing wire gold, and developed this lode into the "Mountain Girl Mine". (Everyone else simply called it the "Porter Mine".) Harry remained here for the next 41 years, going down the canyon to be with his friends at Clair's Camp or Ballarat only when the winter snows got too deep. Harry died at the ripe old age of 86. He is buried in Bishop.

The side trip to the Porter Mine is interesting, but impassable in the winter and early spring when snow lingers long on the north side of the pass. The view north down into the road-less Happy Canyon basin and beyond to the summit of 11,049' Telescope Peak is quite nice. Henry knew how to pick them.

The main road, still Class II, continues on ahead. In a tenth of a mile, the remains of a steam powered four-stamp mill are on the left. This was once a stamp mill operated by a woman, Bessie Hart, during the 1905 period. Ore from Bessie's own mine could not put beans on her table, but her custom milling for others did pay the bills. There is a story that Shorty Harris once proposed to Bessie after seeing the quantity of air she could pump through the blacksmith's bellows down in Ballarat. History does not record her exact answer, but Shorty died a bachelor in 1934.

Also on the left is a Class III side road which goes up the hillside a mile and a half to dead-end at the Cooper Mine, found in 1896 by James Cooper. From different sides of the same ridge, both the Porter Mine and the Cooper Mine tap into the same system of quartz veins which have invaded this very old pre-Precambrian rock. Specimens of the ore can be found along the road. **Timbers shoring up the tunnels are rotting. Stay out of the underground workings.**

The road forks at a point 0.8 miles above Stone Corral. Take either fork; they both go a half-mile ahead and rejoin again. At a point 1.7 miles above Stone Corral, there is another fork. Hidden in the trees here is a weather-tight cabin that is kept unlocked by the National Park Service. Like several other cabins in the Panamints this one, too, can be used by backcountry travelers as an emergency shelter. Please do not use any of the food or water unless it is an emergency!

At this intersection, the right fork makes a steep ascent of six hundred feet in a half mile to cross a pass in the ridge and descend into Middle Park. My recommendation, however, would be to stay left on the main road. It continues up Pleasant Canyon another 1.3 miles. The first mile remains mostly Class II, with the last 0.3 miles an easy Class III.

Then, twelve miles from Ballarat, the road suddenly reaches a saddle on the crest of the Panamint Range. The air is clean and crisp up here, and likely to be cool even in August. Here on this ridge top, a sturdy metal sign reads:

Rogers Pass
El. 7140

Wm Manly & Jn Rogers crossed this pass on the way to get supplies for 49ers trapped in Death Valley. Later, as they led the Bennet & Arcane families to safety, they came here to view the land ahead, looking back, one said, "Goodbye Death Valley!" The date was Feb. 14, 1850. It is believed they crossed the Panamints via Butte Valley & Redlands Cy. They crossed the Slate via Fish & Isham Cy's, then to Providence Spring at Great Falls in the Argus Range. Up Wilson Cy & across the valley to Indian Wells Spring on the way to a Spanish ranch near Newhall. All this party survived. Erected Jan '92 ET Conf. Trona Chapter

On the saddle, the road forks with branches going up the ridge to the left and the right. To the left, a very rocky Class IV road climbs steeply northward towards an antenna site one thousand feet higher. To the right a Class III route climbs the ridgeline to the south, then descends again to another saddle. By turning right, Middle Park is but a couple of switchbacks down the hillside to the west and from there South Park is over the low divide to the south. From Rogers Pass it is nearly twenty miles back to Ballarat via the Class II and Class III roads in South Park Canyon (see Excursion #40). **A word of warning, however. In South Park Canyon, just above Briggs' Camp, is a narrow bridge spanning a chasm in the cliff-side where a portion of the mountain slid away. This bridge has been examined by the Inyo County Road Department engineers who have rated it at no more than 6,000 pounds maximum. If your backcountry vehicle exceeds that weight, do not attempt to descend via South Park Canyon.**

The road down South Park Canyon will be remembered for its steep grades and spectacular narrows. This circle tour can be done from either direction, but the grades going up South Park Canyon are more severe than Pleasant Canyon. Once you are back down and out of South Park Canyon, it is 6.7 miles back to the starting point in Ballarat.

Cacti favor the sunny south facing slopes of Pleasant Canyon

40

Rogers Pass via South Park Canyon

Primary Attraction: Old mines and high Panamint scenery. The loop trip made in combination with Pleasant Canyon makes an interesting camping outing for your family or four-wheel drive club.

Time Required: The loop up South Park Canyon, over the ridge into Middle Park, and back to Ballarat by way of Pleasant Canyon can be done in a single day; however, there is so much country to see, two or even three days would be better.

Miles Involved: It is nearly twenty miles from Ballarat to Rogers Pass by way of South Park Canyon and another twelve miles back to Ballarat by way of Pleasant Canyon.

Degree of Difficulty: In the lower canyon, loose gravel, large rocks and steep grades make the route mostly Class III with several short areas of Class IV. **Water flowing down the road at Colter Spring often freezes during the winter months, making the road so slippery as to be impassable.**

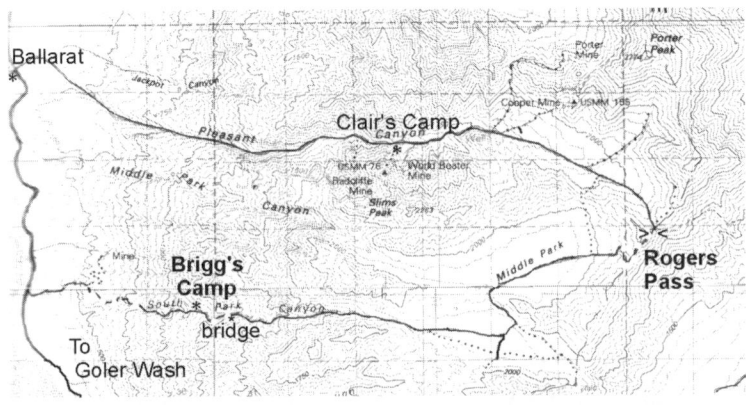

From downtown Ballarat, note your odometer reading and start south on the oiled road in the direction of Goler Wash. In just a half-mile you will pass Post

Office Spring, where in 1850 the second Jayhawker Party is thought to have camped after their perilous escape from Death Valley. The site got the name, not because a post office was ever here, but because local outlaws, in cahoots with certain stagecoach drivers, used the site to stash cash here. The cash would be picked up by the stage driver, who would in turn leave groceries on the return trip.

At a point 3.9 miles south of Ballarat a side road goes left. Although it is not marked, this is the way to South Park Canyon. The Class II road climbs steeply through the fanglomerate of the mesa. Because traction is poor, many will engage their four-wheel drive within a half-mile of leaving the oiled road. Once you top the mesa, however, the grades become gentler and the road improves to Class II again. Stop for a moment at one of the several vantage points. The views down upon Panamint Valley are quite nice.

At a point two miles above the oiled road a second set of steep Class III zig-zags are encountered. They too are only a half-mile long. At a point 2.8 miles above the oiled road, 6.7 miles from Ballarat, you enter South Park Canyon. Immediately the very old metamorphic rocks in the canyon walls close in upon you. The loose gravel in the wash makes it a Class III road for the next half mile, with at least two Class IV sections and one steep Class V grade. The latter is 7.5 miles out of Ballarat and can be easily avoided by a short bypass to the left. At a point 7.8 miles out of Ballarat, the canyon opens up and the road improves. From here on to the crest, it is mostly Class II.

At a point 8.1 miles from Ballarat, a side road to the left steeply makes its way up the north wall of South Park Canyon. This Class III road leads to the Suitcase Mine whose lower workings are but a half-mile above the canyon bottom. In gaining access to their claims, the miners had to carve a series of four switchbacks so severe that the drivers of most vehicles with four wheels will have to see-saw around the hairpin turns. Although this mine is nearly a century old, it has obviously been worked in recent years. This side trip is well worth the effort, as the views down into Panamint Valley are breathtaking.

At a point 8.8 miles from Ballarat, a cluster of buildings adjoining a spring and old millsite is reached. Today the site is called the Briggs Camp, although its history seems to go back long before Harry Briggs ever came to the Panamints, well over a half a century ago. Indeed, the two cabins at the camp are in better condition today than they were twenty or thirty years ago. The C. R. Briggs Corporation allows free use of the cabins on a first come, first served basis, providing the property is duly cared for. The public seems to have reciprocated by maintaining the structures and keeping them stocked with emergency food, bedding, and other amenities of rural life. The fig tree next to the upper cabin has thrived and other landscaping has added to the comfort of this remote outpost.

On occasion bighorn sheep wander through the camp, sampling the tasty green grasses and shrubbery.

One of the cabins at Brigg's Camp

A short distance above the Briggs Camp, South Park Canyon narrows once again. This time the bedrock has created a series of dry waterfalls so high and so severe that no animal, much less vehicle, could ever get over them. To bypass this impassable section of canyon bottom, the early miners carved a road out of the south canyon wall. This road, although marginal, was adequate for nearly 75 years. However an El Niño driven storm in 1983 caused a portion of mountainside to slide away, severing the already precarious road. Passage through South Park Canyon was thus interrupted for a decade until 1994, when miners fashioned a crude but effective bridge out of old utility poles. Inyo County road engineers were less than enthused with the results. They permitted the structure to remain, but limited the weight to 6,000 pounds.

At a point 0.3 miles above the Briggs Camp, the BLM has placed a sign reading:

Narrow bridge ¼ mile ahead
Max. Wt. 3 tons GVW
No turn around

The reader would be well advised to heed the warning. **If your fully loaded vehicle weighs more than 6,000 pounds, go no farther!** Not only could you and your vehicle end up in a crumbled mass of metal four hundred feet below in the bottom of the wash, but your actions could once again sever the road through South Park Canyon for another decade. This is no place for a 7,000 pound Hummer!

The infamous bridge

A tenth of a mile beyond the bridge the road enters the wash again, this time above the dry waterfalls. The canyon opens up and once again the road improves to Class II. In another tenth of a mile, a side road right goes to the Thorndike's Honolulu Mine high on the south ridge.

The Honolulu Mine was discovered in 1907. At first, the richest ore was brought out on the backs of mules. It was not until 1924 that John Thorndike built the steep twisting road up South Park Canyon. He then built a 2,150' tramway from the mine to the canyon bottom, from where he hauled the ore out by truck. The property was last worked between 1942 and 1944 when thirteen hundred tons were taken out.

As a footnote to history, John Thorndike had more on his mind than just mining. He had long dreamed about building a tourist hotel on the summit of 11,049' Telescope Peak. Those plans never materialized for obvious reasons; however, in the 1930s he and his wife did erect a few tourist cabins at 7,500 feet, just below Mahogany Flat. Some of these cabins were still standing when I first climbed Telescope Peak in the 1950s. Alas, Thorndike's Resort did not turn into a second Furnace Creek Inn. The cabins have been subsequently torn down and the site turned into a public campground.

The South Park road continues up the canyon. Notice the cinnamon roll-like swirls of highly metamorphosed rock on the left 0.2 miles above the Honolulu Mine road. In the springtime it is in this area that nature puts on a grand wildflower display. Bright crimson Indian Paint Brush, orange mallow, yellow broom, purple phacelia, white prickly poppy, and long stems of blue lupine all tint nature's pallet.

At a point 10.6 miles from Ballarat at 5,700 feet, Coulter Spring sends its life giving water flowing across and down the road. **In December, January, and February, daytime temperatures in the shady areas are often insufficient to melt the blanket of ice. Under those circumstances, the roadway becomes treacherous and often impassable.** Coulter Spring also marks the boundary of national park lands. From here on into South Park, the roads improve to Class I and II.

At slightly more than eleven miles out of Ballarat, the first pinyons begin to appear. Soon South Park Canyon opens into a treeless basin nearly three miles long by a half-mile wide. This is South Park. At 11.7 miles from Ballarat, the road forks. Both forks run east up the valley and rejoin after a mile and a half. The left fork is less dusty.

At a point 11.8 miles from Ballarat, a crossroads is reached. To the right, a road runs south crossing the dusty landing strip to dead-end in a couple of miles at some prospect holes. By turning to the left off this road, there are several routes eastward up the valley to a 6,500-foot vantage point. Some 3,000 feet below lies Butte Valley and beyond, looking down Anvil Spring Canyon, is the white floor of Death Valley. A little to the right, and a thousand feet below, is Striped Butte with its unique bands. Still farther to the right, the road leading to the summit of Mengel Pass can be seen in the far distance (see Excursion # 9).

Back at the crossroads 11.8 miles from Ballarat, a left turn will soon take you to an abandoned mine and its camp. The main cabin has burned and what is left is an unsightly collection of rusting machinery and refuse. On the hillside above the camp is the tunnel and air compressor building. The rusting artifacts suggest that this mine is of more recent vintage than those far below in South Park Canyon. What appears to be a perfectly straight road running for nearly a mile down South Park is actually a crude airstrip installed to provide easy access to this mine.

It was not mineral wealth that attracted geologist Julia Miller to study this area. It was the very old Precambrian rocks. She found evidence of very old glaciation of the Proterozoic Kingston Peak Formation. This is not the recent Plio-Pleistocene glaciation that started a mere 2.7 million years ago which we are talking about. The traces of glaciation in the Kingston Formation occurred one half a billion years ago!

Rogers Pass Via South Park Canyon

The road continues past the mine camp, doubles back to the northwest and soon tops a 6,400-foot ridge. Spread out below you to the north is Middle Park, a similar basin having an elevation nearly identical to that of South Park. The main road descends from the pass 0.2 miles and then forks. The Class II main road goes right, heading east through Middle Park. In 1.2 miles, a side road goes north to cross the ridge into Pleasant Canyon. My recommendation would be to continue eastward another mile to the crest of the range, and from there turn left, taking a Class III road up the ridge a half mile to drop down onto Rogers Pass. This is the more scenic route. To complete the loop from Rogers Pass, it is but twelve miles down Pleasant Canyon to Ballarat (see Excursion #39 for that route description).

South Park

Middle Park.

41

Mengel Pass via Goler Wash

Primary Attraction:	Typical canyon scenery of the Panamints, and the only remaining through pass over the southern half of the range still open to vehicles. Along the way is a bit of history, both old and new.
Time Required:	The ascent of Goler Wash can take a few hours, or a few days. It all depends on the road conditions of the moment.
Miles Involved:	It is 26 miles from Ballarat to the summit of Mengel Pass. Add two miles for a side trip to Barker Ranch.
Degree of Difficulty:	I have seen Goler Wash when it was no more difficult than Class II, and I have seen it when it was mostly Class IV and V. Over the years the roadbed has washed out many times, and it has been rebuilt many times. How you may find it is anybody's guess. Since the El Niño rains in the winter of 1982-83, the road has been mostly Class III, but with at least four sections of Class IV and sometimes Class V. When it is bad, the four dry waterfalls are generally rated Class IV coming down the canyon going in an east to west direction. Under these conditions, if you choose to go up Goler Wash, expect all four of these bare rock waterfalls to be difficult, with two and possibly three to be Class V. **At its worst, Goler Wash should be attempted only by experienced four-wheelers in short wheelbase vehicles.**

Mengal Pass Via Goler Walsh

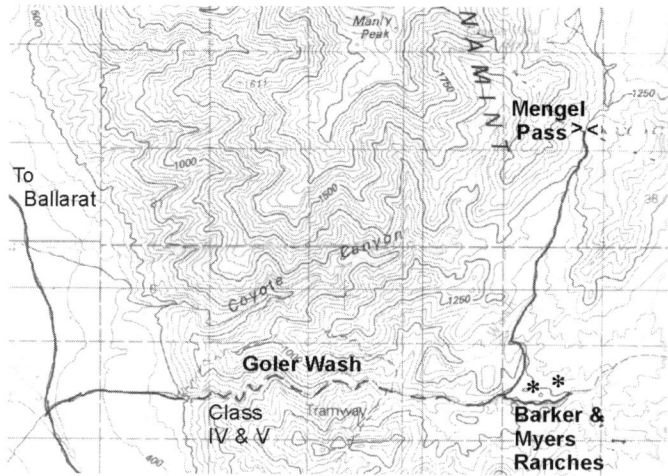

From downtown Ballarat, note your odometer reading, and start south on the oiled road in the direction of Goler Wash. In just a half a mile you will pass Post Office Spring where, in 1850, the second Jayhawker Party is thought to have camped after their perilous escape from Death Valley. The site got the name not because a post office was ever here. It got the name because local outlaws, in cahoots with certain stagecoach drivers, used the site to stash cash which would be picked up by the stage driver, who would in turn leave groceries on the return trip.

At a point 3.9 miles south of Ballarat a side road goes left to South Park Canyon (see Excursion #40). At a point 7.7 miles from downtown Ballarat, you will pass the entrance to the C.R. Briggs Mine operated by the Canyon Resources Corporation. In the late 1990s this mine was one of the five top gold producers in California. This is a new mine, with 1997 being its first full year of operation. In 1998 the mine produced some 80,300 ounces of gold. It has reserves of an additional 653,000 ounces in sight. Unlike many of the mines in the Panamint Range that have played out, this one should be around for a long time.

A crossroads is reached at a point 15.3 miles south of Ballarat; turn left heading up the alluvial fan. Within two miles you will enter Goler Wash and its canyon. Note your odometer reading as you enter the canyon. Within 0.4 miles, in the narrowest parts of the canyon, there is a series of four dry waterfalls that must be ascended. They are all slightly different, ranging in difficulty from Class IV to V. Suddenly the road has become very interesting, immediately turning from Class I to Class V with no transition in between. **Warning: proceed with great caution. Scout the road ahead on foot before attempting to drive over**

these ledges. (Coming downhill from Mengel Pass, I would rate them all at Class IV.) Once over the fourth section of bedrock, the road improves to a much more manageable Class III.

Goler Wash

The rock walls of an old forgotten miner's cabin are on the right 1.7 miles into the canyon, followed in 0.3 miles by a tramline on the left going up to the Lestro Mountain Mine. This was a gold mine tapping into a five-foot quartz vein high on the canyon's wall. In 1940, some six hundred tons of ore came down this tramline on its way to the Golden Queen Mill near Mojave.

At a point three miles into the canyon, the road improves to Class II and the Lotus Mine camp can be seen on the right. The mine itself is actually high on the south ridge at the upper end of a 2,800' tramline. At the contact between a highly metamorphic andesite and limestone bed can be found quartz veins which yielded up to $50.00 per ton in gold. Four tunnels with a combined length of nearly one thousand feet tapped the mineralized zone. Two aerial trams were utilized to bring the ore down. This is the mine that Carl Mengel owned until 1935. The present owners of the Lotus Mine still pay their annual fees to the BLM to retain ownership of the claims.

Mengal Pass Via Goler Walsh

Some careful boulder dodging will have to be undertaken above the Lotus Mine. Vehicles with a short wheelbase should have sufficient maneuverability, but long pickups could encounter some problems. Drivers of SUVs with low running boards should utilize a spotter on foot while twisting through the boulder patch. At a point 4.3 miles inside the canyon, the new park boundary is reached. (Prior to the CDPA of 1994, the boundary was on the summit of Mengel Pass.) A tenth of a mile beyond, the canyon forks. The left fork reaches the summit of Mengel Pass in 3.4 miles.

Before ascending the pass, you might want to make a short side trip to the right. The road swings to the right, abruptly drops down into the wash, and then makes its way eastward under the spreading branches of cottonwood trees. This is Sourdough Spring, so named by Bill and Barbara Myers who lived just up the wash between 1932 and 1960. They claim the name idea came from Carl Mengel, whose idea of a good breakfast was sourdough pancakes and fried liver. A half-mile above Sourdough Spring is the Barker Ranch, built by Bluch and Helen Thomason after Bluch retired from the Los Angeles Police Department. After Bluch died, the property was sold to Jim and Kirk Barker. Just beyond the Barker Ranch is the Myers Ranch.

The Barker and Myers Ranches are places that received quite a bit of notoriety and national press back in 1969. In the very first edition of *Death Valley Jeep Trails* written in 1969, I said, *"During the past year these isolated retreats have been inhabited by a small band of 'hippies', doing whatever hippies do"*. Little did I know that these squatters were Charles Manson and his murdering gang. It was at the Barker Ranch that Charlie was arrested, although at the time his role in the Tate-LaBianca murders was not yet known. (See Appendix F for additional details.)

Charlie moved his band into Barker Ranch sometime in 1968. Mrs. Arlene Barker, who owned the property and whose granddaughter Cathy Gillies was one of Manson's followers, gave permission for Charlie to camp there. She thought he meant only a few days. Manson had other plans. Not only did Charlie move his brood into Barker Ranch, but he had also made plans to kill Mrs. Barker to obtain title through Cathy. By a stroke of luck, the three creeps he sent to do the job had a flat tire in Panamint Valley and never completed the task.

Barker Ranch has once again returned to the peaceful anonymity it once enjoyed. The house is open. The visitor is free to go in and look around. It looks quite comfortable, although someone has filled the toilet with cement to prevent its use. The house could be used as an emergency shelter should a sudden storm arise, but you would not be alone. Your temporary quarters would have to be shared with hundreds of mice and other little rodents. A few ghosts might join you, too. One person who was close to the Manson gang says that there are three bodies buried eight feet deep somewhere on the Barker Ranch. They have never been found.

The road continues up the wash 0.3 miles beyond Barker Ranch to Myers Ranch. Bill and Barbara Myers settled in Goler Wash in 1932, building themselves a comfortable house complete with such amenities as flush toilets, a swimming pool, an orchard, and of course, a garden. They raised three children there: Charles, Pat and Corky. The Myers family reluctantly moved to Fresno in 1960, so that their children could have a better education.

Barker Ranch, where Charles Manson was apprehended in 1969

At one time a faint Class III road went on past Myers Ranch to steeply climb an unnamed pass, then continue on down into Wingate Wash, where it was an easy descent into Death Valley. That entire route has been closed to four-wheelers. Vehicle travel beyond Myers Ranch is now prohibited.

Back down the canyon below Sourdough Springs, the main Goler Wash road goes to the left. For the next 2.5 miles the road is mostly Class II. After leaving the sandy wash, however, the last 0.9 miles is a steep Class III. On the summit is a monument containing the ashes of Carl Mengel, a single blanket prospector who lived just over the pass at Greater View Spring. For a description of the route on the other side, see Excursion #9.

42

Reilly Was a Company Town

Primary Attraction:	A well preserved mining camp reminiscent of Inca ruins in the high Andes.
Time Required:	This is an easy half-day trip out of Ballarat.
Miles Involved:	From downtown Ballarat to downtown Reilly is only 10.5 miles.
Degree of Difficulty:	The dirt road portions are mostly Class II, with only the last mile having a few Class III sections.

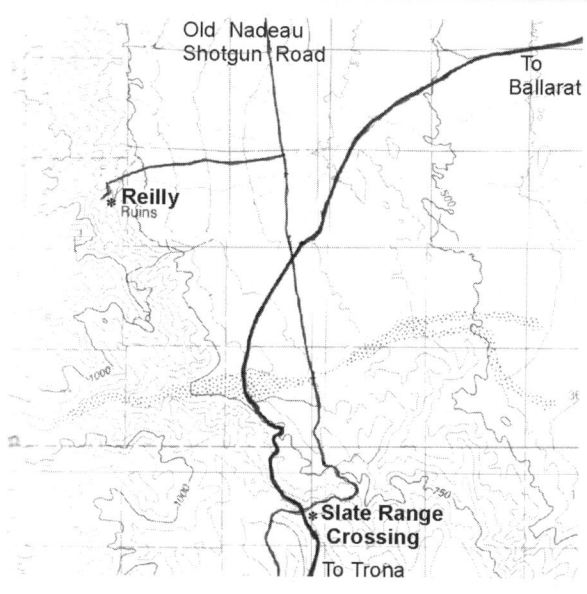

Reilly is another obscure mining camp that never made it into the spotlight during its heyday, and as such has been largely forgotten and overlooked by most historians. Its obscurity and the sturdy stone walls of its buildings have helped to preserve its heritage.

From downtown Ballarat, head west three and a half miles to the Trona Highway. Turn left toward Trona. The "new" (paved) Nadeau Road is passed after 3.8 miles. Just 0.4 beyond, look to the old Nadeau Road crossing the highway; it is not marked. Turn right here. This is the Nadeau "Shotgun Road" a wagon road built by Remi Nadeau in 1877 for his freight wagons going to Lookout. Proceed north for 1.1 miles, where a road to the left begins to climb the bajada. Turn left, leaving the old Nadeau Road and proceed up the bajada for 1.6 miles. The first left turn takes you to the townsite of Reilly. The second road left, 0.1 miles beyond, takes you to the millsite. The third road left, 0.1 miles further, goes a quarter mile up the canyon to one of Reilly's mines.

As a spinoff from the silver strikes at Darwin and Lookout, prospectors were searching every nook and cranny of the Argus Range. Two brothers by the name of Wibbett are supposed to have found some promising silver veins here in 1875. Little mining took place until 1882, when a promoter by the name of Charles Anthony brokered a deal with New York investor, Edward Reilly, who bought the claims. Reilly formed the Argus Range Silver Mining Company and sold stock. With money from stock sales, Anthony had capital for running day to day operations. In late 1882 Reilly set about building a ten-stamp mill and began to block out ore.

To accommodate the employees, who at one time numbered as many as sixty, Anthony put up a boarding house, a large general store, corrals and livery stable. He also built a fine house for himself. If Reilly wanted to profit by the ore, Anthony wanted to profit off Reilly's employees. A post office opened on January 22, 1883, even before the mill was operating. There was no water at the camp, so Reilly spent an additional $40,000 to run a pipeline over from Water Canyon, five miles to the south. Before a single ton of ore was crushed and processed, Edward Reilly had spent $200,000.

Because of numerous delays, however, the mill did not get into operation until September of 1883. Ironically that is also the month the post office closed its doors. Nevertheless, between October of 1883 and February of 1884, the Anthony Mill, as it came to be called, turned out bullion valued at $21,500. This was a far cry from the $200,000 that had been put into the venture. The mine operated another year, and the mill even longer, doing custom milling for other nearby mines. In the end, nobody got rich, not the stockholders, not Edward Reilly, not even Charles Anthony.

Today the mine works are crumbling and unsafe to enter. The mill is gone, leaving only its massive stone retaining walls. The camp of Reilly survives, in part. Remaining are the stone walls of some 23 structures, one with part of its roof still on. Many of these cabins were large enough for a bed and little else. In spite of their small size, these modest workers' lodgings have survived a lot longer than Charles Anthony's fine wooden house.

Only stone walls greet the visitor to Reilly

Trona today

Chapter IX

Trails Out of Trona

Most Death Valley bound visitors zip right on through Searles Valley, not realizing there is some interesting country to be explored here. The author, who grew up here, knows better. Trona lies tucked away in Searles Valley between Mojave and Death Valley. Its reason for being lies in the white mineral deposits of the "dry" lake surface, which have been mined since the 1870s when the Searles brothers began mining borax here. Dozens of chemicals have been extracted from those evaporite deposits, including potash, soda ash, glauber salts, lithium, and the mineral trona itself.

Forty years ago Trona and West End were "company towns" totally owned by the American Potash and Chemical Company and The West End Chemical Company respectively. The town of Trona was then sold off piecemeal in the 1950s, and the community of West End was bulldozed to the ground. Kerr McGee bought and ran the facility for a number of years, followed by North American Chemical Company until the mid-1990s, when IMC bought the operation.

In 1960 Searles Valley had a population of 5,698. By 1990 the population had dropped by 48% to 2,740. The 2000 census will probably reveal that the population has dropped even further. While Trona and its suburb, Argus, have seen better days, they nevertheless remain viable communities where some basic services are still available. There are two gas stations, two markets, a hardware store, an auto parts store, and a motel (one mile north of town).

The Searles Valley Historical Society operates History House at 83001 Panamint Street. Built around 1920, it is one of the oldest houses left in Trona. History House is open by appointment. The Society also operates the Old Guest House Museum at 13193 Main Street. It dates from 1912. The museum is open Mondays, from 9 a.m. to noon, and Saturdays, 11 a.m. to 1 p.m.

43

Remi Nadeau's "Shotgun Road"

Primary Attraction:	Follow portions of the first two wagon roads built in Panamint Valley to service the rich silver mines in the Panamint and Argus ranges.
Time Required:	From Trona one can follow the old Jacobs Road over Slate Range Crossing, and then follow the Nadeau Road to the Minnietta and Modoc Mines in half a day, if no side trips are taken. Some of these side trips are interesting, however, so you had better plan on spending all day.
Miles Involved:	From the old West End Quarry road in Searles Valley to the Minnietta Mine Road in Panamint Valley is some 23 miles.
Degree of Difficulty:	The road is nearly all Class II, except for a couple of places where the road crosses a wash and where it might be Class III. **This road is not suitable for long wheelbase vehicles having a long overhang behind the rear axle.**

One of Remi Nadeau's mule teams (Courtesy Remi Nadeau IV)

The Nadeau Shotgun Road

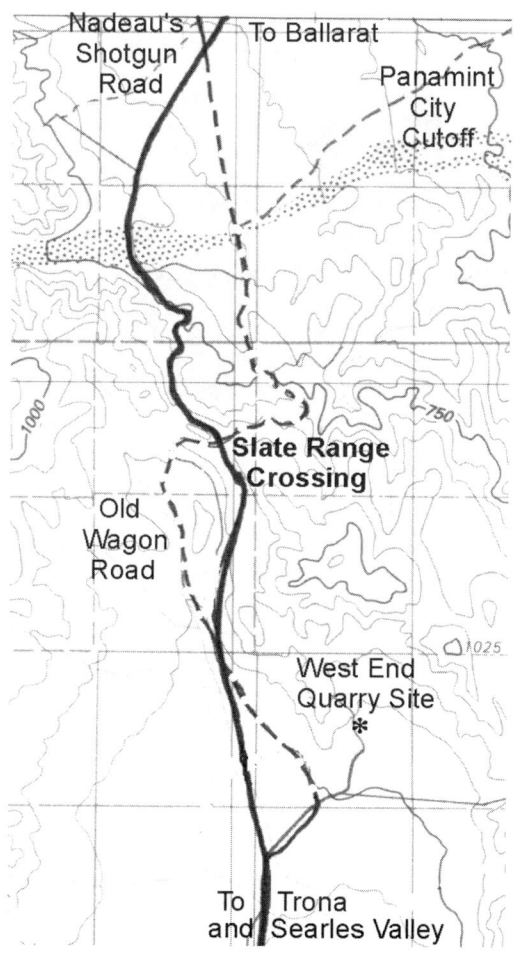

Although the emigrants of 1849 and 50 passed through Panamint Valley after escaping Death Valley, there was to be no wagon road for more than two decades after their passing. That all changed in 1873 when Richard Jacobs and his partner Bob Stewart found a ledge of silver high in Surprise Canyon in the Panamint Range. The following year Jacobs went to Los Angeles in order to raise the capital needed to develop his mine and to build a road to it. Jacobs was a smooth talker. He argued that his rich lode of silver would make everyone rich. Unless the folks of Los Angeles built the road to his mines, the citizens of San Bernardino or Bakersfield would do it. The movers and shakers in Los Angeles responded, and Jacobs had the money to build 60 miles of new road. Several hundred Chinese laborers were engaged and work began in June of 1874.

The old wagon road supported by rock retaining walls is as useable today as it was in 1874

The new road left the Bullion Road to Cerro Gordo near Indian Wells, went east through Poison Canyon, and once in Searles Valley, headed north to a low pass at the western end of the Slate Range. The south side of Slate Range Crossing was relatively easy. The northern slope required several miles of cut and fill, but it, too, was quickly overcome. By August of 1874, the road between Los Angeles and Panamint City was established. One of the first items to be carried over it was a ten-stamp mill going to Jacob's mine. Three years later, French Canadian Remi Nadeau would build his "Shotgun Road" cutting off from the Panamint Road at the northern base of Slate Range Crossing to the mines of Lookout Mountain (see Excursion #35).

The silver booms in Cerro Gordo and Panamint City in the 1870s treated Remi Nadeau quite well. But Remi was not mining silver; rather he was hauling it. In 1861 Nadeau had arrived in Los Angeles driving a team of oxen. He decided to go into the freight hauling business. He borrowed some money from another French Canadian, Prudent Beaudry, bought some mules and wagons, and set off to seek his fortune. It just so happened that Prudent's brother, Victor, was half owner of a very productive silver mine, high in the Inyo Mountains at a place called Cerro Gordo. The mine's smelter was turning out bullion faster that it could be hauled away. In December of 1868, Nadeau was awarded a contract to carry silver bullion from Cerro Gordo, two hundred miles south to the railroad in downtown Los Angeles. In order to keep up, Nadeau increased his transport capacity to thirty-two teams of twelve to eighteen mules per team, with each team pulling two wagons. In 1870 alone, Nadeau's teams moved some seven hundred tons of bullion.

By 1874 it became obvious that Panamint City, with a population of approaching two thousand, would become another Cerro Gordo. In 1875 the

The Nadeau Shotgun Road

twenty working mines in the Darwin area supported a town of seven hundred people, including 78 businesses and two smelters. 1875 was also the year that the mines of Lookout Mountain in the Argus Range were discovered and showed great promise. All of these mines needed their bullion hauled to market, and on the return trip, machinery, supplies and building materials needed to be hauled in. Remi Nadeau was in the right business, at the right place, at the right time. Nadeau set about building roads for his freight wagons, and soon most commerce in Inyo County moved through the hands of his teamsters.

In the spring of 1877 Nadeau built his "Shotgun Road" from the bottom of the Slate Range grade to the Modoc and Minnietta Mines, thus cutting many miles off the previously more circuitous route. As soon as that road was completed he shifted his crews to Wildrose Canyon, where yet another road was built to the base of Lookout Mountain, this one to transport charcoal from the ten newly erected kilns.

The booms at Cerro Gordo, Darwin, Lookout, and Panamint City all faded in time, but Remi Nadeau's mule drawn freight wagons still plied the roads of Inyo County until 1883, when the Carson & Colorado Railroad came into the Owens Valley. Being unable to compete with the railroad, Nadeau then moved his teams to the flourishing new camp of Tombstone in the Arizona Territory, where then he sold the business. Nadeau returned to Los Angeles to build a fine four-story hotel at the corner of First and Spring Streets. Not only was it the tallest building in Los Angeles at the time, it was also the first with a mechanical elevator, and it remained the finest hostelry for years to come.

Remi Nadeau
(Photo courtesy of Remi Nadeau IV)

When I was a youngster, Jacob's old Panamint Road could be picked up at Pioneer Point just north of Trona. However, man's activities of the last fifty years have obliterated it there. To find the old road used by Nadeau's teams, go north out of Trona in the direction of Death Valley. While passing the Trona High School gymnasium at the north end of town, note your odometer reading. At a point 8.2 miles north of the gymnasium the paved Homewood Canyon Road goes off to the left. In another 2.5 miles a paved road turns off to the right. This road goes to the old West End Chemical Company limestone quarry that operated in the 1960s; turn right here. The old Nadeau Road can be seen fifty feet east of today's paved road. After 0.4 miles, the Nadeau Road makes a left turn and crosses Quarry Road. This is where we will pick up the old Panamint Road.

The Westend Limestone Quarry in 1956

Follow the dirt tracks to the northwest as they skirt the base of a low limestone hill. The route is generally Class I, with a few Class II portions at minor washouts. At a point 1.1 miles from Quarry Road, the old Panamint Road crosses the highway to Death Valley. Cross the asphalt and pick it up on the other side.

In another 0.3 miles, the Panamint Road forks; stay left on what appears to be the more traveled route. Within a hundred yards the road forks again. Take either fork; they soon rejoin. At a point 0.6 miles from the highway crossing, the road deteriorates to Class II as it starts up a small wash. At 0.8 miles in from the highway crossing, old campfire rings and scattered pieces of bottles and tin cans suggest this spot has been utilized as a layover for many years. Nadeau's muleskinners probably made this a regular stopping point on their long journey.

At 0.8 miles north of the old campsite, a crossroads is reached. Go straight ahead up the hillside. The top of Slate Range Crossing is but 0.4 miles ahead.

At the summit, the Nadeau Road once again crosses the highway and starts down into Panamint Valley.

Still Class II, the roadway begins its descent across the pink volcanic rocks of Tertiary age. From this lofty vantagepoint, there are good views down into Panamint Valley. To the north, Nadeau's "Shotgun Road" can be clearly seen cutting across the bajadas like a laser beam. As you work your way lower, the rocks soon change from pink to dark basalt. Along the way, the stone retaining walls holding up the road seem just as well built today as they were 130 years ago.

It is only 1.5 miles to the bottom of the grade. In another 0.6 miles there are fifty yards of Class III road as you cross the sandy wash coming out of Water Canyon. On the other side, a fork goes off to the right. This was Jacob's original road of 1874 to Panamint City. The road straight ahead is Nadeau's wagon road of 1877. Some say it was called The "Shotgun Road" because it was surveyed straight across the desert as if one was looking through the barrel of a shotgun.

The Shotgun Road

After another 1.1 miles, the modern highway is crossed again. Note your odometer reading. A BLM sign identifies the route as "P03". Almost immediately on your left a Class II side road goes up the hill a mile and a half to a kitty litter mine, inactive since the 1980s. (There is a lot of flat ground here in the event you are looking for a campsite.)

Needless to say, the Shotgun Road goes straight ahead. In spite of the fact that the Shotgun Road cuts across the grain of the drainage coming off the Argus Range, the road is nevertheless no worse than Class II. The next side road to the left comes after another 1.2 miles. This goes to the old mining camp of Reilly (See Excursion #42).

Continue north another 2.4 miles, where the next major road to the west climbs the fan 2.4 miles to the Onyx mine. Here in marble and limestone is a band of onyx some three to seven feet wide. The onyx quarried here was various hues of brown, cream, red and even green. Some was beautifully banded, some mottled and some cloudy. It would polish very nicely.

The deposit was worked first in 1925 and for about fifty years since. When I first visited the site in the 1950s, the resident caretaker would sell specimens by the pound to rock hounds. The Searles Valley Gem & Mineral Society would come away with boxes of it. When I last visited the site in 1998, the camp was in ruins and it looked like there was none of the good stuff left.

At a point 1.2 miles beyond the Onyx Mine Road, Nadeau's Shotgun Road crosses a deep wash where a stone causeway had to be built. It remains today just as it was in 1877. In the next 3.5 miles, the Nadeau Road crosses four more roads; simply continue heading north. When you have traveled 8.3 miles since leaving the pavement, you will come to the paved new Nadeau Road, which goes to a limestone quarry at the base of the Argus Range. Turn left on the asphalt surface. Stay on the pavement for 2.5 miles; then make a right turn to put you back onto the Old Nadeau Shotgun Road.

The next five miles are a rough Class II, with a few Class III sections encountered when crossing gullies and washes. Eventually, however, the soil turns sandy and the road surface improves. At a point 6.5 miles from the new Nadeau Road, the Shotgun Road reaches the graded Minnietta Road coming in from the right. From this junction you have several options. The road on the left goes one mile to the Minnietta Mine. If you wish to return to the pavement, turn right. The Trona-Wildrose Highway is but 3.6 miles to the east. If you continue straight ahead for a mile, another side road to the left will take you to the site of the Modoc Mine in half a mile, and on to the old Mining Camp of Lookout after another 6 miles (see Excursion #35). All of these sites were ore shipping points for Remi Nadeau's mule drawn wagons. If you continue straight ahead to the north after this second junction, you can access Osborne Canyon (see Excursion #34).

The Minietta Mine in its heyday
(Photo courtesy of County of Inyo, Eastern California Museum)

The Minietta Mine today

44

The Arondo Mine

Primary Attraction: A visit to an old gold mine, with the chance of wild burro sightings along the way.

Time Required: This is a half-day excursion out of Trona.

Distance Involved: The mine is thirty miles round trip from Trona.

Degree of Difficulty: The road in to the mine is no worse than Class III, and there is not much of that.

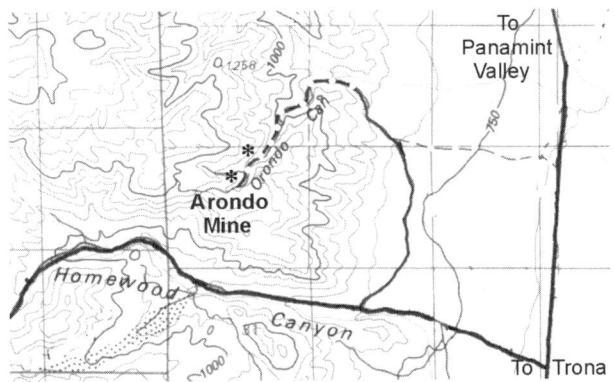

The Arondo Mine, sometimes spelled "Orondo", is situated in a canyon of the same name, on the eastern flank of the Argus Range at the northern end of Searles Valley. It is a pleasant destination for a few hours or a full day.

From Trona take the Death Valley Road north out of town. As you leave town, note your odometer as you pass the Trona High School gymnasium. Proceed north past Pioneer Point and the Valley Wells recreation complex. At a point 8.2 miles beyond the gymnasium, the paved Homewood Canyon Road heads west towards the Argus Range. Turn left here and go west 1.6 miles up the cholla-studded bajada. Just before entering Homewood Canyon, a graded dirt road turns off to the right. A sign reads *"Inyo County Dump"*. In 0.2 miles, pass the refuse transfer point on the left. The road continues on, although it deteriorates to Class I.

Notice the small spot of black basalt lava on the left. In this area the Argus Range is generally Mesozoic granite and quartz monzonite, but, in places such as this, it has been intruded by much younger Tertiary lavas. This little spot of basalt is a reminder of that recent volcanism.

The rough road goes north along the base of the mountains, cutting across the grain of the bajada. The dominate desert shrub here is the ubiquitous creosote. The cholla cactus so common along the Homewood Canyon Road is nowhere to be seen. Another very common plant along the trail here is the desert trumpet or bladderstem, *Ergonum inflatum,* a plant twelve to eighteen inches high with a section of swollen stem near the top.

At a point a mile north of the pavement, the desert road deteriorates further to Class II. Look for a quail guzzler on the left. The California Department of Fish and Game placed these small cisterns throughout California's deserts. The infrequent rains are collected in aprons that channel the water down an inclined ramp, making water available to quail and other desert wildlife long after the rains have passed.

The road swings to the west and enters Bruce Canyon. At a point 2.5 miles from the Homewood Canyon Road, the Class II road forks. The right fork continues up Bruce Canyon a half mile where it dead-ends. A well-worn burro trail continues up Bruce Canyon another mile to Rock Spring. For the Arondo Mine, you will want to keep to the left up Arondo Canyon, a side canyon to the south. The reddish brown soil in the bottom of the wash is distinctly different from the light brown soils on the hillsides. That is because the dirt in the bottom of the canyon is actually the fine waste material which came from the two ore mills more than a mile up Arondo Canyon.

As you ascend Arondo Canyon, you will see an occasional barrel cactus on the hillsides. Wherever they are found, they seem to prefer the well-drained gravel hillsides to the sandy washes.

Soon the road deteriorates even further, to an easy Class III. At a point 3.7 miles from the paved Homewood Canyon Road, there is a fork in the road and an enormous tailings pile. These are the lower workings of the Arondo Mine. The Class III right fork goes up a side canyon another 0.4 miles to dead-end at the "middle workings", the site of a second millsite. The mill has burned, leaving only a huge pile of fine waste which was left over after the ore was crushed and the gold extracted. **Warning: Stay well away from the large open shaft; it is very dangerous to attempt to even peer down into it.**

The left fork remains Class III as it passes a shaft and continues to climb up the canyon bottom. It is another mile to the upper workings of the Arondo Mine. The early history of this mine remains obscure, but it is thought to go back to the 1890s. The property was worked intermittently from 1901 to 1941 and again by several leasees during the period of 1946 to 1950. The gold ore is found in a shear zone in the granitic rocks. While the ounces of gold per ton were relatively low, that gold, which was present, was in a free state, easily extracted by the cyanide leaching process.

When I visited this site in 1959, the main shaft still had its steel headframe, hoist house and several other outbuildings. In the last forty years the headframe has been dismantled, the buildings have collapsed, and only the sturdy ore bunker remains. A protective screen covers the shaft. **Do not attempt to enter any of these old workings; the supporting cribbing is old and rotting.**

The Arondo Mine in 1959

The Arondo Mine in 1999

45

The Gold Bottom Mine and Beyond

Primary Attraction:	This is an opportunity to see the Searles Playa close up, to visit an old mine, and to get a good look at an old Pleistocene beach.
Time Required:	This is an easy half-day trip out of Trona.
Miles Involved:	It is only nine miles from downtown Trona to the Gold Bottom Mine.
Degree of Difficulty:	It is an easy Class I road to the lower workings, Class III to the upper workings, and if you continue on to the overlook into Copper Queen Canyon, the last quarter mile is Class IV.

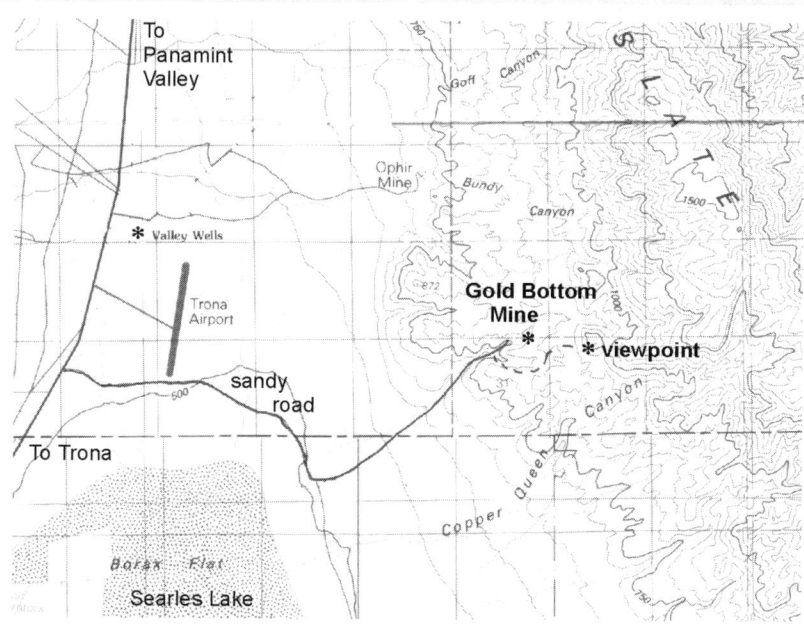

The Gold Bottom Mine, originally called the Copper Queen Mine, lies just inside Inyo County near the northern end of Searles Dry Lake. It is in very old Precambrian rocks on the western slope of the Slate Range. The Death

Valley bound visitor can easily visit the site as a two-hour side trip off the Trona-Panamint Valley Road.

Take the paved highway north out of Trona as if you were going to Death Valley. Note your odometer reading as you pass the Trona High School gymnasium. At a point 2.7 miles north of the school (0.9 miles into Inyo County), look for a wide graded desert road heading east. (If you come to the Trona airport road, you have gone 0.9 miles too far north.) Turn east here and soon you will be passing the south end of the Trona airport runway. There is a little soft sand here, but it should present no problem.

The road skirts the north end of Searles Lake, the fourth in a chain of six Ice Age lakes fed by the ancestral Owens River on its way to Death Valley. When the high Sierra was covered with glacial ice, the Owens River began its journey at Lake Russell (today's Mono Lake Basin), where it flowed south across Adobe Valley and the Owens Valley, picking up volume from the many smaller streams which fed into it. The smallest in this chain, Lake Owens drained to the south. This mighty river must have sent up an enormous cloud of mist, making an awesome roar, as it leaped off the hard basalt cliffs at Fossil Falls. China Lake was the next basin, and then the water turned east to enter Searles Valley by way of today's Poison Canyon. At its peak in the Tahoe stage 75,000 years ago, Ancient Lake Searles was 32 miles long, up to fifteen miles wide, and eight hundred feet deep.

Between the many ice advances in the late Pleistocene, there were interglacial warm periods when the mighty rivers stopped flowing. Without a continuing source of water, lakes like Searles pretty much dried up. The dissolved salts and other minerals became concentrated as the water evaporated. With each renewed wet and dry cycle, successive layers of silt and minerals were deposited on the lake bottom. It is these evaporate minerals that are being extracted today.

Borax was known to be here as early as 1862; however, no serious efforts were made to extract this "white gold" until 1873 when John and Dennis Searles hired a few Chinese laborers and opened a small plant near present day Trona. The operation prospered and by 1890 some fifty workers and fifty draft horses were turning out up to one hundred tons per month. By 1913, long after the Searles brothers had died, the Trona Borax Company bought out the Searles' interests. They sank brine wells in the lake bottom and extracted a wide variety of minerals including potash, soda ash, salt cake, lithium carbonate, glauber salts and the mineral trona. Eventually these holdings became the American Potash and Chemical Company, affectionately known to locals as "AMPOT". A competing operation began at the south end of the lake and this became known as the West End Chemical Company. Both companies developed "company towns" adjoining their plants for their workers. This was the Trona that I grew up in during the late 1940s and 1950s. My parents and I lived in a company house, shopped in the company grocery store, drug store and department store, and frequented the company owned movie theater, community center and bowling alley. In the Trona of that day, only the post office and the school were not operated by the company.

AMPOT eventually sold out to Kerr McGee, and West End sold out to Stauffer. The company town at West End was torn down, and the one at Trona sold off piecemeal to anyone who wanted to buy a house and lot. A few years back North American Chemical Company bought out both companies' operations, giving them control over the entire lake. In the midddle 1990s, IMC bought out North American and they currently operate the plant. At the current rate of production, the estimates are that there are sufficient reserves to last another 150 years.

As you go eastward beyond the playa surface, you will see some tracks going off through the sand on the left, but stay to the right on the main road. Straight ahead you will notice horizontal lines on the hillside, particularly if you come this way in the early morning light. These are wave-cut terraces left by Pleistocene Lake Searles. We will visit one of these ancient beaches on our way to the upper workings of the Gold Bottom mine

At a point 3.1 miles from the highway there is an important road junction. The right fork continues south along the east shore of Searles Lake to come to a locked gate, which marks the boundary of the Naval Air Weapons Station's *Range B*. While there is some interesting country down there, including Layton Pass, unauthorized travel is strictly prohibited by the Navy. Trespassers are treated as spies endangering national security. (If you are somehow able to prove that you are not an agent of a foreign power, then you are simply cited for trespassing and must appear before a Federal magistrate.) **Do not enter the Navy base!** At this fork in the road three miles from the highway, you definitely want to keep to the left.

In slightly more than a mile, this road, still generally Class I, will take you into a small canyon. Within a quarter of a mile, notice the horizontal layers of sand on the hillside to the left. These, too, are remnants of Ancient Lake Searles, probably deposited during the Tioga stage of the Wisconsin period, a mere 20,000 years ago. Although I have found no mega-fossils here, it is deposits like these, at the edge of the old lake, which make good places to look for the remains of large Pleistocene vertebrates: creatures like mastadons, *Camelops*, a llama-like camel, and *Equus,* an early form of large horse. All have become extinct in the last 10,000 to 50,000 years. It's fun to look, but remember that the collecting of such fossils is permitted on BLM administered lands only with a permit.

A half-mile into the canyon, the wash makes a sharp bend, and a side road right climbs the steep hill out of the wash; this is the road to the upper workings. We will want to go there, but for the moment, let's keep to the left and visit the main mine site just around the corner.

Although few records were kept in its early days, the Gold Bottom Mine was one of four important hardrock mines in Searles Valley. (The other three were the Ruth and Arondo Mines across the valley in the Argus Range, and the Ophir Mine just two miles to the north of the Gold Bottom Mine.) In spite of its various names it was lead, not gold or copper, that was the important commodity sought here at the Gold Bottom Mine. Silver and gold were byproducts, however, and were recovered along with the lead in the milling process. The first claims were staked in the 1880s and some ore was produced before 1900. The "lower workings" were developed in 1916 and worked intermittently until 1943.

The important mineralization has taken place here in the very old and highly metamorphosed rocks of Precambrian age. Gold, silver, and lead were recovered from orebodies that were as large as five feet wide and two hundred feet long. An estimated $900,000 to a million dollars was taken out of the ground here. The millsite was outside of the canyon, down by Searles Lake. It is said that the narrow gauge railroad operated by the old Trona Borax Company once came over here.

In his book *Pete Aguereberry,* author George Pipkin says that Jean LeMoigne (see Excursion #13) worked for wages in the Gold Bottom Mine during World War I. Conditions in the mine were so bad that Jean came down with lead and arsenic poisoning, as did many of his co-workers. As if that were not enough, Pete also broke a leg before leaving the mine for good.

As a teenager in the 1950s, I learned all about hardrock mining here, through exploring the 7,500 feet of underground workings. At the time it was like an industrial museum, displaying a wide variety of underground features including adits, shafts, winzes, raises, stopes, drifts, crosscuts, and the like. In those days the mine had been abandoned only ten years previously and the ladders and shoring were still in good condition. Such is not the case today, however. **Under no circumstances should the underground workings be entered. Their danger cannot be over-stated. Six of the many claims here are patented, meaning this is private property where the owner's rights should be respected, even though the site appears to be abandoned.**

It has been my observation that this sheltered and warm south-facing canyon has all the conditions needed for wildflower seeds to germinate early. Among the species seen in bloom as early as January are sand verbena, desert trumpet, chorizanthe, eriastrum, blazing star, four O clock and the lesser mohavena.

The Gold Bottom Mine in 1952

To visit the upper workings, drive back a tenth of a mile to the bend in the canyon. Turn left on the Class II road steeply climbing out of the wash. In a tenth of a mile there are good views of Searles Lake. One can see all the way to the Trona Pinnacles at the south end of the valley. Look around at the soil, which consists of rounded rocks. 20,000 years ago this was a Tioga stage shoreline. There may have been more sand between the cobbles then, but it is easy to imagine the waves lapping up on the beach here.

The road deteriorates to Class III as it ascends a layer of dark basalt lava, just above the marine terrace. In just a half mile from the bottom of the wash, the road forks. The right fork goes a short distance to the upper workings. The left fork passes a couple of prospect holes (get out and look for malachite and other greenish colored copper minerals) and then goes on another two miles to dead-end on a rounded granite hilltop overlooking the badlands of Copper Queen Canyon. The last quarter mile is a steep Class IV with very poor traction. The views of the Slate Range and of Searles Valley are quite good from this lofty perch.

A steep section of Class III road above the Gold Bottom Mine

46

Those Curious Pinnacles

Primary Attraction:	Curious lake-bottom geologic features left over from the last Ice Age.
Time Required:	This is an easy two to three hour excursion out of Trona.
Miles Involved:	The heart of the Pinnacles is only thirteen miles out of Trona, and only seven miles off State Highway 178.
Degree of Difficulty:	In dry weather the dirt access road is an easy Class I. Once you are there, many of the roads through the pinnacles are Class II. **Drivers of conventional vehicles should stay out of the sandy wash that divides the two portions of the North Group.**

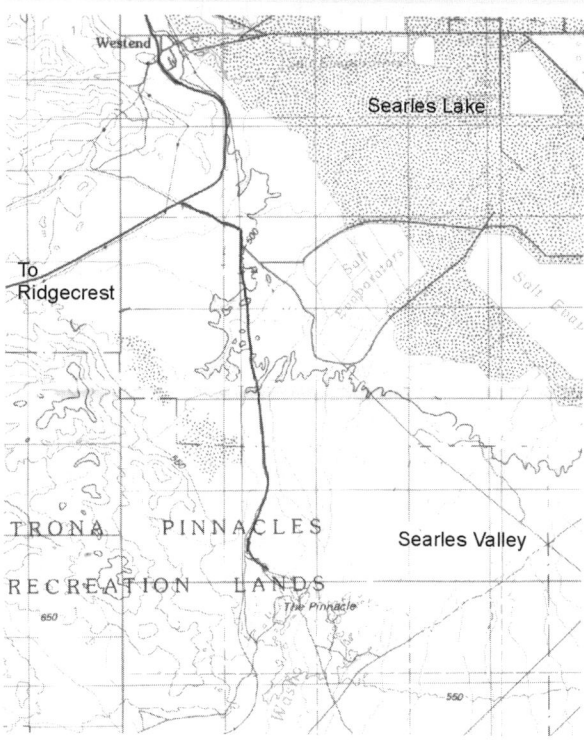

As you travel State Highway 178 between Ridgecrest and Trona, you cannot help but notice a series of rock spires off in the distance in the south end of Searles Valley. If the access roads are dry, which they usually are fifty weeks a year, a brief side trip is worth the hour or two that it takes.

A prominent BLM sign marks the turnoff, which is 6.5 miles south of downtown Trona. If you are coming the other way, the turnoff is 14.2 miles from the county line at the eastern edge of Ridgecrest. The graded road heads southeast for the first half mile, and then turns south.

At this first curve in the dirt road was the site of *Magnesia*, the western terminus of a 28-mile long monorail that operated between 1924 and 1926. This unique single rail railroad carried epsom salts from Wingate Pass down into the southern end of Panamint Valley, then up and over the Slate Range by way of Layton Canyon to this point. Here it was transferred to a conventional rail car of the Trona Railroad. The line was expensive to build, the equipment suffered frequent breakdowns, and the quality of the product being mined deteriorated with depth. Because of these factors, the monorail operation lasted only two years. While advanced in its concept, the project was considered a failure.

The Trona Railroad, on the other hand, had its first section of track laid in September of 1913 with the last spike nail in March of 1914. It has carried saline products along its 31 mile course to the Southern Pacific tracks at Searles Station ever since.

Years ago, when I took my young bride on her second camping trip to the desert (we spent our honeymoon camping in the Sahara), we had agreed to rendezvous with some friends just off the road to the Trona Pinnacles. We arrived after dark on a moonless night and set up our makeshift camp on a convenient flat spot a couple of miles south of the highway. Soon our friends arrived and as the hour was late, we all retreated to our tents for the night. We were sound asleep when suddenly a blinding light illuminated our tents. The sudden light was accompanied by a deafening roar which, even in our drowsy stupor, we recognized as a diesel locomotive. It was close and getting even closer. Everyone instantly became wide-awake and in full panic mode. Had we set up camp on railroad tracks without realizing it? Just as we tumbled out of our tents we came to discover that the low berm just behind our camp, was not a berm at all, but the roadbed of the Trona Railroad. We had camped 25 feet away from the tracks without realizing it. We were quite safe, but the railroad's single train a day, which went through at midnight, was very startling.

As you continue south on the graded road, notice the parallel terraces cut horizontally into the hillsides to the west. These are marine terraces, cut by wind-driven waves going back to the times when the floor of this valley was filled with water. The highest terrace seems to be at the 2260-foot contour line.

Those Curious Pinnacles

Over time, as the lake level dropped, a series of new wave cut terraces were created down lower on the hillside.

The road into the Trona Pinnacles is generally Class I

The so-called Plio-Pleistocene Ice Age began in late Pliocene times, about three million years ago, when the Northern Hemisphere turned cooler and wetter. Large accumulations of snow covered what is now Canada, the northern part of the United States, and the mountains of the west. The weight of the snow compacted into great masses of ice which, under the force of gravity, moved slowly downhill. The "Ice Age" was not a single event lasting millions of years, but a whole series of at least seven advances and retreats of the ice, with interglacial warm periods between. At the peak of these glacial periods, there was so much water on the land in the form of ice that the world's oceans were three hundred feet lower than today. As the cycle reversed and the mighty glaciers began to melt, the great glaciers of the Sierra Nevada were sending a great river of meltwater down into the Owens Valley. This mighty Owens River roared as it passed over a basalt ledge known today as Fossil Falls. The great river next filled the China Lake basin, creating a broad shallow lake, which drained eastward through Poison Canyon to form yet another large lake here in Searles Valley. Eventually ancient Lake Searles drained into Panamint Valley and then went on to make Lake Manly in Death Valley. However, our story about these curious pinnacles has its beginning when ancient Lake Searles filled this valley. At its peak during the Tahoe phase of the Pleistocene, about 75,000 years ago, ancient Lake Searles was 32 miles long, fifteen miles wide, and up to eight hundred feet deep. At that time even Poison Canyon was inundated, and China Lake and Lake Searles were joined by a thin channel.

But so much for the prehistoric lake. Let's move on down the road and see what those pinnacles are all about. At a point six miles south of Highway 178, the dirt road forks. The right fork generally follows the railroad south into the Spangler Hills and the BLM's off-road vehicle playground. For the next nine miles along this road, two major clusters of pinnacles are passed, the middle group with about one hundred spires, and the south group with about two hundred. These are the oldest ones, dating from the highest water levels in the Tahoe phase. They are also the most badly weathered and least impressive.

Take the left fork for the north group. It contains two hundred of the youngest and best preserved of the pinnacles. They were formed along an elongated fissure during the Tioga phase, about 20,000 years ago. Most are no higher than fifty feet, but at least one is 120 feet tall.

These rock spires of tufa were formed underwater at the mouth of springs, possibly hot springs. The spring water rose out of cracks in the lake bottom, carrying dissolved calcium minerals. When the warm spring water suddenly came in contact with the cold lake water, the dissolved minerals precipitated out. The calcium minerals built up at the vents and, with time, built these columns underwater. The warm spring water also attracted algae, leaving much organic matter in the tufa. At the end of the Ice Age, as the lake dried up, these columns rose up out of the ever-lowering lake. Now the water is gone, but the pinnacles remain. In 1968 the Department of the Interior designated the Trona Pinnacles as a *National Natural Landmark*.

As you wander around the pinnacles, notice the predominate plant. It is Desert holly, *Atriplex hymenelytra*, a very salt tolerant plant. It will grow and flourish in soils much too salty for many other species. Take a close look at its leaves to appreciate where it got its name. The plant also produces a bright red berry-like flower that gives it all the more holly-like appearance.

The BLM permits people to drive around the pinnacles. Camping is also permitted, although there are no facilities (pack your trash out). Hollywood has discovered the area, too. A minute or so of *Star Trek V* was filmed here, and more recently, the Walt Disney Studios chose the Trona Pinnacles as a set for their blockbuster hit *Dinosaur*. Unfortunately one stagehand was electrocuted here on location during the filming.

While this strange underwater stalagmite phenomenon has been observed a few other places in the world, nowhere can it be seen easier than here near Trona.

Those Curious Pinnacles

Our SUV is dwarfed by the giant pinnacles

Appendix A

A Glossary of Geologic and Mining Terms Used in the Text

Adit: a horizontal tunnel.
Alluvial Fan: the cone-shaped deposit of sand and gravel washed out of a canyon.
Andesite: a brown, reddish, or gray volcanic rock with a mineral composition equivalent to granite.
Arkostic: having a significant amount of feldspar.
Arrastra: a crude animal-powered device in which gold ore is crushed.
Ash: very fine rock particles thrown out by explosive volcanic eruptions.
Bajada: the slope of sand and gravel where two or more alluvial fans have coalesced.
Basalt: a hard black volcanic rock, sometimes containing gas bubble holes.
Batholith: a large mass of igneous rocks still deep within the earth.
Bedrock: solid rock exposed at the surface of the ground.
Breccia: angular fragments of volcanic rock held together by finer material.
Bunker: a hopper-like structure in which ore is stored while awaiting transport or processing.
Cinder Cone: the accumulated pile of ash and cinder at the mouth of a volcano.
Collar: the rim surrounding the top of a shaft.
Conglomerate: a sedimentary formation of various rocks having a wide variety of particle size and shape.
Dacite: a light colored volcanic rock high in quartz (silica) and feldspar.
Dike: an intrusion of molten igneous rock into a crack or joint.
Dolomite: a metamorphic form of limestone, containing magnesium carbonate and calcium carbonate.
Epoch: a unit of geologic time within a "period" (example: the Pleistocene epoch of the Quaternary period of the Cenozoic era).
Era: the largest subdivision of geologic time (example: Mesozoic era).
Fanglomerate: conglomerate deposited and cemented together, as in an alluvial fan.
Fault: a crack in the earth's surface with one side moving in relation to the other side.
Feldspar: a very common rock-forming mineral containing silica and aluminum oxides.
Galena: lead sulfide, a common ore of lead.

Glaciation: the formation and movement of ice masses.
Glory hole: a pocket of very rich ore.
Gneiss: a very hard, often banded metamorphic rock.
Granite: a coarse-grained igneous rock containing quartz, feldspar and mica as the principal minerals.
Granodiorite: an igneous rock of similar composition as granite, except it contains more plagioclase feldspar than granite.
Headframe: the structure over a shaft, which supports a pulley, used to hoist ore buckets.
Hornfels: a dense metamorphic rock, often formed when slate (another metamorphic rock) has come in contact with hot igneous rocks such as granite.
Ice Age: a long period of cold climate, where snowfalls on the land accumulated vast areas of ice because precipitation exceeded melting. Ice ages have occurred as early as the Precambrian and as recently as the Holocene epochs.
Igneous rock: molten rocks formed deep within the earth that have been forced to the surface.
Iron pyrite: a crystalline form of iron sulfide, sometimes called "Fools Gold" which can be mistaken for gold by the untrained.
Lagging: Smaller cross-timbers supported by stulls.
Lava: magma that comes to the earth's surface by volcanic action.
Limestone: sedimentary rock of calcium carbonate formed in the sea bottom by the accumulation of shells and other organisms.
Lode: a vein or deposit of valuable minerals in solid rock.
Magma: deep-seated molten rock.
Marine Terrace: a flattened natural terrace on a hillside originally formed by wave action on the shoreline.
Metamorphism: the alteration of older igneous or sedimentary rocks by great heat, pressure, or chemical changes, resulting in the changing of the original rock into something different.
Metasediments: sedimentary rocks that have been subjected to great heat and pressure causing them to become metamorphic rocks. Their original sedimentary composition may no longer be recognized.
Mica: a group of minerals characterized by their separation into thin, shiny plates or flakes.
Mine: a place where a mineral commodity has been extracted and processed for its economic value.
Mining claim: The mining law of 1872 permits a person who finds valuable minerals on Federal land to claim the right to mine it. Each lode claim measures 1500' long by 600' wide. Each placer claim covers 20 acres. Multiple claims are permitted. Improvements must be performed annually. In recent years more

restrictions have been imposed on the staking of mining claims.
Monzonite: a granite-like igneous rock rich in both plagioclase and orthoclase feldspar and ferro-magnesium minerals, but having little quartz.
Obsidian: a black volcanic glass that has formed by very rapid cooling of volcanic lava.
Orebody: a sufficient concentration of valuable minerals to warrant the expense of mining.
Quartz: a common rock-forming mineral of silicon dioxide often found in a crystalline state.
Quartzite: a metamorphic form of sandstone.
Quartz latite: a volcanic rock rich in feldspar and quartz.
Quartz monzonite: a granite-like rock, except it is rich in quartz as well as the feldspars.
Patented Claim: a mining claim of sufficient value that a legal process has been gone through which gives the owner not only mineral rights, but ownership of the land with all rights of use.
Period: a unit of geologic time within an era (example: Jurassic period of the Mesozoic era).
Placer: sand or gravel deposits containing gold or other valuable minerals.
Playa: a flat dry lakebed in an enclosed desert basin.
Pluvial: caused by the action of heavy rains.
Pluton: a mass of deep-seated igneous rock that intrudes the crust of the earth and slowly cools.
Potassium-argon dating: a method of dating rocks based on the decay of the potassium-40 isotope to argon-40.
Prospect: a place where an economically valuable mineral has been found, and explored for; however, no mining has (yet) taken place.
Pumice: a light-colored, lightweight frothy volcanic rock, often having enough air holes in it to permit it to float.
Pyroclastic: rock fragments formed by a volcanic explosion.
Rhyolite: a volcanic rock similar in mineral composition to granite.
Richter scale: a system for measuring the intensity of earthquakes. It is a log-rhythmic scale, meaning each numerical increase represents a tenfold increase of intensity.
Schist: a metamorphic rock, rich in mica that easily splits into plates or flakes.
Sedimentary rock: rocks formed by the accumulation of rock or organic material in the sea bottom or on top of the ground.
Seismic: earthquakes or man-made vibrations of the earth.
Stope: an underground opening above a tunnel from which ore is extracted.
Stull: large timber in a tunnel which supports the rock, thus preventing a

cave-in.
Sulfide: the presence of sulfur, chemically bonded with other (metallic) minerals.
Tactite: a contact metamorphosed calcareous rock.
Tailings: A pile of waste rock at a mile tunnel or shaft. May also be finely ground ore left over after the milling process has extracted the valuable minerals.
Talc: a very soft, white mineral found in zones of some metamorphic rock.
Trilobite: a primitive and long extinct marine animal that lived on the bottom of Paleozoic seas.
Tuff: a rock formed from compacted volcanic ash.
Unconformity: a surface of erosion representing a gap in time between the older rocks below and the younger rocks above.
Vein: any mineral deposit that has filled a fissure or fracture. A relatively few contain valuable minerals, but most do not.
Volcanic ash: fine rock material ejected from a volcano.
Wave cut bench: see Marine Terrace.

Appendix B
Geologic Time Chart

Era	Period	Epoch	Million years ago
Cenozoic	Quarternary	Holocene	
		Pleistocene	2-3
			12
	Tertiary	Pliocene	
		Miocene	26
		Oligocene	37-38
		Eocene	53-54
		Paleocene	
			65
Mesozoic	Cretaceous		
			136
	Jurassic		
			190-195
	Triassic		
			225
Paleozoic	Permian		
			280
	Pennsylvanian		
			310
	Mississippian		
			345
	Devonian		
			395
	Silurian		
			435
	Ordovician		
			500
	Cambrian		
			570
Proterozoic	Keweenawan		
	Huronian		1,000
Archeozoic	Timiskaming		
	Keewatin		1,800

Appendix C
The Plio-Pleistocene Ice Age

Epoch (Present Time)	Sierra Nevada Phase	Years Ago	Significance
	Matthes	700 to present	
Holocene	Recess Peak	2000 to 2600	Bow & arrow replaces atlatl. Grinding stones first used. Pottery introduced. All desert lakes are now mostly dry.
Neoglacial		6,000	Ubehebe Crater blows it's top
	Hilgard	9000 to 10,500	Earliest human artifacts found in Death and Panamint Valleys.
		15,000	High water in Lakes China, Searles Panamint, Manly & Rogers. Lake Hill was a large island. Most Trona Pinnacles were formed.
	Tioga	20,000	Maximum ice in the Sierra.
Wisconsin	Tenaya	45,000	Maximum ice in the Sierra.
Pleistocene	Tahoe	75,000	Greatest known water depths in inland lakes. China & Searles were joined together. Lake Hill was a small island. Water poured down Wingate Wash into Lake Manly.
Illinoian	Mono Basin	130,000	
Kansan	Casa Diablo	400,000	Maximum ice in Sierra.
Nebraskan	Sherwin	700,000	Lake Tecopa starts to dry up.
	McGee	2,600,000+	Continental glaciation begins in North America.
Late Pliocene	Deadman Pass	2,700,000 to 3,100,000	Oldest known Plio-Pliestocene glaciation in California.

Appendix D

Ice Age Lakes in the Death Valley Area
(after Snyder, Hardman and Zdenck, 1964)

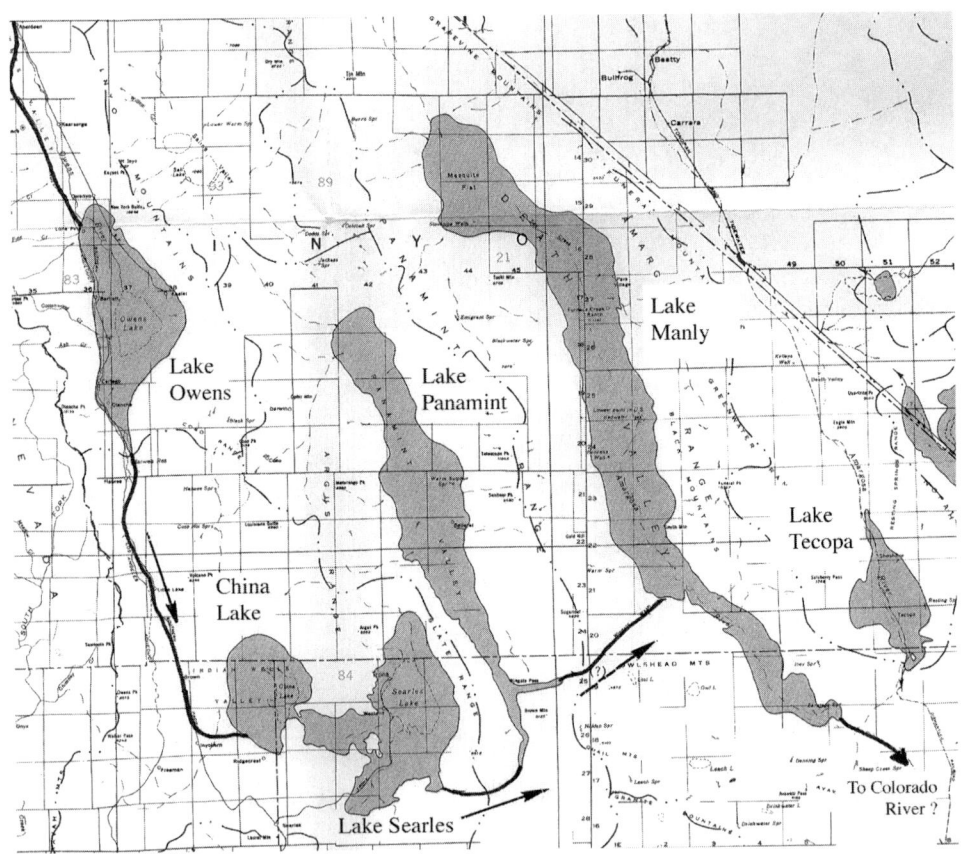

Appendix E
Early Man in the Death Valley Area

Years Ago	Time Period Name	Artifacts Found	Place Found
Present day	**Historic**		
1769			
500	*Saratoga Spring Culture*	pottery, clay figurines	Saratoga Spring
1100	Death Valley IV	pottery, fine arrowheads grinding stones pictographs & petroglyphs	sand dunes salt pans Greenwater Canyon
	Pacific		
2,000	Death Valley III	metates, manos shell beads clay figurines bows & arrows house rings petroglyphs	Amargosa River sand dunes many places
4000			
5,000	Mesquite Flat Culture	stone circles grinding stones	
	Death Valley II	fluted points	gravel terraces
	Archaic	Fluted points, scrapers	Death Valley Lake Panamint China Lake
	Pinto Basin Tradition	Fluted points, house rings rock scrapers	Little Lake Lake Manly
	Lake Mohave Tradition		Lake Manly
9,000	*Nevares Spring Culture*	scrapers, choppers	Lake Manly
	San Dieguito Tradition		Death Valley?
11,000			
	Paleo-Indian	Fluted points stone scrapers	Lake Manly Lake Panamint China Lake Owens Lake
	Death Valley I	Atlal points, house rings stone scrapers spear points	Lake Manly Lake Rogers Lake Mohave
30,000? 40,000? 50,000?		Crude stone Scrapers?	Calico site?

Appendix F

Strange Happenings in Goler Wash

During the early morning hours of August 9, 1969, five people including Folger's Coffee heiress, Abigail Folger, and the very pregnant actress, Sharon Tate, were viciously murdered at a residence in the posh Benedict Canyon section of Los Angeles. Thus began a bizarre series of events that would involve dozens of people, and hundreds of crimes, drawing national attention to Goler Wash, a previously unheard of and forgotten corner of Death Valley. Within three months, the name Charles Manson was known worldwide.

Charles Manson's downfall started on September 9, 1969, with his senseless vandalizing of a National Park Service front end loader that was parked near the Race Track. This really upset the rangers, particularly one Dick Powell. A group of hippies in a red Toyota and a dune buggy had been seen in the vicinity. A couple of weeks later Powell spotted a red Toyota in Panamint Valley, complete with a band of hippies in it. By this time Powell was aware of a group of squatters living at Myers and Barker Ranches in upper Goler Wash. On September 29th, he and Jim Pursell, a CHP officer out of Bishop, made a friendly call at the Barker Ranch. Ultimately they found nine young women in their late teens and early twenties, and, very carefully camouflaged, the red Toyota and a dune buggy. No arrests were made at that time, but checks later revealed both vehicles had been stolen.

Early on the morning of October 9th, Ranger Powell and Officer Pursell returned to the Barker Ranch. This time they brought some friends with them: a small army of Park Service rangers, CHP officers, Inyo County Sheriff deputies, and even a state game warden. A pre-dawn sweep of the two ranches netted three males, ten females and two infants, along with various weapons. All were transported to Independence and booked into the Inyo County Jail on a variety of charges.

Even though thirteen members of this band had been arrested, it was thought that there were still more out there. Three days later the ranches were raided again, this time in the late afternoon. By this time Powell and Purcell were very familiar with the area and went ahead of the main force to reconnoiter. They observed four males entering the Barker Ranch house. In a lightning raid, the hippie-hunting duo burst through the door with guns drawn and arrested the four men plus three females. Still, the group's leader was not among those taken into custody.

After this second group had been cuffed and moved down canyon, Officer Pursell checked the house once again. In the darkness, he reached in a cabinet under the bathroom sink, and upon feeling a mass of greasy hair, he pulled on it.

Out tumbled Charlie Manson, the group's leader. The raid of October 12th had netted ten more suspects. The Inyo County Jail in Independence was filling up.

Conversations among some of the arrested women, overheard by deputies, suggested that some of those being held in jail might have had something to do with the murders in Los Angeles. The Inyo County Sheriff then tipped off the Los Angeles Police Department. The telephone lines between Independence and Los Angeles began smoking as officers of the two agencies began comparing notes and putting the pieces together.

Between July 27th and August 26th, Charles Manson and his gang of misfits butchered at least nine people. Gang member, Sandra Good, once bragged that the total number of murders committed by Manson's group was 35-40. That may be correct. Manson himself bragged of killing 35 people. After detective work put Manson at the Tate-LaBianca crime scene, Charles Manson was charged with the Tate-LaBianca murders on December 9, 1969. Inyo County gladly released Charlie to the Los Angeles authorities.

The same Thanksgiving weekend that the Los Angeles Police Department and the Inyo County Sheriff Department were finding they had a mutual interest in Charles Manson, some backcountry friends, Herbie and Jane Horne, Tom and Diana Jones, and Bob Boyd, and I decided to visit Barker Ranch ourselves, to check out first hand the strange doings in Goler Wash. By this time Inyo County District Attorney Frank Fowles, his Deputy Buck Gibbens and investigator Jack Gardner along with five LAPD sergeants and Los Angeles Deputy District Attorney Vincent Bugliosi had been in there to search the place thoroughly. Surely all the useful evidence had been found and our presence would cause no harm.

Nevertheless, on a hillside near the ranch house, half under a bush, but in plain sight, Herbie found a large metal can containing a marijuana pipe and a jar in which there appeared to be marijuana seed. So much for the DA's thorough search! We left the evidence where we found it, and notified the proper authorities.

On June 15, 1970, Charles Manson, Patricia Krenwinkel, Leslie Van Houton, and Susan Atkins, were all put on trial for the Tate-LaBianca murders. On March 29, 1971, the jury came in with a guilty verdict against all four defendants. The sentence was death, but later, in 1972, the death penalty was ruled to be unconstitutional by a very liberal California Supreme Court under Chief Justice Rose Bird. The quartet is still incarcerated in prison. Charles Manson has had nine parole hearings since 1978, and the next one is scheduled for the year 2002. Will Charlie ever be released? If that should ever happen, will Manson ever return to Goler Wash? Only time will tell. In the meanwhile, he still resides in Cocoran State Prison in the San Joaquin Valley.

If you want to check on Charlie's current status, one of his "family" members, Sandra Good, maintains a Charles Manson web page. You can access it at http://www.ATWA.Com. Be prepared for some weird stuff.

Herb Horne points to a can containing drug paraphenalia halfway hidden beneath a bush

Appendix G
Common Wildflowers You May Encounter

Common Name	Scientific Name	Places Seen
Predominately Yellowish		
Lesser Mohavea	*Mohavea breviflora*	Gold Bottom Mine
Panamint Daisy	*Enceiliopsis agrophylla*	anywhere from Goler Wash to Jail Canyon
Coreopsis	*Coreopsis calliopsidea*	Common: Ibex, Argus & Funeral Mtns
Bladderpod	*Isomeris arborea*	Very common: floor of Death & Panamint Valleys
Heart-leaved Primrose	*Oenothera cardiophylla*	Argus & Panamint Mtns, Slate Range
Desert Trumpet	*Eriogonum inflatum*	Common everywhere below 6,000 feet
Stinkweed	*Cleomella obtusifola*	Alkaline flats of Searles, Panamint & Saline Valleys
Rock-Pea, Desert Deerweed	*Lotus rigidus*	Panamint, Saline & Eureka Valleys
Goldenhead	*Acamptopappus sphaerocephalus*	Saline Valley, Darwin Canyon
Rabbitbrush	*Chrysothammus nauseosus*	Common everywhere
Burroweed	*Franseria dumosa*	Common: it grows anywhere mesquite does
Predominately Creme or Whitish		
Desert Daisy	*Erigeron pumilus*	Hunter Mountain
Evening Primrose	*Oenothera caespitosa*	Common: Argus, Panamint, Black & Funeral Mtns.
Verbena	*Verbena goodingii*	Common: Grapevine, Black & Panamint Mtns.
Wild Buckwheat	*Erogonum*	Very common, found everywhere, many sub-species
Desert Holly	*Atriplex hymenelytra*	Common near salt flats, Searles & Death Valleys
Pickleweed	*Allenrolfea occidentalis*	Another common salt flat inhabitant
Predominately Pinkish or Reddish		
Indian Paint Brush	*Castilleja chromosa*	Common: Echo, Cottonwood &, Darwin Canyons
Scarlet Locoweed	*Astragalus coccineus*	Panamint, Argus, Black, & Grapevine Mtns

True Phlox	*Phlox stansburyi*	Hunter Mountain
Arizona Lupine	*Lupinus arizonicus*	Panamint, Saline & Eureka Valleys
Sand Verbena	*Boerhaavia annulata*	Panamint & Death Valleys

Predominately Bluish or Purple

Gilia	*Gilia cana triceps*	Panamint & Hunter Mtns.
Wild Heliotrope	*Phacelia crenulata*	Common: Panamint & Death Valleys
Thisle Sage	*Salvia carduacea*	Panamint, Searles, Saline, & Eureka Valleys
Bladder Sage	*Salazaria mexicana*	Panamint, Searles, Saline & Eureka Valleys
Desert Aster	*Machaeranthera tortifolia*	Panamint, Searles, Saline & Eureka Valleys
Indigo Bush	*Dalea fremontii*	Panamint, Saline & Death Valleys
Eriastrum	*Eriastrum eremicum*	Panamint, Saline & Death Valleys

Appendix H
Standard Checklist of items that should be in every SUV at all times

Documents

Current vehicle registration (required by State law)
Proof of current liability insurance (required by State law)
Campfire permit (free, obtain one annually)
Map of the specific area you are in, the more detailed the better.
Shop manual for vehicle involved

Personal Safety & Comfort Items

First Aid Kit (the bigger the better)
Extra medications used by anyone present
Water, 2 gallons per person
Pot, cooking, small
Canteens, with carrying case, 2 minimum
Lightweight day or fanny pack
Extra food (sealed MRE's are good for emergencies)
Warm clothing, jacket & hat for all
Compact disposable space blanket, 1 per person
Work gloves, 1 pair minimum
Flashlights, 2 minimum, with fresh or extra batteries
Citizens Band radio, or better yet, 2 meter radio transceiver
Compass
Swiss Army knife or equivalent (with can opener)
Fire extinguisher
Plastic tube tent
Matches (in waterproof container)
Whistle, shrill, emergency signaling
Toilet paper roll
Female sanitary pads, 2 each (can double as trauma dressings)
Notebook, small, with lead pencil
Highway flares, 2 minimum
Sun screen
Insect repellent
Poncho, 1 minimum
Tarp, plastic, small or medium size
Bucket, canvas, collapsible, (a required item in some National Forests)

Extrication Equipment

Shovel, folding GI type, or preferably long handle (required item in some National Forests)
Nylon tow strap
Hi-Lift jack
Hydraulic jack, 4 ton
Come-along, 4 ton rating (minimum)
Tire chains (may be a seasonal item)
Hatchet, or preferably, full size ax
Saw, small

Automotive Tools

Socket set, SAE & metric, recommended
Spark plug socket for above
Open end wrench set, SAE & metric
Crescent wrench set, 3 sizes recommended
Screwdriver set, slot and Phillips
Pliers assortment
Wire cutters
Hammer
Battery post & terminal cleaner
Battery jumper cables
Hack saw with extra blades
Lug wrench
Mini-air compressor
Small funnel
Tire pressure gauge

Spare Automotive Parts

Spark plugs, 2 minimum
Spark plug wire material
Coil
Points set with condenser
Brake fluid, 1 pint
Power steering fluid, 1 pint
Motor Oil, 2 quarts minimum
ATF Fluid, 1 quart
Oil filter
Fuse assortment
Fan belts of appropriate sizes
Tire boot & inner tube
Hose bandage tape

Field Expedient Supplies

Duct tape, 1 roll
Electrical tape, 1 roll
Bailing wire, 1 roll
Electrical wire, 1 small roll, 16 gauge
Sealant, radiator (Stop Leak)
Gasket sealant
Tube, siphon, 5' minimum
Cord, nylon, 50' minimum
Hand Cleaner (waterless)
Paper towel roll
Plastic trash sack

Optional Non-Esstential Items which are nice to have along

Camera with film
Binoculars
Glass cleaner
Bar soap, small
Plastic bags, small, resealable
NOAA Weather radio receiver
GPS receiver
Spare fuel container with spout
Cellular telephone
Family radio service transceivers, one pair

Appendix I
Some Useful Addresses

Superintendent's Office
Death Valley National Park
Death Valley CA 92328
(760) 786-2331
(760) 786-2330 (after hours emergency, other than 911)

Death Valley National Park
Beatty Information Office
Main Street
Beatty NV 89003
(775)553-2200

Death Valley National Park
Shoshone Information Office
Shoshone CA 92384
(760) 852-4308

Bureau of Land Management
Ridgecrest Resource Area
300 So. Richmond Road
Ridgecrest, CA 93555
(760) 384-5400

Bureau of Land Management
Bishop Field Office
785 No. Main Street
Bishop CA 93514
(760) 872-4881

Bureau of Land Management (Nevada areas surrounding the Park))
1553 So. Main Street
P. O. Box 911
Tonopah NV 89049
(775) 482-7800

Eastern California Museum
155 No. Grant Street
(P.O. Box 206)
Independence CA 93526
(760) 878-0258

Maturango Museum
100 E. Las Flores Ave.
Ridgecrest CA 93555
(760) 375-6900

Death Valley Natural History Association
P.O. Box 188
Death Valley CA 92328
(760) 786-3285

Searles Valley Historical Society
P.O. Box 630
Trona CA 93592
(760) 372-4800, 372-5230, or 372-5064

Historical Society of the Upper Mojave Desert
100 E. Las Flores Ave.
Ridgecrest CA 93555
(760) 375-6900

Beatty Chamber of Commerce
P.O. Box 956
Beatty NV 89003
(775) 553-2424

Death Valley Chamber of Commerce
Highway 127
Shoshone CA 92384
(760) 852-4524

Lone Pine Chamber of Commerce
126 So. Main Street
Lone Pine CA 93545
(760) 876-4444

Big Pine Chamber of Commerce
126 So. Main Street
(P.O. Box 23)
Big Pine, CA   93515
(760) 938-2114

References

Alltucker, Ken, "Nevada Mining Feels Pain from Gold's Global Decline", Reno Nevada: *Reno Gazette-Journal*, September 26, 1999.

Anon, *Death Valley*, Boston and New York: American Guide Series, Houghton Mifflin Co., 1939.

_____, "Geologic Map of California", *Death Valley Sheet*, San Francisco CA: California Division of Mines, 1958.

_____, "Geologic Map of California", *Mariposa Sheet*, Sacramento CA: California Division of Mines and Geology, 1967.

_____, *Romantic Heritage of Inyo-Mono*, California Interstate Telephone Company, 1966.

_____, "California Fossil Discovery Reveals New Species of Camel", *California Geology*, Sacramento CA: California Division of Mines and Geology, January and February 2000.

Albers, J.P, and J.H. Stewart, *Geology and Mineral Deposits of Esmeralda County, Nevada*, Reno NV: Nevada Bureau of Mines and Geology Bulletin 78, Mackay School of Mines, University Of Nevada, 1972.

Ashbaugh, Don, *Nevada's Turbulent Yesterday*, Los Angeles: Westernlore Press, 1963.

Bailey, Edgar H. (Editor), *Geology of Northern California*, San Francisco: California Division of Mines and Geology Bulletin 190, 1996.

Belden, L. Burr, *Mines of Death Valley*, Glendale: La Siesta Press, 1966.

_____, *Old Stovepipe Wells*, San Bernardino CA: Death Valley '49er Keepsake Publication #8, Inland Printing & Engraving Co., 1968.

Betancourt, J.L., with T.R. Van Devender and P.S. Martin (eds.), *Packrat Middens: The Last 40,000 Years of Biotic Change*, Tucson AZ: University of Arizona Press, 1990.

Billeb, Emil W., *Mining Camp Days*, Berkeley: Howell-North Books, 1968.

Blanc, Robert P. and George B. Cleveland, "Pleistocene Lakes of Southern California" (Parts I & II), *Mineral Information Service*, San Francisco: California Division of Mines, April and May 1961.

Brandt, Roger G., *Titus Canyon Road Guide, A Tour Through Time*, Death Valley: Death Valley Natural History Association, 1992.

Brott, Clark W., Daniel F. McCarthy, Kathlyn Obendorfer-McGraw, and Mary Obendorfer, *Archaeology in Panamint Dunes, 1983*, Ridgecrest CA: prepared under contract for Bureau of Land Management, 1984.

Bryan, T. Scott, and Betty Tucker-Bryan, *The Explorer's Guide to Death Valley National Park*, Niwot CO: University Press of Colorado, 1995.

Bugliosi, Vincent, and Curt Gentry, *Helter Skelter*, Toronto, New York, London: Bantam Books, 1974.

Burchfiel, B. Clark, *Geology of the Dry Mountain Quadrangle, Inyo County, California*, San Francisco: California Division of Mines and Geology Special Report 99, 1969.

Caruthers, William, *Loafing Along Death Valley Trails*, Pomona CA: P.B. Press Inc., 1951.

Clark, William B., *Gold Districts of California*, Sacramento CA: California Division of Mines and Geology Bulletin 193, 1970.

Clements, Lydia, *Death Valley Indians*, Los Angeles: Hollycrofters, 1954.

Clements, Thomas, *Geological Story of Death Valley*, Palm Desert CA: Death Valley '49ers, Inc. Publication No. 1, Desert Magazine Press, 1954.

Chalfant, W.A., *Death Valley : The Facts*, Stanford CA: Stanford University Press, 1936.

_____, *The Story of Inyo*, Bishop CA: Piñon Book Store, 1933.

_____, *Gold Guns & Ghost Towns*, Stanford CA: Stanford University Press, 1947.

Chartkoff, Joseph L. and Kerry Kona Chartkoff, *The Archeology of California*, Stanford CA: Stanford University Press, 1984.

Cronkhite, Daniel, *Death Valley's Victims*, Morongo Valley CA: Sagebrush Press, 1981.
Crowe, Richard D., "Sourdough Pancakes and Fried Burro Liver", *Proceedings Fourth Death Valley Conference On History and Prehistory*, Jean Johnson, editor, Death Valley CA: Death Valley Natural History Association, 1996.
Davis, Emma Lou, and Christopher Raven, editors, *Environmental and Paleoenvironmental Studies in Panamint Valley*, San Diego: Great Basin Foundation, 1986.
DeDecker, Mary, "The Search For The Bullfrog Wild Pea", *Proceedings First Death Valley Conference On History & Prehistory*, Richard Lingenfelter & James Pisarowicz, editors, Death Valley CA: Death Valley Natural History Association, 1991.
Digonnet, Michel, *Hiking Death Valley*, Palo Alto CA: privately published, 1997.
Downs, Theodore, *Fossil Vertebrates of Southern California*, Berkeley and Los Angeles: University of California Press, 1968.
Elias, Scott A., *The Ice-Age History of Southwestern National Parks*, Washington and London: Smithsonian Institution Press, 1997.
Elliott, Russell, R., *Nevada's 20th Century Mining Boom*, Reno NV: University of Nevada Press, 1966.
Evans, James R., and Gary C. Taylor, John S. Rapp, *Mines and Mineral Deposits in Death Valley National Monument, California*, Sacramento CA: California Division of Mines and Geology Special Report 125, 1976.
Gath, Eldon, "Quarternary Lakes of the Owens River System", *Geology And Mineral Wealth Of The Owens Valley Region*, Santa Ana CA: South Coast Geological Society, 1987.
Goodwin, J. Grant, *Lead and Zinc in California*, San Francisco CA: California Division of Mines Volume 53, 1957.
Grant, Campbell, et.al., *Rock Drawings of the Coso Range, Inyo County, California*, Ridgecrest CA: Maturango Museum Publication No. 4, Maturango Press, 1968.
Grayson, Donald K., *The Desert's Past, A Natural History of the Great Basin*, Washington & London: Smithsonian Institution Press, 1993.
Greene, Linda W., *Historic Resource Study, A History of Mining in Death Valley National Monument*, Denver CO: Parts 1 and 2 of Volume I, National Park Service, Western Service Center, March 1981.
Gudde, Erwin G., *1000 California Place Names*, Los Angeles and Berkeley: University of California Press, Second Revised edition, 1959.
_____, *California Gold Camps*, Berkeley & Los Angeles CA: University of California Press, 1975.
Hall, Clarence A., editor, *Natural History of the White-Inyo Range Eastern California*, Berkeley, Los Angeles, & Oxford: University of California Press, 1991.
Hall, Wayne E., with E.M. MacKevett, *Economic Geology of the Darwin Quadrangle, Inyo County, California*, San Francisco CA: California Division of Mines Special Report 5, 1958.
Hall, Wayne E. and Hal G. Stephens, *Economic Geology of the Panamint Butte Quadrangle and Modoc District, Inyo County, California*, San Francisco CA: California Division of Mines and Geology Special Report 73, 1963.
Hall, Wayne E., *Geology of the Panamint Butte Quadrangle, Inyo County, California*, Washington DC: Geological Survey Bulletin 1299, U.S. Geological Survey, 1971.
Henderson, Randall, *On Desert Trails*, Los Angeles CA: Westernlore Press, 1961.
Henry, Donald J., *California Gem Trails*, Long Beach CA: Lowell R. Gordon, 1957.
Hubbard, Paul B., et.al., *Ballarat*, Lancaster CA: published by the author, 1965.

Hunt, Charles B., *Plant Ecology of Death Valley California*, Washington DC: Geological Survey Professional Paper 509, U.S. Geological Survey, 1966.
_____, *Death Valley: Geology, Ecology, Archaeology*, Berkeley, Los Angeles, London: University of California Press, 1975.
Jaeger, Edmund C., *The California Deserts*, Stanford CA: Stanford University Press, Revised Edition, 1938.
_____, *The North American Deserts*, Stanford CA: Stanford University Press, 1957.
_____, "River of Bitter Waters", *Desert Magazine*, Palm Desert CA: Desert Press, Inc., July, 1958.
_____, *A Naturalist's Death Valley*, Bishop CA: Death Valley '49ers Publication No. 5, (Revised Edition) Chalfant Press, 1979.
Jahns, Richard H., editor, *Geology of Southern California*, San Francisco CA: California Division of Mines Bulletin 170, 1954.
Johnson, Leroy and Jean, *Escape From Death Valley*, Reno & Las Vegas: University of Nevada Press, 1987.
_____, "The Bennett-Arcan Long Camp and Manly's Sulphur Water Well", *Proceedings First Death Valley Conference on History & Prehistory*, Death Valley CA: Death Valley Natural History Association, 1991.
Kirk, Ruth, *Exploring Death Valley*, Stanford CA: Stanford University Press, 1965.
Kohler-Antablin, Susan, "California Non-Fuel Minerals – 1998", *California Geology*, Sacramento CA: California Division of Mines and Geology, September/October 1999.
Lanner, Robert M., *The Pinyon Pine, A Natural and Cultural History*, Reno NV: University of Nevada Press, 1981.
Larson, Peggy, and Lane Larson, *A Sierra Club Naturalist's Guide to the Deserts of the Southwest*, San Francisco CA: Sierra Club Books, 1977.
Latschar, John A., Historic Resource Study, *A History of Mining in Death Valley National Monument*, Denver CO: Parts 1 and 2 of Vol. II, National Park Service, Denver Service Center, 1983.
Leigh, Rufus Wood, *Nevada Place Names*, Salt Lake City UT: Deseret News Press, 1964.
Lingenfelter, Richard E., *Death Valley & The Amargosa*, Berkeley and Los Angeles: University of California Press, 1986.
Likes, Robert C. and Glenn R. Day, *From This Mountain - Cerro Gordo*, Bishop CA: Chalfant Press, 1975.
Lofinck, Sewell "Pop", *Mojave Desert Ramblings*, China Lake CA: Maturango Museum Publication 2, Maturango Press, November 1966.
Long, Margaret, *The Shadow of the Arrow*, Caldwell ID: Caxton Printers, 1950.
McAllister, James F., *Rocks and Structure of the Quartz Spring Area, Northern Panamint Range, California*, San Francisco CA: California Division of Mines Special Report 25, 1952.
_____, *Geology of the Mineral Deposits in the Ubehebe Peak Quadrangle, Inyo County, California*, San Francisco CA: California Division of Mines Special Report 42, 1955.
McKee, Edwin H., *Geology of the Magruder Mountain Area, Nevada-California*, Washington DC: Geological Survey Bulletin 1251-H, U.S. Geological Survey, 1968.
McWhorter, Frank, "True Greasewood Is Full Of Grease", *Desert Magazine*, Palm Desert CA: Desert Magazine, January 1978.
MacKevett, Edward M., *Geology of the Santa Rosa Lead Mine, Inyo County, California*, San Francisco CA: California Division of Mines Special Report 34, 1953.
Marcom, Geron, "An Introduction To Death Valley's Hidden Legacy", *Proceedings Fourth Death Valley Conference On History & Prehistory*, Jean Johnson, editor, Death Valley CA: Death Valley Natural History Association, 1996.

Maxson, John H., *Death Valley, Origin and Scenery*, Death Valley CA: Death Valley Natural History Association, 1963.
Merriam, Charles W., and Wayne E. Hall, *Pennsylvanian and Permian Rocks of the Southern Inyo Mountains, California*, Washington D.C: U.S. Geological Survey Bulletin 1061-A, U.S. Government Printing Office, 1957.
Merriam, C.W., *Geology of the Cerro Gordo Mining District, Inyo County, California*, Washington D.C: U.S. Geological Survey Professional Paper 408, U.S. Government Printing Office, 1963.
Miller, Julia M.G., *Geologic Map Of A Portion Of The Manly Peak Quadrangle, Southern Panamint Mountains, Inyo and San Bernardino Counties, California*, Sacramento, CA: California Division of Mines and Geology Open-File Report 85-9, 1985.
_____, "Tectonic Evolution of the Southern Panamint Range", *California Geology*, Sacramento CA: California Division of Mines and Geology, September 1987.
Mitchell, Roger, "Saga of Cerro Gordo", *Four Wheeler Magazine*, Tarzana CA: Ames Publishing Company, September 1965.
_____, "Exploring Cottonwood Canyon", *Desert Magazine*, Palm Desert CA: Desert Magazine, November 1967.
_____, "The Legend of Lookout", *Desert Magazine*, Palm Desert CA: Desert Magazine, April 1968.
_____, "Riddle of the Racetrack", *Desert Magazine*, Palm Desert CA: Desert Magazine, November 1968.
_____, "15 Backcountry Trips", *Desert Magazine*, Palm Desert CA: Desert Magazine, November 1969.
_____, *Death Valley Jeep Trails*, Glendale CA: La Siesta Press, 1969, revised edition 1975.
_____, *Inyo-Mono Jeep Trails*, Glendale CA: La Siesta Press, 1969.
_____, "Exploring the Saline Valley", *Desert Magazine*, Palm Desert CA: Desert Magazine, November 1971.
_____, *Western Nevada Jeep Trails*, Glendale CA: La Siesta Press, 1973.
Mordy, Brooke D. & Donald McCaughey, *Nevada Historical Sites*, Reno NV: University of Nevada, Desert Research Institute, 1968.
Morton, Paul K., *Geology of the Queen of Sheba Lead Mine, Death Valley, California*, San Francisco CA: California Division of Mines and Geology Special Report 88, 1965.
Munz, Philip A., *California Desert Wildflowers*, Berkeley and Los Angeles: University of California Press, 1962.
Myrick, David F., *Railroads of Nevada*, Berkeley CA: Volumes 1 & 2, Howell-North Books, 1962.
Nadeau, Remi, *City Makers*, Los Angeles CA: Trans-Anglo Books, 1965.
_____, *Ghost Towns and Mining Camps of California*, Los Angeles CA: Ward Ritchie Press, 1965.
_____, *The Silver Seekers*, Santa Barbara CA: Crest Publishers, 1999.
Norman, L.A. & Richard M. Stewart, *Mines and Mineral Resources of Inyo County*, San Francisco CA: California Division of Mines Volume 47 Number 1, January 1951.
Norwood, Richard H. and Charles S. Bull, *A Cultural Resource Overview of the Eureka, Saline, Panamint and Darwin Region, East Central California*, Riverside CA: prepared for California Desert Planning Staff, Eric W. Ritter, editor, under Bureau of Land Management contract, 1980.
Page, Ben M., *Talc Deposits of Steatite Grade, Inyo County, California*, San Francisco CA: California Division of Mines Special Report 8, 1951.

Paher, Stanley W., *Nevada Ghost Towns & Mining Camps*, Berkeley CA: Howell-North Books, 1970.
Pipkin, George C., *Pete Aguereberry, Death Valley Prospector & Gold Miner*, Trona CA: Second Edition, Murchison Publications, 1982.
Raven, Christopher, *Landscape Evolution and Human Geography in Panamint Valley*, San Diego CA: Contributions of the Great Basin Foundation Number 1, Great Basin Foundation, 1985.
Reed, Lester, *Old-Timers of Southeastern California*, Redlands CA: Citrograph Printing Co., 1967.
Rinehart, C. Dean, and Donald C. Ross, *Economic Geology of the Casa Diablo Mountain Quadrangle California*, San Francisco CA: California Division of Mines Special Report 48, 1956.
Romero, Miriam A., editor, with John M. Sully and Robert D. Smith, *Amargosa Canyon-Dumont Dunes Proposed Natural Area*, a report submitted to the Bureau of Land Management by the Pupfish Habitat Preservation Committee, 1972.
Ross, Donald C., *Geology of the Independence Quadrangle, Inyo County, California*, Washington D.C: U.S. Geological Survey Bulletin 1181-O, Government Printing Office, 1965.
Sadovich, Maryellen V., *Your Guide to Southern Nevada*, Carson City NV: Nevada Historical Society Guidebook Series, State Printing Office, 1976.
Schumacher, Genny, *Deepest Valley*, San Francisco CA: Sierra Club, Vail Ballou Press, Inc., 1963.
Sharp, Robert P., *Geology: Field Guide to Southern California*, Dubuque IA: Regional Geology Series, Wm. C. Brown Company, 1972.
Sharp, Robert P. and Allen F. Glazner, *Geology Underfoot in Death Valley and Owens Valley*, Missoula MT: Mountain Press Publishing Co., 1997.
Smith, George C., with Bennie W. Troxel, Clifford H. Gray, and Roland von Huene, *Geologic Reconnaissance of the Slate Range, San Bernardino and Inyo Counties California*, San Francisco CA: California Division of Mines and Geology Special Report 96, 1968.
Snyder, C.T., George Hardman, and F.F. Zdenek, *Pleistocene Lakes In The Great Basin*, Washington D.C: Misc. U.S. Geological Survey, Geologic Investigations Map I-416, 1964.
Stinson, Melvin C., *Geology of the Keeler 15' Quadrangle, Inyo County, California*, San Francisco CA: California Division of Mines and Geology Map Sheet 38, 1977.
Strong, Mary Francis, "Amargosa Gorge", *Desert Magazine*, Palm Desert CA: Desert Magazine, November 1975.
_____, *Desert Gem Trails*, Mentone CA: Gem Books, 1996.
Trexler, Dennis T., and Wilton N. Melhorn, "Singing and Booming Sand Dunes of California and Nevada", *California Geology*, Sacramento CA: Division of Mines and Geology, July 1986.
Troxel, Bennie W., editor, *Geologic Features, Death Valley, California*, Sacramento, CA: California Division of Mines and Geology Special Report 106, 1976.
Tuohy, Donald R., *Nevada's Prehistoric Heritage*, Carson City NV: Nevada State Museum Popular Series, 1965.
Vredenburgh, Larry M., "Reilly: The Well Preserved Ruins Of An 1880's Mining Camp", *Proceedings First Death Valley Conference On History & Prehistory*, Richard Lingenfelter & James Pisarowicz, editors, Death Valley CA: Death Valley Natural History Association, 1991.
Von Huene, Roland, *Fossil Mammals of the Indian Wells Valley Region and How to Collect Them*, Ridgecrest CA: Maturango Museum Publication #5, Maturango Press, 1971.

Wagner, David L., and Eugene Y. Hsu, *Reconnaissance Geologic Map of Parts of Wingate Wash, Quail Mountains, and The Manly Peak Quadrangles, Inyo and San Bernardino Counties, Southeastern California*, Sacramento CA: California Division of Mines and Geology, 1987.

Wallace, William J. and Edith, *Ancient Peoples and Cultures of Death Valley National Monument*, Ramona CA: Acoma Books, 1978.

Weight, Harold and Lucile, Rhyolite, *The Ghost City of Golden Dreams*, 4th Edition revised, Twentynine Palms CA: Calico Press, 1953.

Weight, Harold, *Twenty Mule Team Days in Death Valley*, Twentynine Palms CA: Calico Press, 1955.

_____, *Greenwater*, Twentynine Palms CA: Calico Press, 1969.

Wheelock, Walt, *Desert Peaks Guide, Part I*, Glendale CA: La Siesta Press, 1964.

_____, *Desert Peaks Guide, Part II*, Glendale CA: La Siesta Press, 1975.

Wilson, Neill C., *Silver Stampede*, New York: The Mcmillan Company, 1937.

Wright, Lauren A., and Bennie W. Troxel, *Geology of North Confidence Hills 15' Quadrangle, Inyo County, California*, Sacramento CA: California Division of Mines and Geology Map Sheet 34, 1984.

Yoshino, Kimi, "Manson returns to Corcoran prison after discipline", *The Fresno Bee*, Fresno CA: June 13, 1998.

Zanjani, Sally, "Jack Longstreet In The Death Valley Region", *Proceedings First Death Valley Conference On History & Prehistory*, Richard Lingenfelter & James Psarowicz, editors, Death Valley CA: Death Valley Natural History Association, 1991.

Index

A Mine of Her Own (book), 52
A-10 Warthog, 100
Aa (lava), 180
Abronia villosa, 136
Acamptopappus sphaerocephalus, 289
Adobe Valley, 268
Aguereberry, Pete, 270
Aguereberry Point, 11, 31, 34-35
Algae, 276
Allenrolfea occidentalis, 37, 289
Alvord, Charles, 54-55
Amargosa Borax Works, 168
Amargosa Canyon, 12, 145, 149-151
Amargosa Chaos, 131
Amargosa City, Nevada, 99
Amargosa Gorge, 148-149, 151
Amargosa River, 102, 127, 131, 146-147, 149
Amargosa Valley, 20, 113
Amateur radio, 140
American Potash and Chemical Company, 255, 268-269
Amhibole, 88
Ammonite fossils, 87
AMPOT (see American Potash & Chemical Corporation)
Anaconda Corporation, 195
Andy Hills, 87
Anglesite, 212
Anthony Mill, 252
Anthony Mine, 234
Anthony, Charles, 221, 234, 252
Antimony, 35
Anvil Spring, 54-55
Anvil Spring Canyon, 51, 244
Archeological Resources Preservation Act of 1979, 4, 7, 8
Area of Critical Concern, 193
Argus Range, 6, 210, 213, 216, 219, 252, 259, 262, 264
Argus Range Silver Mining Company, 252
Argus Range Wilderness, 220
Argus, California, 221, 229, 255
Arizona lupine, 290
Arondo Mine, 264-266, 270
Arrastra, 42, 53, 62, 219, 278
Arsenopyrite, 220
Artesian Road, 168
Asbestos, 88
Ash Hill, 210, 214

Ashford Canyon, 129, 131
Ashford, Harold, 131
Ashford, Henry, 131
Ashford, Louis, 131
Astragalus coccineus, 289
Astragalus lentiginous micans, 158
Atkins, Susan, 287
Atolia, California, 34
Atriplex hymenelytra, 22, 276, 289
Auguereberry, Pete, 55
Automobile Club of Southern California, 66, 79, 125
Avawatz Mountains, 142
Azurite, 27, 34
Badwater Road, 32, 45
Badwater, 193
Baker, California, 134, 158
Bakersfield, California, 257
Bakersfield Trail Blazers 4x4 Club, 229
Ballarat, California, 203, 221-224, 233-234, 240-241, 244
Bank Panic of 1875, 231
Bank Panic of 1907, 114-115, 119
Barchan dunes, 146
Barite, 199
Barker, Jim, 249
Barker, Kirk, 249
Barker Ranch, 246-247, 249-250, 286-287
Barrel cactus, 234, 239
Barrick Corporatiom, 112
Barstow, California, 115
Basin and Range Province, 94
Basketmaker Culture, 137
Bats, 66
Beatty, Nevada, 20, 26, 91-93, 102-104, 112-113, 153
Beaudry, Prudent, 258
Beaudry, Victor, 258
Beavertail cactus, 24, 45
Beetles, 158
Belden, Burr, 115
Bendire, Lt. Charles, 54
Benedict Canyon, 286
Bennett-Arcan Party, 41, 52, 54, 132
Bennett's Long Camp, 40
Beveridge Canyon, 167-168
Beveridge, California, 167
Big Bell Mine, 116
Big Dune, 118

Index

Big Four Mine, 12, 185, 188-189
Big Pine, California, 84, 153-156, 163-164, 175, 181, 199, 208
Big Silver Mine, 169
Big Talc Mine, 51-52
Bighorn sheep, 109, 127-128, 242
Billie Borax Mine, 5, 26
Bi-Mettalic Mine, 102
Bird, Rose, 287
Birney, Fred, 27
Bishop, California, 140, 154, 181, 237
Black Mountains, 25, 30, 125-127, 130-131
Bladder sage, 290
Bladderpod, 289
Blazing star, 270
BLM Desert District Office, 9
BLM Ridgecrest Resource Office, 3, 6, 9, 295
BLM Tonopah Office, 6, 77, 295
Blue Monster Mine, 166
Blue sage, 172, 201
Blythe, California, 67
Bodie, 195, 213
Boerhaavia annulata, 290
Bonanza King Formation, 33, 59, 158, 179
Bonanza, Nevada, 99
Bonnie Claire playa, 206
Bonny Mine, 45, 134
Borax, 41, 71, 168
Borden, Alexander Shorty, 37
Bornite, 34
Boyd, Bob, 287
Brachiopod fossils, 33-34
Briggs' Camp, 239, 241-242
Briggs, Harry, 241
Bristlecone pine, 164
Britt, Henry, 62
Broom, 244
Brown, Charles, 30
Bruce Canyon, 265
Bryan, Scott, 142
Bugliosi, Vincent, 287
Bullfrog Goldfield Railroad, 26, 29, 91
Bullfrog Mine, 91, 98, 106, 112,
Bullfrog Mining District, 91
Bullfrog, Nevada, 25, 37, 91, 99, 102, 112
Bullion Road, 258
Bungalette City, 57
Bunker Hill Mine, 166
Burchard, H.C., 174, 199

Burchfiel, B. Clark, 180
Burgess Mine, 167
Burro Spring, 88
Burros (feral), 69, 73, 87, 170-173, 179, 184, 220
Burroweed, 289
Butte Valley, 50-51, 53, 244
C.R. Briggs Corporation, 241
C.R. Briggs Mine, 247
Cal Tech radio telescopes, 156, 164
Calcite, 199
Calico, California, 8, 213
California Department of Fish & Game, 87, 169, 265
California Desert Protection Act, 4, 10-11, 61, 70, 94, 153, 156-157, 160-161, 164, 219, 225, 249
California Native Plant Society, 159
Calochortus kennedyi, 172
Camel, 150
Camelops, 269
Camping, 5, 6
Candalaria, Nevada, 26
Canyon Resources Corporation, 247
Carbonate Lead Mines Inc., 48
Carbonate Mine (Argus Range), 216
Carbonate Mine (Panamint Range), 48-49
Carbonate, (site), 47-49
Carrara Formation, 33, 158, 179
Carson & Colorado Railroad, 26, 29, 156, 164, 259
Caspian Sea, 147
Cattle grazing, 171-173, 201
CDPA (see California Desert Protection Act)
Centennial Exposition of 1876, 79
Cerro Gordo, California, 115, 174, 195, 201, 206, 258-259
Cerrusite, 48, 212
Chalcopyrite, 220
Chilopis lineras, 234
China Garden Spring, 193-194
China Lake, 8, 186, 268
China Lake Basin, 130, 275-276
China Lake Naval Weapons Center, 214
Chinese, 193, 257, 268
Chloride City, Nevada, 111-116
Chloride Cliff (site) 112
Chloride Cliff Mine, 116
Chloride Junction, 114

Index

Cholla cactus, 142, 179
Chorizanthe, 270
Chris Wicht's Camp, 12, 43, 227-229
Chrysothammus, nauseous, 289
Chuckawalla Canyon, 38
Chuc-Walla newspaper, 29
Chukar partridges, 87, 171, 208
Cinnibar, 115
Citizens band radio, 140
City of Los Angeles, 154, 287
Civilian Conservation Corps, 57
Clair, W.D., 235
Clair's Camp, 234-236
Clark, Patsy, 27
Clements, Tom, 85
Cleomella obtusifola, 289
Clinton, Bill, 10
Clovis points, 188
Cole, Ken, 138-139
Collecting, 5, 7
Colorado River, 67
Colter Spring, 240, 244
Comstock Lode, 231
Conn & Trudo Borax Works, 168
Convict Lake, California, 77
Cooper Mine, 238
Cooper, James, 221, 238
Copper, 35, 49, 127, 193, 206, 270
Copper Basin, 127
Copper Bell Mine, 206
Copper Queen Canyon, 267, 272
Copper Queen Mine, 267
Corcoran State Prison, 287
Corcoran, Bill, 73
Coreopsis, 289
Coreopsis, calliopsidea 289
Corona Mine, 225-226
Cottontop cactus, 24, 33, 77, 179, 210, 214
Cottonwood Canyon Road, 5
Cottonwood Canyon, 11, 64-69, 116, 204
Cowhorn Valley, 156, 165
Coyote, 74
Crackerjack (site), 141-142
Crampton, Frank, 72
Crater (site), 157
Cravenocerus ammonite, 87
Creasor, Phil, 27
Creosote, 17, 93, 265
Crinoid fossils, 87

Cripple Creek, Colorado 231
Cross, Ed, 99
Crystal Spring Formation, 46, 51, 134, 136
Cuervo Smelter, 195
Curious Butte, 54
Curran, Jack, 225-226
Currie Well, 93, 97-100
Cycads, 150
Cyprindon nevadensis, 136
Cyprus Industrial Minerals, 136
Daisy Canyon, 169, 171
Dalea fremontii, 290
Dante's View Road, 30
Dante's View, 26
Darwin, California, 115, 174, 190-191, 193-195, 199, 214, 216, 228, 252
Darwin California (book), 195
Darwin Canyon, 183
Darwin Falls, 192-193
Darwin Mines, 195
Darwin Wash, 192-193, 198
Darwin Zinc Mine, 193
Daunet, Isadore, 71-72, 168
Daylight Pass, 98, 112-113
Dayton, Jim, 41
Dead Sea, 147
Deadman Pass, 25, 29, 122-124
Death Valley Expedition of 1890, 95
Death Valley in 49 (book), 72
Death Valley Jeep Trails (book), 2, 61, 236, 249
Death Valley Junction, California, 29-30, 123
Death Valley Natural History Association, 296
Death Valley Railroad, 26
Death Valley Scotty, 73
DeDecker, Mary, 95, 158
DeDecker, Paul, 95
DeDeckera Canyon, 155, 158-159, 175
Dedeckera eurekensis, 158
Deep Springs Valley, 158
Deer, 107
Defense Mine, 214
Defiance Smelter, 195
Denning Springs, 141-143
Denning, Frank, 142
Desert aster, 290
Desert Bighorn sheep, 69
Desert daisy, 289
Desert deerweed, 289

Index

Desert gold, 134
Desert holly, 22, 276, 289
Desert Magazine, 177
Desert Mariposa lily, 172, 201
Desert pavement, 71
Desert trumpet, 41, 265, 270, 289
Desert willow, 234
Devil's Gate, 156, 164
Devil's Golf Course, 32, 40
Devil's Playground, 157-158
Digonnet, Michel, 38, 59, 193
Dodder, 37
Doe Spring, 94
Dove, 171, 208
Dow Corning, 181
Dumont Dunes, 6, 12, 133-134, 145-147. 151
Dune primrose, 202
Eagle Borax Works, 41, 71, 115, 168
Earthquake fault, 37, 41, 187
Earthquake, 115
East Mojave Scenic Area, 10
Eastern California Museum, 295
Echinocactus polycephalus, 24, 33
Echinocereus engelmani, 33
Echinocerus mojavensis, 24, 33
Echo Canyon, 11, 16-20
Echo Pass, 12, 16-20, 117-118, 120, 127
Echo Wash, 12
Eclipse Talc Mine, 134
Eichbaum Toll Road, 57
Elliott, Russell, 25
Ely Springs dolomite, 33, 88, 186
Emigrant Canyon, 60
Emigrant Mine, 174, 199
Emigrant Ranger Station, 71
Emigrant Wash, 61, 71
Empress Mine, 193
Enceiliopsis agrophylla, 289
Engelman's hedgehog cactus, 33
Engineer Ophir Mine (see Ophir Mine)
Enterprise Mill, 78
Ephedra funerea, 106
Ephedra nevadensis, 106
Ephedra viridis, 106
Ephedra, 93, 106, 236-237
Epsom salts, 274
Equus, 269
Eriastrum eremicum, 271, 290
Eriastrum, 270, 290

Erigeron pumilus, 289
Eriogonum fasciculatum polifolium, 159
Eriogonum inflatum, 41, 265, 289
Esmerada County, Nevada, 81
Eureka dune grass, 158
Eureka Dunes, 146, 155, 157, 181
Eureka evening primrose, 158
Eureka quartzite, 33, 186
Eureka Valley Road, 157-158
Eureka Valley, 11, 155-158, 175-176, 192, 208
Evening primrose, 289
Exotic species, 37, 87, 135-136, 177, 193
Eye of the Needle, 16-18
Fairbanks, R.J., 30
Fairview, Nevada, 25-26
Ferge, Charles, 221-222
Finley, Henry, 119
Firearms, 5, 6
Fires, 5, 6
First Grotto, 59
Fish Lake Valley, 156-157
Folger, Abigail, 286
Fort Irwin, California, 142
Foss, A.L., 212
Fossil Falls, 268, 275
Fossils, 33-34, 86-87, 107, 145, 150, 205, 269
Four-O'Clock, 136, 270
Fowles, Frank, 287
Franklin Mine, 115
Franklin, A.J., 115
Franseria dumosa, 289
Fremont xeraside, 172, 201
Fremont, John C., 149
Fremont's Second Expedition of 1844, 149
French, Darwin, 194
Frenchman's Canyon, 232
Frenchman's Flat, Nevada, 91
Frisco Mine, 116
Funeral fanglomerate, 23
Funeral Formation, 130
Funeral Mountains, 6, 16-17, 19, 106, 113, 115, 119
Funeral Peak, 125
Funston, Frederick, 95
Furnace, California, 18, 25-27, 124-125
Furnace Creek Campground, 15
Furnace Creek Copper Company, 27, 29
Furnace Creek Fault, 23
Furnace Creek Formation, 17, 22

Index

Furnace Creek Inn, 15, 21, 32, 40, 243
Furnace Creek Ranch, 15-17, 21-22, 25, 31, 36, 40, 44, 47
Furnace Creek Wash, 21
Furnace Mine, 19
Galena, 212, 235
Galena Canyon Road, 44-45
Galena Canyon, 44-46
Gardner, Jack, 287
Gastropod fossils, 33-34
Gem Mine, 225-226
General Management Plan, 3, 177-178
Geoglyphs, 137, 150, 187
Geologist's Cabin, 54-55
Geraea canescens, 134
Ghost Towns and Mining Camps of California (book), 142
Giant Talc Mine, 134
Gibbens, Buck, 287
Gilia cana tricepts, 290
Gilia, 201
Gilia, 290
Gillies, Cathy, 249
Glauber salts, 255, 268
Gold, 43, 49, 115, 127, 165, 174, 199, 220, 225, 234, 247, 270
Gold Bar, 97, 99
Gold Bottom Mine, 267-272
Gold Bug Mine, 234
Gold Center (Nevada), 26
Gold Dollar Mine, 116
Gold Hill Mine, 53
Gold Key Mining Company, 131
Gold Mountain, Nevada, 76-79
Gold Point, Nevada, 76, 80-82
Gold Valley, 25, 30, 123, 125-128
Goldbelt Spring, 67, 203-204
Golden Canyon, 193
Golden Lady Mine, 218-219
Golden Queen Mill, 248
Golden Treasure Mine, 130-131
Goldenhead, 289
Goldfield Consolidated Mines, 47
Goldfield, Nevada, 25, 28-29, 91-92, 125
Goldsworthy brothers, 127
Goler Wash, 12, 50, 240, 246-250, 287
Good, Sandra, 287
Goodsprings, California. 149
Grantham Mine, 52

Grantham, Louise, 52
Grapevines, 202
Grapevine Canyon, 171-172, 201-202, 208
Grapevine Mountains, 93-95, 97, 106, 113
Grapevine Peak, 94
Grapevine Ranger Station, 75-76, 84
Gray Eagle Mine, 166
Greasewood, 93
Great Salt Lake, 149
Great Western Mine, 80-81
Greater View Spring, 50, 55-56 , 250
Green Sticker vehicle, 10, 146
Greenwater, California, 25-30, 121, 123-125, 127, 203
Greenwater Canyon, 11, 66
Greenwater & Death Valley Copper Co., 29
Greenwater Miner newspaper, 29
Greenwater Valley Road, 26, 30, 126-127
Grey, Fred, 222
Grotto Canyon Road, 5
Grotto Canyon, 58-59
Gudde, Erwin G., 142
Hall Canyon, 11, 224, 226
Hall, Wayne, 186
Hanaupah Canyon, 36-39
Hanaupah fan, 37
Hanging Mesa, 79
Happy Canyon, 11, 237
Harmony Borax Works, 115, 168
Harris, Frank Shorty, 25, 37, 41, 55, 99, 237
Harrisburg Flats, 31
Harrisburg, California, 62
Harry Wade Road, 141-142
Hart, Bessie, 237
Hart, Orpha, 231
Hayseed Mine, 119
Hearst, George, Senator, 215
Heart-leaved primrose, 289
Hidden Valley, 197
Hidden Valley dolomite, 86, 88, 205
Hiking Death Valley (book), 59, 193
Historical Society of the Upper Mojave Desert, 296
History House Museum, 255
Hitchcock, Leo, 95
Hole in the Wall, 11, 21-24
Homestake Dry Camp, 5
Homestake Mine, 99
Homewood Canyon Road, 260, 264-265

Index

Honolulu Mine, 243
Hoover, Herbert, 10
Horne, Herb, 287-188
Horne, Jane, 287
Hornsilver Herald, 81
Hornsilver, Nevada, 80
Horse Thief Canyon, 156
Hot springs, 121, 175
Huhn, Ernest Siberian Red, 52
Hungry Bill, 42
Hungry Bill's Ranch, 40, 42, 232
Hunter Mountain, 197-198, 200-202
Hunter Mountain Road, 164, 170, 172, 197, 202-204, 208
Hunter, Bev, 73, 203
Hunter, William, 203, 206
Huntley Industrial Minerals Inc., 88
Ibex Mine, 135, 142
Ibex Mountains, 134
Ibex Spring, 133-135
IMC Chemicals Inc, 254-255, 269
Independence, California, 28-29, 140, 287
Indian paintbrush, 42, 172, 201, 244, 289
Indian Ranch Road, 224-225, 228, 234
Indian Wells, California, 258
Indigo bush, 290
Inventory of Rare and Endangered Plants of California, 96
Inyo black toad, 158
Inyo County, 239, 242, 259, 268, 286-287
Inyo County Sheriff's Department, 286-287
Inyo Mine, 5, 16, 19
Inyo Mono Jeep Trails (book), 2, 153
Inyo Mountains, 156, 159, 164, 166, 169, 171
Inyo-Mono SUV Trails (book), 164, 167, 169
Iron pyrite, 220-221
Isomeris arborea, 289
Jackass Creek, 202
Jackass Flats, 165
Jackpot Canyon, 234
Jacobs, Richard, 257, 260-261
Jail Canyon, 11, 224-226
Jayhawer Party, 241, 247
Jeager, Edmund, 17
Jellyfish, 34
Johns-Manville Products Inc., 46, 52
Johnson, Albert, 75, 84
Johnson, Bessie, 84
Johnson Canyon, 36, 38, 40-43

Johnson, Leroy, 54
Johnson, William, 42
Jones, Tom & Diana, 287
Joshua Flat, 156
Joshua Tree National Park, 10
Joshua trees, 77, 160, 172, 198, 201
Jubilee Pass, 129
Julian, Charles, 107-108
July gold, 158
Juniper, 93, 166
Juniperous californica, 93
Juniperous osteosperma, 93, 166
Kawich, Nevada, 26
Keane Spring, 114
Keane Wonder Mine, 116
Kearsarge Station, 29
Keeler Canyon Formation, 188, 210
Keeler, California, 29, 212
Kelly, V.C., 195
Kelso Dunes, 157-158
Kerr McGee Corporation, 255, 269
Kingston Peak Formation, 244
Klare Spring, 107-108
Knob Mine, 234
Kramer, Count, 131
Krenwinkel, Patricia, 287
Kuma River, 147
Kuntz, 25, 27-28, 124
Kunze, Arthur, 27
Lake Hill, 186-188
Lake Manly, 130, 136, 146, 187, 275
Lake Panamint, 38, 187
Lake Rogers, 85
Lake Russell, 268
Lake Searles, 186, 268-269, 275-276
Lake Tecopa, 134
Lamphier, John, 221
Lang, Ted, 221
Larrea tridentata glutinosa, 17
Las Vegas & Tonopah Railroad, 26, 91, 93, 97, 99, 112
Las Vegas, Nevada, 26, 140, 149
Last Chance Range, 158, 161
Lathyrus hitchcockianus, 95-96
Lathyrus paluster, 95
Latimer (California), 206
Layton Canyon, 274
Lead, 35, 48-49, 72, 115, 174, 188, 193, 195, 199, 206-207, 212, 215, 234-235, 270

Index

Lead Canyon, 166
Leadville (site), 107-108
Leadville Chronicle, 108
Leaky, Dr. L.S.B., 8
Leavitt, Chet, 127
Lee Annex, 118
Lee (California), 18, 20, 26, 117-119
Lee, Dick, 119
Lee, Gus, 119
Lee (Nevada), 118-119
Lee Flat limestone, 211
Lee Flat, 170, 172, 174, 198, 201
Lee Herald, 119
Lee Mines, 174, 199-200, 202
Lee Pump, 202
Leeland (site), 118-119
Lee's Camp Road, 117
Lee's Camp, 119-120
Lemoigne Canyon, 11, 72
LeMoigne, Jean Cap, 70-73, 270
Lesser mohavena, 270, 289
Lestro Mountain Mine, 248
Limber pine, 94-95
Lime Point, 80-81
Limestone Spring, 230
Lingenfelter, Richard, 42, 49, 54, 77, 206
Lippencott Grade, 12, 165, 170-171, 196-197, 207-208
Lippencott Lead Mine, 207
Lithium, 255, 268
Little Hebe Crater, 85
Little Sand Spring, 77
Lone Pine, California, 167, 174
Longitudinal dunes, 141
Lookout (site), 115, 210, 213-217, 228, 252, 262
Lookout Mountain, 209-210, 213-217, 219, 258-259
Los Angeles, California, 149, 154, 257-259
Los Angeles County Museum, 150
Los Angeles Police Department, 287
Lost Burro Formation, 86, 174, 199, 205
Lost Burro Gap, 83, 86, 205
Lost Burro Junction, 87-88
Lost Burro Mine, 5, 86, 204-205
Lost Gunsight Mine, 194
Lost Gunsite Lode, 72
Lost Mexican Mine, 237
Lotus Mine, 55, 248

Lotus rigidus, 289
Lower Warm Springs (Saline Valley), 3, 161, 166-167, 175-178
Lucky Boy Mines, 166
Ludlow, California, 148
Lupine, 244
Lupinus arizonicus, 289
Machaeranthera tortifolia, 290
Magnesia (site), 274
Mahogany Flat, 38-39, 243
Malachite, 27, 34, 220, 272
Mallow, 172, 201, 244
Mammoth City, 195
Mammoth Mine, 45, 136
Manhattan, Nevada, 26
Manly Peak, 6
Manly, William, 41, 54, 132
Manson, Charles, 249, 286-288
Many headed barrel cactus (see Cottontop)
Marble Bath, 180-181
Marble Canyon (Inyo Mountains), 165
Marble Canyon (Panamint Mountains), 11, 64, 66-68, 204
Marcom, Geron, 66
Marine terraces, 130, 272, 275
Mariposa lily, 172, 201-202
Mastadons, 269
Mattinson, Ernest, 127
Maturango Museum, 296
Mayflower Mine, 100-104
McAllister, Jim, 204
McBride Camp, 35
McCausland, Benjamin, 131
McCausland, Ross, 131
McCormick, Hugh, 54
McGarry, L.P., 118
McSweeney Junction, 29
Mengel, Carl, 55-56, 248, 250
Mengel Pass, 50, 54-56, 244, 246-250
Merry Christmas Mine, 220
Mesquite Flat Culture, 285
Mesquite Spring, 75
Mesquite trees, 84, 179
Mesquite Well, 52
Messina, Paula, 206
Middle Park, 233, 238, 240, 244-245
Midvale, Utah, 48
Mill Canyon, 172, 174, 199, 201
Miller Spring, 194

Index

Miller, Julia, 244
Mines of Death Valley (book), 115
Mining in Parks Act, 5
Mining, 5, 7
Minnietta Mine, 210, 213-214, 216, 219, 256, 259, 262-263
Minnietta Road, 210, 213, 218, 262
Minnows, 158
Mistletoe, 166
Modoc Mine, 214, 216, 219, 256
Mohave aster, 172, 201
Mohave Desert, 201
Mohavea breviflora, 289
Mojave National Preserve, 10
Mojave River Museum, 53
Mojave, California, 195, 221, 248, 255
Monarch Canyon, 114
Monarch Mine, 114
Monarch Talc Mine, 136
Mongolian Mine, 45
Mono Lake Basin, 268
Montgomery Hotel, 103
Montgomery, Bob, 91
Moorehouse Talc Mine, 135
Mormon Point, 130
Mormon tea, 93, 106, 236
Mormons, 55, 172, 201
Morning Glory Mine, 35
Morton, Leander, 77
Mound cactus, 24
Mount Ophir, 194
Mountain Boy Mine, 237
Mountain Girl Mine, 237
Moyer, Wendell, 180-181
Mt. Whitney, 111, 116
Mushroom Rock, 130
Myers, Barbara, 55, 249-250
Myers, Bill, 55, 249-250
Myers, Charles, 250
Myers, Corky, 250
Myers, Pat, 250
Myers Ranch, 247, 249-250, 286
N.O.T.S., 51
Nadeau, Remi (IV), 1, 142, 195
Nadeau, Remi, 210, 213 215, 252, 256
Nadeau Shotgun Road, 210, 213-214, 219, 251-252, 256-262
National Antiquities Act of 1906, 7, 8
National Herbarium, 95

National Natural Landmark, 157, 276
National Register of Historic Places, 108, 169
Natural arch, 62
Naval Air Weapons Station, 4, 269
Naval Ordnance Test Station, China Lake, 4
Nazca Peru, 67, 187
Nelson, E.W., 187
Neotoma, 138
Nepheline, 89
Nevada Oryctes, 158
Nevada Street, 118
New Coso Smelter, 195
New Discovery Mine, 225
New Nadeu Road, 251-252
New York Butte, 167
Newhall, California, 41
Noble, Levi, 131
Noonday dolomite, 48
Noonday Mine, 150
Nopah Formation, 33, 158-159, 179, 188
North American Chemical Company, 255
North Pass, 172
NOTS Range B, 11
Nova Formation, 59, 61
Novack Camp, 228
O.B. Joyful Mine, 225
O'Brien Canyon, 89
Oenothera caespitosa, 289
Oenothera cardiophylla, 289
Oenothera avita eurekensis, 158
Off-Road driving, 5, 6
Olancha Dunes, 6
Olancha, California, 174
Old Camp, 79
Old Deperndable Mine, 35
Old Guest House Museum, 255
Old Spanish Trail, 150-151
Old Timers of Southeastern California (book), 203
Ontario Canada, 89
Onyx Mine Road, 262
Onyx, 262
Opal Canyon, 165
Opal Mine, 165, 270
Opuntia basilaris, 24, 45
Opuntia echinocarpa, 24
Oriental (Nevada), 76,79
Oriental Mine, 79
Oriental Wash, 77

Index

Orion, Nevada, 99
Oro Fino Mine, 55
Orondo Mine (see Arondo Mine)
Oryctes nevandensis, 158
Osborne Canyon, 209-212, 262
Osborne, J.L., 212
Ovis canadensis nelsoni, 69, 128
Owens Lake, 169, 268
Owens River, 154, 156, 186, 268, 275
Owens Valley Formation, 188
Owens Valley Indian Wars, 153
Owens Valley, 156, 202, 259, 268, 275
Owl, 220
Pabuna village, 52
Pacific Coast Borax Company, 24
Pack rat, 138-139, 204
Paddy's Pride Talc Mine, 134
Pahoehoe lava, 180
Pahrump Group, 46, 135
Paiute Indians, 52, 115, 234, 237
Palazzo, Robert, 195
Palm Spring, 3, 178-179
Palm trees, 175-176
Panamint Basin, 130
Panamint Butte, 188
Panamint City (site), 3, 12, 42, 115, 195, 207, 215-216, 221, 227-232, 258-259, 261
Panamint daisy, 289
Panamint Dry Lake, 186
Panamint Mountains, 159, 186-187, 214
Panamint Pass, 232
Panamint Road, 260-261
Panamint Russ, 54
Panamint Springs Resort, 174, 183, 185-186, 191-192, 198-199, 208-210, 213, 218, 224
Panamint Tom, 52
Panamint Valley sand dunes, 171-172, 187-188, 202
Panamint Valley, 41, 186, 193, 201, 215, 221, 274-275
Papoose Flat, 156, 164
Pentstamen, 42
Perdido Formation, 68, 87-88, 211
Pershing, Blackjack, 95
Petrified wood, 7, 150
Petroglyphs, 7, 11, 66- 67, 79, 109, 156, 180, 204
Pets, 5, 6
Pfizer Inc., 45, 134, 136

Phacelia crenulata, 290
Phacelia, 32, 41, 210, 214, 244
Phinney, Charles E., 93
Phinney Canyon, 11, 92-97, 100
Phinney Canyon Road, 93, 100
Phinney, F.C., 93
Phinney Mine, 94
Phlox stansburyi, 290
Phlox, 41, 159, 290
Phoradendron juniperium, 166
Pickleweed, 37, 289
Pinnacles (see Trona Pinnacles)
Pinto Basin Culture, 187, 285
Pinus aristata, 94
Pinyon pine, 166,180
Pioneer Mine, 104
Pioneer Nevada, 101-104
Pioneer Point, California, 260, 264
Piper Mountain, 6
Piper Mountain Wilderness, 156
Pipkin, George, 270
Pleasant Canyon, 12, 221, 233-240, 245
Pleasanton Talc Mine, 136
Plio-Pleistocene Ice Age, 95, 128, 134, 139, 146, 179, 244, 268, 273, 275-276
Pogonip Series, 33
Poison Canyon, 186, 258, 268, 275-276
Popcorn flower, 42
Porter brothers, 114
Porter, Henry Clay, 237
Porter, John, 206
Porter Mine, 237-238
Post Office Spring, 240-241
Potash, 255, 268
Powell, Dick, 286
Pray, Chester, 48
Prehistoric Indians, 109,180
Prickly pear cactus, 77, 142, 179
Prickly poppy, 244
Primrose, 41
Prince's Plume, 160, 172, 201
Pueblo Culture, 137
Pupfish, 136, 158
Pursell, Jim, 286
Pyromorphite, 212
Quail, 171, 208, 265
Quarry Road, 260
Quartz, 199
Quartz monzonite, 171,192, 202, 210-211, 264

Index

Queen of Sheeba Mine (Argus Range), 216
Queen of Sheeba Mine (Panamint Range), 47-49
Rabbitbrush, 289
Racetrack playa, 3, 85, 170, 198, 206, 286
Racetrack Road, 5
Radiocarbon dating, 8, 138
Rainbow Canyon, 198-199
Ramsey, Nevada, 25
Randsburg, California, 34, 213
Ratcliff, Henry, 221, 234
Ratcliff Mine, 221, 234, 236
Rawhide, Nevada, 25
Red Amphiteater, 24
Red Pass, 105, 107
Redlands Canyon, 54
Reed, Lester, 203
Reilly (site), 251-253, 261
Reilly, Edward, 252
Rest Spring Gulch, 87
Rest Spring shale, 87
Rest Spring, 87-88, 204
Resting Spring Range, 6
Revel, James, 95
Rhyolite, 18, 25, 27, 61, 91, 98-99, 102, 106, 112-114, 125
Richardson, Wade, 237
Ridgecrest, California, 140, 274
River Jordan, 147
Rob Roy Talc Mine, 136
Roberts, George D., 77-78, 100
Rock hounding, 5
Rock Spring, 265
Rock-pea, 289
Rogers Pass, 233, 240
Rogers, John, 41, 54, 132
Roosevelt, Franklin D., 81, 235
Round Mountain, Nevada, 26
Russian thistle, 136
Ruth Mine, 270
Ryan (site), 26, 106
Saddle Cabin, 16, 19
Salazaria, mexicana, 290
Salina City (site), 206
Saline Preservation Association, 178
Saline Range, 179-180
Saline Valley Road, 163-169, 175, 199-200, 208
Saline Valley sand dunes, 167

Saline Valley Salt Marsh, 169
Saline Valley, 3, 8, 11, 155-156, 164, 192, 197, 201-202, 207-208
Saline Warm Springs, 176
Salsberry Pass, 48, 129
Salsberry, Jack, 48-49, 206
Salsberry, John, 107-108
Salt Creek, 73
Salt tram, 169-170, 208
Salt, 169-170
Salvia carduacea, 290
Samson, R.J., 226
San Bernardino, California, 257
San Dieguito Culture, 8, 285
San Francisco, California, 29, 115, 174, 199, 215
San Francisquito Ranch, 41
San Lucas Canyon, 168, 174, 201
Sand verbena, 136, 270, 290
Santa Ana, California, 207
Santa Rosa Flat 199
Saratoga Spring, 133, 136-139, 142
Saratoga Springs Culture, 136-137, 285
Sarcobatus Flat, 93, 99-100
Sarcobatus vermiculatus, 93
Scarlet locoweed, 289
Scheelite, 34, 235
Schwab (site), 16, 18-20, 26
Schwab, Charles M., 18, 27
Scott, Walter, AKA Death Valley Scotty, 75, 84
Scotty's bungalow, 84
Scotty's Castle, 74-75, 76, 83-84, 157, 172, 206
Searles Lake, 130, 267-268, 270-271
Searles Station, 274
Searles Valley, 41, 255-256, 258, 264, 275
Searles Valley Gem & Mineral Society, 262
Searles Valley Historical Society, 255, 296
Searles, Dennis, 268
Searles, John, 268
Seif dunes, 146
Seldom Seen Slim (see Charles Ferge)
Senator Mine, 80
Shaw, Tom, 77, 79
Sherwin phase, 134
Shining locoweed, 158
Shining milk-vetch, 158
Shoreline Butte, 130

Index

Shorty's Well, 36, 40
Shoshone, California, 26-27, 30, 44, 121, 134, 153
Shoshone Indians, 33, 169
Siberian Red, 52
Sierra Nevada Range, 202, 275
Silver, 35, 49, 115, 174, 188, 195, 199, 206-207, 212, 215, 225, 252, 257, 270
Silver Crown Mines, 83, 89
Silver Peak, Nevada, 226
Silver Reid Mine, 174, 199
Silver Spur Mine, 165
Simpson, Ruth, 8
Skidoo, 61-62, 72, 221
Slate Range Crossing, 256-258, 261
Slate Range, 258, 267, 272, 274
Slate Ridge, 78, 80
Sleeping circles, 137, 150
Smith Mountain, 127
Smith, Borax, 148, 168
Snow Canyon, 209, 218-220
Snow Flake Talc Mine, 167-168
Sober-up Gulch, 102
Soda ash, 255, 268
Soldier Pass Canyon, 156
Sorensen, Walter, 222
Sourdough Spring, 249-250
South Park Canyon, 233, 239-245
South Park, 233, 238-239
South Pass, 172, 174
Southern Pacific Railroad, 108, 274
Southworth, John, 72
Spangler Hills, 6, 276
Spanish American War, 95
Spaulding, Geffrey, 166
Sperry, Grace, 148
Sperry Station, 148-149
Sperry Wash, 133, 149-150
Springdale, Nevada, 92, 104
Squaw tea, 93, 106, 236
St. George Mine, 220
Stanleya pinnata, 160
Stateline (Nevada), 77
Stateline Mill, (Nevada) 78, 100
Stateline Mine (California), 119
Stateline Mine (Nevada), 77-78
Stauffer Chemical Company Inc., 269
Steatite, 45

Steel Pass, 11, 155, 160-161, 175-176, 181, 208
Stephens, Hal, 186
Sterling quartzite, 34
Stewart, Bob, 257
Stinkweed, 289
Stone Canyon, 214
Stone Canyon Road, 210, 214
Stone Corral, 233, 237-238
Stovepipe Wells, 3, 57-58, 65, 174
Strawtop Cholla cactus, 24
Striped Butte, 53-55, 244
Suitcase Mine, 241
Sulfur, 157
Sunset Campground, 15
Surprise Canyon, 12, 43, 227-233, 257
Surprise Mine Camp, 211
Surprise Mine, 212
Swallenia alexandrae, 158
Swansea (site), 169
Syenite Junction, 89
Syenite, 88
Sylvania Mountains, 6
Sylvania Wilderness, 156
Talc, 44-46,
Tamarisk, 37, 136
Tapirs, 107
Tarantula Mine, 34-35
Tate, Sharon, 286
Tate-LaBianca murders, 249, 287
Teakettle Junction, 5, 85-86, 197, 205, 207-208
Tecopa, California, 26, 121, 149
Telephone Canyon, 59, 61
Telephone Spring, 62
Telescope Peak, 38-39, 214, 225, 237, 243
Texas Spring Campground, 15, 17
Thistle sage, 290
Thomason, Barbara, 249
Thomason, Bluch, 249
Thompson Canyon, 218
Thompson, Shotgun Mary, 231
Thompson, Robert, 139
Thorndike, John, 243
Timbisha Shoshone, 8
Tin Mountain, 85
Tin Mountain limestone, 85-87, 89, 174, 199, 204-205, 211-212
Titanothere Canyon, 106-107

Index

Titus Canyon, 11, 105-110
Titus Canyon Formation, 107, 109
Titus Canyon Road, 5
Titus, Morris, 106
Tokop, Nevada, 76, 80
Tombstone, Arizona, 259
Tonopah & Tidewater Railroad, 29, 91, 108, 118, 121, 148-149
Tonopah and Goldfield Railroad, 26-27, 48
Tonopah BLM Office, 6
Tonopah, Nevada, 25, 28-29, 48, 91, 125, 236
Tonopan Junction, 29
Tow trucks, 294
Towne's Pass, 174
Trail Canyon, 11, 31-35, 40
Transverse dunes, 146
Tremolite, 88
Trilobite fossils, 17, 33-34
Trona (mineral) 255, 268
Trona Borax Company, 268, 270
Trona, California, 174, 210, 213, 218, 229, 254-256, 260, 264, 267-269
Trona pinnacles, 271, 273-277
Trona Railroad, 274
Troster, 226
Tuber Canyon, 225
Tucki Mine, 12, 59, 60, 62-63
Tufa, 276
Tule Canyon, 77-78
Tule Spring, 40
Tungsten, 34, 235
Twenty Mule Team Canyon, 21
Twenty Mule Teams, 51, 137
U.S. Forest Service, 164
Ubehebe Crater, 77, 83-85, 170, 172, 197, 205
Ubehebe Lead Mine, 5, 206
Ubehebe Mining Company, 206
Ulida Flat, 204
United States Army, 54
United States Navy, 51, 214, 269
Upper Warm Spring, 179-180
Ural Emba River, 147
Valley View Road, 20, 118
Valley Wells, 264
Van Houton, Leslie, 287
Vegetables, 42, 193
Verbena goodingi, 289
Verbena, 289
Victory Tungsten Mine, 34
Villa, Pancho, 95
Virginia City, Nevada, 231
Visitor's Center, 15
Walt Disney Studios, 276
War Eagle Mine, 188
Warm Spring Mine, 52
Warm Springs (Saline Valley) 166-168
Warm Springs Canyon, 5, 44, 46, 50-51
Warm Springs, 52-53
Warm Sulfur Springs, 187
Water Canyon, 252
Water Supply Paper #24, 100
Waucoba Wash, 166
Weaver, Charles, 226
Weight, Harold O., 27
Welles, Florence, 128,171
Welles, Ralph, 128, 171
Wells, Phillip, 166
West End Chemical Company, 255, 260, 268-269
West Frontier Street, 118
West Side Road, 5, 32, 34, 37-38, 40-41, 45, 48,
Western Lead Mines, 107-108
Western Nevada Jeep Trails (book), 2
Whippoorwill Canyon, 166
Whippoorwill Flat, 165
White Eagle Mine, 45, 166
White Mountains, 156, 164
White Pass, 105-106
White Top Mountain, 83, 87-88, 159, 204
Whittier, A.D., 206
Wibbett brothers, 252
Wicht, Chris, 222, 229
Wild heliotrope, 290
Wild-buckwheat, 159, 289
Wildrose, 202
Wildrose Canyon, 215, 259
Wildrose Canyon Road, 210, 213, 218
Wildrose charcoal kilns, 215-217
Willow Creek (site), 127
Willow Creek Camp, 166
Willow Creek Mining District, 127
Willow Spring, 127
Wingate Pass, 274
Wingate Wash, 11, 38, 51, 130, 187, 250
Winters, Aaron, 168
Witherell, Joe, 127
Wonder Mine, 174, 199

Index

Wonder, Nevada, 25
Wood Canyon (Argus Range), 218-219
Wood Canyon (Panamint Range), 54
Wood Canyon Formation, 17, 33, 179
Wood rat (see Pack Rat)
Woodcock, Deborah, 166
World Beater Mine, 236-237
World War I, 73, 207
World War II, 207
WPA Federal Writer's Project, 18
Wynog Mine, 193
Wyoming Mine, 232
Yucca brevifolia, 172, 201
Yucca Flats, Nevada, 91
Yucca Mountain, Nevada, 91
Yucca whipplei, 166
Yucca, 166
Zabriske quartzite, 179
Zabriskie Point Formation, 33
Zabriskie, California, 27, 48
Zanjani, Sally, 52
Zinc Hill, 191, 193
Zinc, 35, 174, 188, 193, 195, 199, 206-207, 212, 225
Zurich siding, 156, 164